International
Environmental
Action

Thomas W. Wilson, Jr.

International Environmental Action

A Global Survey

DUNELLEN

Contents

LIST OF APPENDIXES

Foreword

Early in 1970, the "crisis of the environment" entered the public discourse with dramatic speed and impact. Many seemed to sense that the human race was faced with something new, complex, poorly understood – and somehow fateful.

Belatedly, society began to stir: government agencies, legislatures, universities, foundations, industries, professional and other groups began to face up to the fact that something had gone wrong – if not irreversibly, perhaps dangerously so, in man's relations with nature. Students across the country reacted by proclaiming Earth Day. The United Nations began preparations for a World Conference on the Human Environment to be held under UN auspices in Stockholm in the early summer of 1972.

The Aspen Institute for Humanistic Studies and the Anderson Foundation (Robert O. Anderson, Chairman) felt that new perspectives and new approaches to decision-making in the environmental field would be needed if human society is to adjust to the coming to terms with the natural system on which all life depends. Perhaps a new organization should be formed to monitor and stimulate such perspectives and approaches to the environmental crisis.

But first it seemed essential to know more about the reactions of existing governmental and nongovernmental institutions, both here and abroad. The Anderson Foundation therefore made available a grant for as comprehensive a survey as could be mounted over a four-month period. The interest and assistance given to this project by John W.

Musser, President of the General Service Foundation and Trustee of the Aspen Institute, is gratefully acknowledged.

The survey was completed by mid-year under the supervision and principal authorship of Thomas W. Wilson, Jr.

Some of the materials produced for the survey – notably an introductory essay – were then tested as tools for provoking thought and discussion. They were introduced into the deliberations of the Executive Seminar Program of the Aspen Institute for Humanistic Studies, which for the past two decades has involved business and other leaders in the mainstreams of basic humanistic thought. More recently, in the Executive Seminar Program, great attention has been given to include scientists, artists, and representatives of minority groups and youth.

The discussions which ensued in the Executive Seminar in the summer of 1970 encouraged the Aspen Institute to adapt its ongoing program to include a strong emphasis on fundamental environmental issues. More specifically, the Aspen Institute, in cooperation with the Aspen Center for Physics and the Council for Biology in Human Affairs of the Salk Institute, decided to sponsor annually an intensive summer study of some specific environmental problem of international concern. The first of these, to be held in 1971, will bring outstanding participants from the major areas of the world to Aspen, Colorado, for an urgent study of eight to ten weeks on how the world community can best be organized to deal with environmental management problems on the international plane. The study and recommendations that will emerge from it will be directly relevant to the proceedings of the UN Conference on the Human Environment.

Other parts of the Aspen Institute-Anderson Foundation survey – the international section in particular – were also shown to selected groups for reaction and comment.

As an outcome of these tests and inquiries, it became clear that many of the materials assembled for the survey would evoke wide interest and provide a valuable reference work, despite the fact that many gaps still exist in the range of desirable information. It therefore was decided late in 1970 to shorten and revise the original survey for publication in its present form.

It is contemplated that this book will be the forerunner of an annual volume expanding and bringing up to date the highlights of environmental affairs around the world, together with the key documents that will make the volume a working tool for organizations and individuals who need, or just want, to stay abreast of how men and institutions are responding to the crisis of the environment. It is hoped it will be a type of strategic balance sheet on what has and has not been done each year. Meanwhile, action has gone forward on the major recommendation of the Anderson Foundation survey: that a small, independent, non-governmental organization be established to stimulate, synthesize, and communicate contemporary information and opinion about the environmental crisis – including its social-political-economic-institutional implications and especially in its international context. As this is written, steps are being taken, after a period of trial activities, to launch on an ongoing basis this new organization, the International Institute for Environmental Affairs.

This book, then, can be looked upon as an instrument and part of a process which already has helped to stimulate institutional adaptation to the environmental crisis and to launch a new organization to enrich public debate about the novel and pressing issues which arise from it.

The Anderson Foundation and the Aspen Institute for Humanistic Studies are deeply convinced that intelligent management of the human environment will require major social adaptations for which experience provides few guidelines – and that such adaptations cannot be made successfully without public understanding and participation. We trust that this book will make some small contribution to that end.

J. E. Slater
President
Aspen Institute for Humanistic Studies
Anderson Foundation

December 1970

Preface

This book is an unforeseen by-product of a survey directed by the editor and principal author of the present volume. The survey was intended to take the measure of public and private reaction to the sudden explosion of interest in the state of the human environment -- to get a snapshot of who is doing what about it.

Population growth and urbanization – major factors in the environmental crisis – were eliminated from the range of the inquiry as an arbitrary device for keeping it within manageable bounds.

Needless to say, we found governmental and nongovernmental institutions characteristically in a state of ferment about the condition of the environment and how to cope with it; the landscape was dotted with moving targets.

We also found that many information-reporting networks that keep tabs on what's going on within major constituencies had not yet cranked up machinery for following environmental affairs. Information about what other national governments are doing unilaterally was so fragmentary as to be almost valueless.

These information gaps will be filled over time; for example, the national reports which are being prepared for the upcoming UN Conference on the Human Environment will provide a starting point for country-by-country review.

In the meantime, it appears that the survey has brought together in one place the most comprehensive overview currently available of actions, reactions, and plans on the national and international levels for beginning to cope with the new awareness of environmental crisis.

The editor wrote Part 1, comprising the introductory material; Part 3, on the international scene; and the final postscript. Part 2 is derived mainly from papers prepared by survey team members Richard K. Chalmers, Donald Mabie, and George E. Arnstein. Edgar N. Pike is the principal author of Part 4. The bibliography is the work of Paul Mahany. Dana Orwick has helped prepare the manuscript for publication. The undersigned is solely responsible for editing and for decisions as to what to retain and what to delete from the original survey report, which ran to approximately 1,000 pages.

T. W. W., Jr.
Washington, D.C.
December 1970

Part 1

The Environment:
Too Small a View

The current confusion about the "crisis of the environment" is a compound of extremely limited factual data and similarly limited perceptions of the potential impact of this crisis upon national and international society.

What follows immediately is an effort to cut through some underbrush in search of some ground to start from. The result, at best, takes the form of tentative and unfinished notes. If they lack cohesion, it is because the author hoped that a certain amount of jumping about might, paradoxically, help make the point that everything is tied together.

T. W. W., Jr.

There is room for argument about the "crisis of the environment"—how serious, how imminent, how real is the peril of continued exploitation and degradation of the Biosphere.

On the one hand, the ambient atmosphere is being charged with pollutants which, singly or in combination, might have serious adverse effects on human health; on the other hand, nobody can prove at this point that prolonged exposure to present levels of mid-city carbon monoxide does any biological harm, or that small quantities of DDT in his soup will make anyone sick or shorten his life.

On the one hand, we are learning that the components of natural systems are intricate, complex, interrelated, and interacting; on the other hand, we know, by virtue of being alive, that any working biological system is tough, resilient, adaptive, and designed for survival.

We can deplore the slow extinction of rare species or give thanks for the slow emergence of new ones, without in either case knowing for sure whether the future variety of life has lost or gained by some tiny fraction over recent decades.

We can predict ecological disaster by statistically extrapolating trends or we can recall that unpleasant phenomena, like pollution and genetic defects, have been taken for granted as facts of life for millennia. Or we can take another tack and note that the one sure thing about the future is that it will not be a straight-line projection of the past.

The uncertainties derive from a simple lack of adequate knowledge about the ecology and how it works. To characterize the present state of ignorance, it is enough to quote a single sentence of a report prepared by a study group for the National Academy of Sciences: "At present, we do not systematically, comprehensively, or regularly measure environment quality, nor do we know how and to what extent it is changing and has already changed." [1]

The optimists, the pessimists, and those in between agree, then, that a vast amount of research needs to be done——and the sooner the better. With a serious effort, it appears that hard data could be assembled in some research areas bearing upon biological effects of important chemical compounds within five years. In other areas, experiments remain to be designed, techniques are not at hand, and research results could be twenty, thirty, or forty years away, even if started tomorrow.

But these are scientific and technical questions. And to keep the debate on those grounds is to risk repeating, at a higher level of abstraction, the error of those now condemned for thinking only in terms of "industry" or "agriculture" or "economics" or "biology." Ecology needs to be studied in a scientific and technological framework. But there is much more to the "environmental crisis" than that.

The phenomenal thing about this year's concern for the quality of the environment is not a quantum jump in last year's incidence of environmental insults. Something exploded. What happened?

There is room for argument about this, too. Plainly, the conservationist groups have prepared the ground over the years with patient and valuable work. The conservationist movement has its pioneers and heroes——and its victories, too.

Yet not many people were turned on by the impending fate of the California Condor or the Blue Whale, even if they hoped the Whooping Cranes would make it. *Our Plundered Planet* came out, without much impact, years before *America the Raped,* and the Population Reference Bureau was looking hard for an audience for a long time before the *Population Bomb* appeared.

So current concerns for environmental integrity were sparked by something more than evolving enlightenment about the need to conserve natural resources, though the knowledge gathered by the conservationists provided fuel for the movement, once it got going.

---

1. Report of the Environmental Study Group to the Environmental Studies Board of the National Academy of Sciences, National Academy of Engineering, "Institutions for Effective Management of the Environment" (Part I, Washington, D.C.: NAS, January 1970), p. 4.

One factor, which is difficult to weigh but not too difficult to see, is this: various groups of people who have become unhappy about various things rather suddenly began to reformulate their concerns and redirect their frustrations in terms of environmental degradation. The most obvious groups are among the young discontented about the Establishment, or the system, or the bureaucracy, or the Vietnam war, or the military-industrial complex, or bigness, or the dehumanization of life, or crowding, or what-not. Since the quality of the environment bears directly on the quality of life, pollution is a handy symbol of what's wrong with society's values, and a potentially workable instrument for reform.

It may well be that another large if unmeasurable group that transferred its target of concern to environmental quality is made up of those who had reached a point of saturation in the capacity to be interested in world affairs, and a breaking point in their frustration at not being able to do anything about complex problems and crises which appeared to be in the hands of grey, faceless people in the Department of State who could not even be identified——much less held accountable for their failure to impose a tolerable order upon world affairs. A twenty-year public consensus about U.S. foreign policy was beginning to break down but no new consensus was emerging: there was no agreement about what different policies could be formulated and followed for European security ... nuclear weapons ... foreign aid ... the Middle East. ... There seemed to be nothing that a citizen could do about such tangled issues even if he thought he knew what should be done——except demonstrate against the war in Vietnam or in support of the President and our troops.

Yet any citizen could see the gook in the rivers and the junk on the landscape; he could taste——or thought he could taste——the carbon monoxide; he could hear the noise of the jets and feel the crush of the crowds.

Everyone knew what ought to be done and felt that he might be able to do something about it. A belching industrial chimney is a marvelously visible target. An individual could bomb it or picket it; he could talk to an officer of the company or the trade union; he could join a committee, sign a petition, write a letter, go to a meeting, stuff envelopes, pass out handbills.

One of the triggers of the explosion in public concern about the quality of environment, then, may be traced to the much-discussed malaise in American society. The new concern has a potential for uniting, in common cause, conservatives and militants, the young and not-so-young, housewives and professionals; it also has a potential for adding to existing frustrations, for deepening divisions between the races, for turning away from responsibilities in the world at large——and for turning into a passing fad.

Yet it is difficult to get away from the conviction that another trigger of the sudden environmental awareness was the view of Earth from outer space——the visual confirmation of what previously could be grasped only intellectually: that Earth indeed is small, lonely, unitary, finite, and vulnerable. After Apollo 9 the perception of Spaceship Earth no longer was a figure of speech or a flight of the imagination.

Regardless of how many people see the space program as evidence of distorted national priorities——regardless of the future of manned space exploration——the view of Earth from outer space is now a part of man's experience which he cannot expunge and which must in some measure affect the way he looks upon the eco-system on which his survival depends.

Against that image, familiar facts and steep projections begin to take on meaning: Earth is becoming dangerously crowded; resources are running out; wastes are piling up; pollutants are fouling the life-support system of the human race.

In the new view of Earth and the new awareness of the environment, then, there is the potential for an emergent and unifying world outlook with political, moral, and spiritual implications of the first magnitude.

The Growth of Technology

How did we get into this mess? By the simple process of unknowingly or unconscionably passing on the environmental bill to future generations——throughout the whole of human history. In retrospect this is not too surprising.

There is a tendency these days to foster the notion that Nature is in perpetual peace and in perfect balance at all times and everywhere——gentle, friendly, and inherently benign in its relations with living species. As though a tornado could not level Lubbock as the A-bomb leveled Hiroshima; as if there were no tidal waves or floods or droughts or hailstorms or volcanic eruptions to threaten the survival of early man and still kill and destroy in the twentieth century. Man had to survive the violent side of Nature and still suffers from environmental events to which he is an innocent party.

And for a long time there was no great problem about the gross availability of water and land and forest: they were there to be taken, used, consumed——even if, at times and in places, Nature's resources were ravaged and destroyed through the ignorance or rapacity of human tribes.

We are being reminded lately that this indifference——even arrogance ——toward Nature found explicit religious sanction in Judeo-Christian culture. Having created Man, says Genesis, God bade him:

Be fruitful, and multiply, and replenish the earth and subdue it; and have dominion over the fish of the sea, and over the fowl of the air, and over every living thing that moveth upon the earth.

On top of that came the "frontier spirit" in the New World: if the soil got tired or the timber ran out, there was plenty more of it over the horizon with water aplenty and minerals to boot. And the New World was peopled with movers and shakers.

Then there is the so-called "Puritan work ethic," which has no equivalent in many cultures, to compound religious sanction and the illusion of infinite resources.

Out of all this, and perhaps much else, came an unquestioning faith in growth——in production, consumption, and population——until Stewart Udall described the per capita Gross National Product as our Holy Grail.

Somewhere along the line, we must have slipped inadvertently into assuming that "the greatest good for the greatest number" was a simple addition of individual "goods," though Bentham had something more in mind in his definition of "the good society."

Yet if Americans have been possessed with the search for material things——if they have made their decisions too exclusively on the basis of quantitative criteria——if they have measured their presumed state of well-being with numbers that take little or no account of social and human costs, it is still pertinent to note that most of us thought the name of the game was "a decent standard of living" for all, which is a goal not without social or moral or humanistic content.

It is also pertinent to note that the one product of western civilization which has turned out to have universal appeal is not our religions or philosophies or political principles or social systems but our technology. Modern technology, which is almost exclusively Western in origin, is wanted everywhere in the world and for the same reason it has been pressed into service in the West: to create a "decent standard of living for all."

Non-Western philosophical perceptions of harmony between man and nature did not withstand the "revolution of rising expectations," once increased per capita consumption appeared to be a feasible proposition. As the political leadership in nation after nation made economic growth its first priority, fatalism about natural forces and the human condition began to fade as the prevailing mood in most of the world.

One does well, then, to look beyond philosophies to the five-year plans for economic development——and to the smog, traffic jams, noise and crowding in Seoul, Bangkok, New Delhi, or the trash and garbage piled around the picnic grounds on Mount Fuji. The position of man-in-the-landscape in old Chinese painting is often cited as evidence of the spirit of harmony between man and nature. So there may be a bit of irony in the point that the greatest collection of Chinese painting in the world is in Taiwan——which also has one of the world's highest rates of sustained growth in Gross National Product, something which doesn't happen unless there is a "will to develop," which in turn involves human intervention in natural systems.

Neither environmental pollution nor addiction to growth is, as it turns out, an American or a Western phenomenon. Search for the Holy Grail of rising per capita Gross National Product is near-universal. And in that pursuit the newly industrializing countries are making most of the mistakes made by those who brought off the industrial revolution in the first place. This may lay a special burden on the shoulders of the highly industrialized, but hardly justifies self-flagellation about the sins of "materialism."

It is being said by some that the capitalist system, with its addiction to profit and perpetual expansion, is the real devil of the piece. It's a simple, straightforward explanation, but it doesn't help at all. About a decade ago, Nikita Khrushchev gave a famous interview to William Randolph Hearst, Jr., which was widely misread at the time. "We will bury you," Mr. Khrushchev said at one point, and the threat was taken as a military or ideological one. Not at all. What the Chairman of the Communist Party of the Union of Soviet Socialist Republics was saying was that socialism would bury capitalism by out-producing capitalist countries in consumer products: meat, butter, radios, refrigerators, vacuum cleaners——the whole consumer durable goods bit.

The fact that this has not happened, or come close to beginning to happen, is not cited in defense of free enterprise or to poke fun at socialist planning. The point is that even Mr. Khrushchev was running after the Holy Grail——even though he stood Karl Marx on his head in the process.

In 1968, Soviet delegates to the UNESCO Conference on the Biosphere surprised many by distributing a long study of water pollution problems in the Soviet Union. Two years later they were prepared to discuss problems of atmospheric pollution as well.

National planning has helped many nations make more rational allocation of resources. But neither Marx's "scientific" vision of social history, nor the obsession with state planning that followed Lenin, prevented the world's leading socialist society from making a mess of its environment any more than have free enterprise and mixed economic systems. State managers, like private entrepreneurs, it appears, have had their eyes fixed on quantitative, physical production without much regard to economic externalities, social or aesthetic costs, or the impact upon environmental quality.

No doubt the search for devils will go on and no doubt industry will be the principal goat.

No one is likely to blame the scientists and technicians and doctors who figured out how to lengthen life expectancy, and thus set off the population explosion.

Not many will blame farmers who in places add more pollution to rivers and lakes than does industry. Much farming in this country is now known as agro-industry, but people still think of a farmer as a little guy who works hard at an essential occupation.

Government, except for the military, will not be blamed so much because its failures are, at bottom, failures on the part of the public.

The consumer is not likely to see himself as the major culprit, no matter how many cans are strewn around the country or cars abandoned on the streets.

Industrial pollution is highly visible; industry is seen to be big, bureaucratic, and greedy. So while it might be more objective to conclude that there are no devils in this story——or alternatively that just about everybody shares the blame——the chances are that industry is in for a large part of the pollution rap.

Economic Growth vs. Ecology
There is a simple approach to the task of breaking the human race of its

historic habit of exploiting and degrading the natural environment.

Swear off. Quit. Stop. Don't do it!

And this, unhappily, appears to be about as far as most people, including some professional conservationists and many activists, have gone in their thinking so far. This attitude may be good enough to prevent the filling of an estuary to put up a high-rise apartment, or to divert an expressway that road engineers want to drive through urban neighborhoods, or to save a wilderness from destruction by a jetport ——to mention a few specific cases in which environmentalists have won signal victories in the recent past.

Much more of this will be done and will itself induce far-reaching changes in decision-making. Already the courts have granted "standing" to suits brought on the basis of public interest without proof or claim of financial damage to individuals. It may well be that constitutional grounds exist for asserting the "right" of the public to a decent environment. Competent legal aid to "defend the environment" is rapidly becoming available, and so are expert witnesses for law suits to estop some proposed project. It may be prophesied safely that the traditional protection afforded by the law to the right of a man or a corporation to do whatever he wants to do with personal property unless it causes calculable damage to others is about to be a thing of the past.

It probably would be impossible, even if it were desirable, to stop "economic growth" as conceived in the past. Automatic stimuli of dynamic growth deliberately have been built into the system over the past thirty years——usually, incidentally, for respectable social ends, such as high employment. No-growth ignores the effect of compound interest; and Edwin Dale has written in *The New York Times Magazine* that "we are almost 'condemned' to a rise in our total output of four percent."

We may redirect economic growth more into services than manufactures; we may shift our notions of what constitutes a "decent standard of living;" we may to some extent downgrade the virtue of "affluence;" we may reorient, among other things, product research, marketing methods, advertising, and concepts of cost and profits.

But it is politically, socially, and morally unthinkable that we shall abandon all forms of economic growth——or that we shall create major unemployment in the name of a cleaner environment. "Affluence" has arrived for no more than about half the population. The ghettos are still there, the poor are still with us, and they are unlikely to respond to the notion that this is their permanent status because economic growth is wasteful of resources, an insult to the environment, and therefore wicked.

Yet at the risk of offending well-intentioned and constructive people, it must be said that some conservationists appear to reverse the distortions of the past by putting the interests of Nature above the interests of man. They appear to be as unconcerned about the human side-effects of protecting the environment as others have been about despoiling it——as arrogant toward Man as others have been arrogant toward Nature. They would deny that they dream of returning to a pastoral society in which Nature is secure from artificial interventions and the people can enjoy the blessings of even-handed poverty, but at times they sound as though this would be a logical conclusion to be drawn from what they say.

Don't-do-it and take-them-to-court may be a necessary and valuable tactic to contain indiscriminate bulldozing of the landscape and mindless paving through the cityscape——a holding action and even a forge for the shaping of social and aesthetic criteria for injection into decision-making processes. But it is not a viable long-term strategy.

A Reassessment of Priorities

Pollution has been with us for a long time. Someone has pointed out that the drinking water was becoming polluted in Rome during the first century B.C. Spanish explorers landing along the Pacific Coast noted that smoke from Indian fires hung in the air above what is now Los Angeles. Not to mention the man-made deserts where forests once grew in the Middle East and North Africa. Or the dust-bowl in mid-America.

The head of the biology department of a major university points out that the air in most of the major cities of the northern hemisphere is less polluted today than it was thirty or forty years ago——because in the interim it has become more economical to burn oil than soft coal. So it can be denied that there is an "environmental crisis" in the sense that some vast and irreversible ecological disaster is on the near horizon.

But to deny or doubt the existence of a "crisis" is to miss the main points. In the narrowest context, the main point is that the proliferation and combination of pollutants in air, water, and soil raises sufficient potential hazards to human and other life, and enough of a danger of temperature and other climatic changes, so that prudence demands that industrialized societies take urgent steps to minimize the hazards.

In a wider context, there is the immutable fact that the ecology is a permanently closed system with finite resources which will not support indefinitely rising curves of population growth and production-consumption-disposal cycles; so prudence also demands that the human race as a whole cease and desist from its age-old habit of passing the buck to future generations. There is little doubt that some form of disaster would become inevitable on the assumption that we all continue to do indefinitely what we have been doing in the past, especially since the first industrial revolution.

Yet it is inconceivable that the human race would knowingly and deliberately destroy its own life-support system. And this is where the inner character of the "crisis of the human environment" begins to be exposed: The trade-offs between action and side-effects henceforth must be made in the here and now.

If there is to be no likelihood of choking to death in our own waste, we must change our ways. To change our ways, we must make decisions on different sets of criteria than we have been using before. To do that we have to adapt traditions and traditional ways of looking at things and weighing their values. This means social change——perhaps pervasive enough to be called "cultural mutation."

Technology is needed; money is needed; but so are new ways of calculating "costs," defining "progress," measuring "growth," and making economic, social, and political decisions in the course of which attitudes, values, and even philosophical and religious perceptions will come into question.

Assuming that there is, in fact, something like a national consensus to the effect that the environmental buck stops here, the "crisis" has more to do with economic-political-social change than with more and better sewage treatment and smoke abatement, essential though these may be. It is a crisis not just for the environment but for traditions and institutions as well.

And if there is not a working national consensus——and ultimately an international one——then the task of fostering the understanding essential to such a state of mind is itself one of crisis proportions.

The Question of Environmental Management

Faced with finite resources and unable to turn back the clock, we must identify a radical solution of the resources problem before long.

One place to start might be with the proposition that Man can alter Matter but he cannot destroy it. In this sense, nothing is "consumed," and "nonrenewable" resources like minerals are used but not "depleted."

This makes an urgent case for a massive research and development program on the technological possibilities for recycling and reusing resources now effectively "consumed" in industrial processes.

For the short term, a wide variety of new measures may be needed: a requirement on biodegradable materials; an end to planned obsolescence; inclusion of disposal costs in price calculations; new methods of using or recovering wastes; a moratorium on the launching of some types of new products; power rationing, etc.——all of which will have pervasive effects on traditional thought about economics, social policy, relations with government, and other matters difficult to identify at this point.

But unless finite resources ultimately can be reused more or less infinitely, there is a traumatic barrier somewhere down the road which the world is currently traveling. Whether the "fusion torch" holds a large part of the answer remains to be seen. Meanwhile, it is not unreasonable to demand, as *Science* magazine did recently, that "the next industrial revolution" must take place in the area of new technology for reusing and recycling the materials we extract or divert from Nature.

In gearing up for such an effort, it might be useful to think of the whole process as one of converting the economy from a "dirty" to a "clean" production-consumption-disposal system. This may turn out to be more difficult and prolonged than the conversion of the economy from a peace-time to a war-time footing in the early 1940's. But the analogy may not be wholly useless; we learned how to allocate resources to priority tasks very efficiently indeed. The catch is that the war-time system was highly authoritarian——which brings up something close to the ultimate question: how to devise democratic participation in decision-making on the use of limited resources.

It is possible, if not probable, that the present focus on air and water pollution and solid waste disposal will induce the public illusion that the problems can be solved by money and technology, legislation and litigation. The pervasive impact of environmental management on decision-making processes and criteria may remain out of view. But not for long.

It seems more likely that the value changes predicated by the need for environmental management are more likely to emerge from hundreds of separate decisions in public and private life, as one decision after another requiring trade-offs comes up for action, than from the meditation of scholars. The two-dimensional, either-or choices posed by the don't-do-it approach will have to give way when it is recognized that neither excessive pollution of Lake Erie nor the abolishment of 2,000 jobs in Port Huron are acceptable alternatives and that better answers must be found.

What may be even more misleading than confusing the job of pollution abatement with the more fundamental socio-political-economic impact is the danger of losing sight of the global implications of a unitary environment. Noise in New York, carbon monoxide in St. Louis, sewage in the Potomac, mercury in the Missouri: these may appear to be, and often are, local problems——like smog in Seoul and sulphates in the Rhine. Public concern so far has tended to be narrowly parochial.

And if the image of Spaceship Earth was a trigger for environmental awareness, that image remains in gross conflict with parochialism——the root of some large fraction of human traditions in all societies. It can be argued that concern for "the human environment" should extend to the environment surrounding the individual family——and that attachments to sub-cultures as well as to national groups should be maintained in the essential interest of cultural diversity. But parochialism too often turns around a concept of "interests" which implies competition and rivalry; and these can indeed be dangerous.

The concept of conflicting parochial interests is close to the heart of international discord and the institution of war. The traditional doctrine is simple——and deadly: national societies, especially great powers, have "national interests;" these interests inherently conflict; the interests of A can only be served at the expense of the interests of B; A and B are thus concerned about their "security" in the pursuit of their interests; security is served by being militarily "superior" to nations with conflicting interests; therefore, rival-interest states and groups of states arm themselves and——in the nuclear age——the result is a "balance of terror." This may only be a scary way of describing a *pax atomica,* but it is a state of affairs which, at best, is ludicrously anachronistic when viewed from the perspective of outer space.

In some profound sense, Man has reached a point in his relations with the environment at which national traditions, rooted in parochial concepts of interests, are anachronistic, irrelevant, and obstructive if not ultimately fatal to those who retain them.

When the Second World War was over and the atomic age was born, many people concluded that the nation-state was an obsolete institution in the war-and-peace context. It can be said now that the nation is not a viable unit for coping with the socio-political side effects of modern science as a whole.

Yet it does not follow, as too many have concluded, that nations and their concepts of sovereignty must be abolished in favor of world government, even if that were a practical or desirable proposition.

What is needed, rather, is somehow to pull together the major functional institutions of the world community, to infuse their leaders with an ecological point of view, and to turn toward the solution of the environmental problems rooted in modern science. Out of this could emerge a more rational world community, bearing little likeness to the world governments dreamed of by the constitution-drafters but more relevant to the natural world, which values diversity.

What has to be suppressed is not national governments but the spirit of national rivalry rooted in the notion that differences imply competitiveness and competitiveness implies dominance. What has to be cultivated and nourished is diversity and the respect of diversity——the honoring and not the exploitation of difference——or at least a tacit decision in the interest of survival to put up with people who are different , whether one likes it or not.

A new ethic for international conduct might well begin by insisting more upon tolerance of diversity than upon the concept of brotherhood which has come to rest upon the similarities-despite-the-differences among men.

Neither tribes nor nations need become one to cope with their common and unitary life-support system. And since the natural world is hostile to monocultures, an ecologically-oriented world might learn to become more hospitable to the notion of cooperation among diverse peoples and cultures——even if some still insist on holding their noses in the process.

Security and Progress

Institutions are seldom responsive to the observable obsolescence of their traditions. In 1953, J. Robert Oppenheimer foresaw that the day would come when a nation with 20,000 thermonuclear bombs would not necessarily be superior in any real strategic sense to a nation with only 2,000 thermonuclear bombs——that the numbers would no longer measure useable military strength——that the whole pattern of military and political traditions that historically had led nations into competitive programs of armament would no longer be relevant to societies in possession of large numbers of atomic weapons which would impose a qualitative balance of strategic military power. He was excommunicated from the institutions he served. Seventeen years later, there was some reason to hope that Soviet and American leaders were beginning to accept the concept of a qualitative parity; yet they approached the Strategic Arms Limitation Talks armed with computer-processed data, presumably in search of quantified trade-offs.

In 1963, Lynton Caldwell, Professor of Government at the University of Indiana, published an article in *Public Administration* in which he analyzed with extraordinary clarity the impact of environmental problems upon planning and policy processes, upon values and institutions. [2] He is said to have been chided by academic colleagues for imagining relationships which did not exist. Seven years later, at least two newspapers noticed the coincidence between Earth Day and the birthday of Nikolai Lenin, and concluded that the environmental crisis was a communist invention.

Somewhere deep in the corpus of the present predicament is the accelerating rate of scientific discovery in conflict with stubborn traditional attitudes. One is tempted to paraphrase Pogo: We have met the enemy and it is our traditions.

To believe that the human race is unlikely to choke to death or be submerged in its own waste in the next thirty years is not to disbelieve that the next thirty years may well be the most critical period in human history.

There are some things you don't see from outer space——things you have to know if that view is to liberate the mind from the deadweight of tradition and prepare the way for the emergence of a world point of view free from the distractions and distortions of suffocating alleyways of specialized knowledge and thought.

One has to know, for instance, that the multiple major world crises have similar origins and analagous characteristics. All have begun with significant achievements of the human intellect; all are the by-products

2. Lynton K. Caldwell, "Environment: A New Focus for Public Policy," *Public Administration Review*, XXIII, 3 (September 1963), pp. 132-139.

of human success; all began as amoral and apolitical events which were to have side effects rarely foreseen and seldom even recognized until now:

. A revolution in medical technology greatly increased life expectancy——and largely created the population explosion.

. Successive industrial revolutions relieved whole populations of arduous physical labor and provided them with undreamed-of material standards of living; they also led to a prodigal exploitation of natural resources and a sinister fouling of the natural environment.

. A revolution in agricultural technology permitted less than 10 percent of the U.S. population to raise enough food for itself and the other 90 percent, to export large quantities, and to give away more; it also sparked a mass migration of people from land to city which became a major cause of urban crowding and decay.

. A revolution in international communications and transport technology——coming at a time when over 100 million people were being released from colonial status—— increased the interdependence of nation-states; they also helped stimulate leaders in a hundred or more countries to want to "develop" essentially along the lines of the industrialized West.

. A revolution in the science of physics converted matter to energy, opened up vast new sources of power——and led to a mutual capacity for mutual destruction on the part of the two most powerful nations in the world.

These paradoxes and ambiguities all arise from man's historical struggle against disease, hunger, poverty, war, and ignorance: they are by-products of the classical pursuit of "security" and "progress." What is new is the speed with which each of those trends has come to the point of crisis in the twentieth century. And in a fundamental sense, it is all the same crisis: in its population dimension——in its urban dimension——in its nuclear weapons dimension——in its environmental dimension, the overall crisis represents the social fallout of modern science.

In this perspective, the question of whether the greatest danger to human health comes from the tires, brake linings, or exhaust pipe of an automobile is a technical quibble: even "the Environment" is too narrow a framework for thinking about the total impact of science upon society.

Cooperation in Crisis

Fear can set people at each other's throats——or unite them against a threat that is perceived to be common to them.

The single life-support system on which all men depend is under sufficient threat to warrant a united defense by the tribes of man. For the first time it can be said——not just rhetorically but in a hard, objective sense——that all Earth's peoples are truly in the same boat whether they know it yet or not.

There can be little doubt that the nations of the world are about to start up an enterprise which ultimately should lead to global management of Earth's environment——a task for which their experience has not prepared them and their institutions are not adequate. There is hope in the recent fact that international cooperation between states which have seen themselves as political rivals has not depended upon the emergence of good will and mutual trust, but upon technological imperatives and mutual needs. Yet ideology, tradition, mistrust, rivalry, secrecy, inexperience—— all stand as obstacles to success for a common enterprise of such scale and ramification that it would force an historic break in the way nation traditionally has related to nation.

What's more, the fear of unacceptable damage to the unitary life-support system is not shared everywhere. The fear of starvation and malnutrition——concern for economic development goals——dominate the thoughts of political leaders in almost all the countries in early stages of development. A suddenly discovered concern for the quality of the environment thus could have a bitterly divisive impact on international relations, if the cures appeared to be at the expense of economic development goals.

In the global framework, which is the only context in which Earth's environment can fit, a priority task of extraordinary political and psychological complexity emerges: to maximize the unifying effects and minimize the divisive effects of our new awareness of Earth's environment and the need to manage our relations with it in the interests of the human race.

If this should fail, a new version of the Apocalypse begins to emerge ––one that is perhaps more realistic than sudden disaster through a nuclear exchange or a precipitate ecological collapse. This is the gloomy prospect of a slow but accelerating slide into unmanageable social chaos.

Uncontrolled and interacting population growth, urbanization, resource depletion and environmental degradation––compounded by cultural trauma, massive unemployment, political inexperience, and institutional breakdown––accompanied by alienation, crime, violence, corruption, and addiction: this *could* be the vicious cycle alternative to a rational and cooperative international response to the "crisis of the human environment."

It is not yet clear exactly what the term "environmental management" will turn out to mean. It is even less clear how the costs of it will be divided within the international, regional, and national societies. Whatever thinking has been done about it so far has been applied to aspects involving the arrest of increased pollution, a measure of "clean-up" to meet emerging standards, and the indefinite maintenance of undefined levels of environmental quality. However the burden is shared, this will be a very costly business.

Yet this may be only the beginning of it. Public demand may go well beyone "reparations" for past damages to Nature. The environmental movement conceivably could burst into a much wider dimension embracing aesthetics––in natural settings, in cityscapes, in neighborhoods, in architecture, in roadsides, in harbors and bridges, in landscape design, in products, even in advertising.

If something like this is the ultimate dimension of "environmental awareness," and if political leadership is serious about being responsive, then enormous costs will be involved for a long time to come. Any conceptions of "environmental quality" such as those just mentioned are, of course, exercises in futility in the absence of a radical reduction in defense spending.

Those who are really serious about the quality of the environment would do well, as an intensely practical and directly relevant matter, to address themselves to the tangled issue of arms control. New questions need to be asked:

Why can't intelligence-gathering satellites be adapted to monitoring arms control agreements?

Are strategic conclusions drawn from geopolitical analysis really valid in the age of nuclear weapons and space travel? For example, is the "strategic bridge" between Africa, Asia, and Europe in the Middle East as strategic as it was in Mahan's time, and what are the implications for the Sixth Fleet?

In the age of overkill, is it really true that a measure of unilateral disarmament would hand a military advantage to the other side?

Have both sides grossly exaggerated what the other would consider "unacceptable damages?"

Could it even be argued that any nation which launched a massive nuclear attack would itself suffer damage——in terms of environmental injuries——that would be considered unacceptable to rational men, even if there were no nuclear retaliation at all?

Such questions need answers quite apart from concern for financing improvements in environmental quality. But it is not inconceivable that a new awareness of the vulnerability of Earth's life-support system might suggest some new handles on the arms control problem which traditionally has been approached within either an impractical moral framework or a narrow military one which has lost touch with reality.

Present Indications of Change

Without reference to peace protests or "student unrest" or underground movements, it may well be that the current chorus in favor of new values and social changes is already out of date. We may, in fact, be deep in an unmeasurable and unpredictable process of transformation in traditions and value systems:

One can state in respectable society today that "the automobile must go" without being accused of being drunk, and noise has become a current topic for dinner conversation.

There is open talk of enforced limitation of families, and little doubt that abortion will be legalized generally.

Several hundred conservation cases are pending before the courts, many involving injunctions against projects which even months ago would have been welcomed by almost everyone as sure signs of "progress."

Lawyers are boning up on "environmental law" and scientists are rallying to the side of the environment in the name of the public interest.

The "zero growth" movement finds adherents.

The Los Angeles Chamber of Commerce confronts an organization called "For a Lesser Los Angeles."

A majority of industrial leaders polled by *Fortune* are in favor of Federal establishment and enforcement of nationwide air and water pollution standards and oppose the introduction of new products without adequate testing of their possible side-effects. [3]

More or less radical young lawyers argue cases supported by local chapters of the DAR and retired Admirals.

Citizens are no longer sure that they want their community or county or even their country to continue to grow.

It can be argued that widespread public demand for change comes to the surface only after the forces of change already are in motion and moving irresistibly. Whether or not this is always true, there is considerable evidence that the sudden explosion of public concern for environmental quality follows rather than precedes the unleashing of forces of social change, related or unrelated to specific environmental issues.

Thus the "value" problem may not be one of engineering changes in attitudes but of shaping actions in accord with attitudinal changes already in process.

A Global Effort

In 1946 the government offered to make a dramatic and radical political adjustment to a revolutionary development in the science of physics. The so-called Baruch Plan proposed, in effect, to build a special international house as the exclusive abode for nuclear physics research and development in order to obviate the dangers of national competition for atomic weapons. Unhappily, it was not accepted.

3. Robert S. Diamond, "What Business Thinks About Its Environment," in "The Environment, A National Mission for the Seventies," by the Editors of *Fortune* (New York, Evanston, and London: Harper and Row, Publishers, Perennial Library No. P-189, 1970) pp. 55-64.

There were powerful historical, national, ideological, and political reasons for the failure of the Baruch Plan. These were greatly compounded by the fact that the first technological application of the New Physics took the form of a military weapon; weapons are the symbols of international discord; and international discord stems from an assumption that the interests of major nation-states inherently conflict. Thus political tradition survived the impact of a major breakthrough in science, and man began to live with a new fact of life: he had acquired a capacity to destroy himself.

The intervening quarter-century has brought a succession of new scientific breakthroughs and the development of associated technologies——in medicine, agriculture, industry, transport, communications, and space travel. In a large sense these culminate in what we now call the "crisis of the human environment"; and inherent in that crisis lies another human capacity for self-destruction, not in an instant of blast and fire, but through long neglect and a lack of enlightened political will.

Yet the perception of an environmental crisis offers a new and more hopeful chance on a world scale to adapt politically and socially to the achievements of modern science.

Unlike the nuclear weapons problem, environmental management does not require the yielding of national sovereignty over an area of activity emotionally associated with historic conceptions of security. It does not require a single, sudden break with tradition but can proceed step by step from research to cooperation to institution building. It rests on technical rather than political analysis and judgment, and on relatively easy recognition of common interests. The gradual reform of political tradition inherent in technical cooperation would be a subtle process and need not be explicitly recognized as part of any agreement.

This is not to say there will be no political problems or politically based institutional problems. It is to say that the world has a fresh chance to rebuild and strengthen the United Nations system so it can keep the peace not by using armies to repair it in the breach, but by providing services so valuable to all nations that the corrosive tradition of national rivalry gradually will wither and someday die on the vine, unnoticed and unlamented——the best thing that could happen for the human environment.

Part 2

The Environmental Crisis and the Federal Government — An Interpretive Overview

The environment is an intricate physical system; doing something about it is a complex political problem.

While scientists are looking for hard data which are not yet available, political leaders are looking for concepts, plans, programs, and priorities for which there is no experience and little to go by. Both are only at the beginning of their quest, but one thing is sure: political decisions cannot await conclusive scientific data on the ecosystem and its inter-play with human life. Many of those decisions will have to be made by the Federal Government – often without being sure what the side-effects will be.

In early 1971, any judgment on the adequacy or inadequacy of the Federal Government's reaction to the environmental crisis is necessarily subjective and tentative. And the stimulus-response pattern of public opinion, Congressional initiative, and Executive action obviously inter-acts and is difficult to unravel.

The conservationist viewpoint has been represented in Congress for a long time; indeed, the first concept of "national parks" found expres-sion in the Yellowstone Act, passed by the Congress in 1872. Many Federal agencies have had long-standing interests and obligations for the protection of natural resources.

Yet, generally speaking, when conservationists tangled with develop-ers on the Federal Government level, they usually have lost for reasons which have now become familiar.

What has happened in Washington in recent months is what has happened elsewhere: a sudden surge of interest and activity – part response and part stimulus to a rising public awareness of a pervasive threat, not just to Redwoods or Whooping Cranes or wilderness areas, but to "the environment" which sustains all life on Earth.

Benchmarks for the new awareness in Washington can be assigned arbitrarily – for example, the passage by Congress of the Federal Water Pollution Control Act of 1956 or the Clean Air Act of 1963 or the first establishment of exhaust emission standards for 1968 model automobiles. These and other events were part of the background and build-up to the great explosion of public interest that occurred around the turn of last year.

January 1, 1970, however, is as good a date as any for starting to measure Federal response to the newly-recognized crisis of the environment. On that day President Nixon signed into law the National Environmental Policy Act of 1969 which, among other things, brought into being the Council on Environmental Quality (CEQ). At that point, it could be said that the Federal Government was seized with the environmental issue and, as in the case of pregnancy, this could hardly be a casual or limited condition.

In its broadest form, the political issue posed by the environment and related issues is whether governmental institutions, conceived under other circumstances and dedicated to other goals, can adapt to the requirements of environmental management – whether the decision-making processes can ingest new concepts, viewpoints, and values broadly enough and quickly enough to sustain confidence that the institutional system can still work. Some already have concluded that established bureaucracy is inherently and literally incapable of such reform – though more would insist that it be given a chance.

Somewhat more concretely, the general political issue can be framed this way: can or will the Federal Government mount a sustained national effort adequate to cope with the environmental predicament? The question suffers the liability that no one knows just what the environmental predicament is; but it can be suggested that such an effort would require these basic ingredients:

> Public support
> An overall policy
> A set of priorities
> Action programs
> Institutional mechanisms

Money
The political will to initiate, act and persevere.

Against these criteria, one can look at the brief record between January 1, 1970, and the end of the year.

It is not difficult to conclude that the Federal Government is not doing enough about the environment – perhaps not doing nearly enough; or that sharper policy direction is needed; or that priorities are misguided or missing; or even that rhetoric masquerades for understanding and commitment. But it is self-deluding to begin with the premise that next-to-nothing is being done, because that premise is wrong. Quite a lot is being done; more is in the works; much more is being researched or planned or just brooded about.

Public Support

Early fears that public concern for environmental quality would turn out to be just another passing fad ignored a basic point: the problem is real and will not go away by itself. Indeed the task of environmental management is permanent and, since even successes create new problems, it can be concluded that general public interest in environmental quality – no doubt with erratic highs and lows and with shifting points of focus – will remain as a continuing factor in public opinion that elective officials must take into account.

But the clear and unanswered question is: environmental quality at what price? The cause of clean air, pure water, and uncluttered landscape per se is about as popular as an early spring in New England. Yet the focus on these symptoms of the environmental issue has left the costs, except in purely financial terms, largely unexplored in the public discourse.

An emerging energy crisis may well force the question of alternatives and concomitant trade-offs to the forefront of public debate in the very near future. At that point, a split in public opinion could develop between the haves and have-nots. There was a foretaste of this in mid-1970 when a coalition of Puerto Rican organizations banded together to support Consolidated Edison's proposal to expand its Astoria generating plant in Queens, a step which would raise the level of air pollution in New York City. In Queens as in East Asia, energy is valued above environmental quality by those who feel they have not shared in the present supply. "Power to all the people" could turn out to be a slogan with a new dimension.

Advocacy of plentiful power will not, of course, come only from the poor. When Consolidated Edison restricted power deliveries in New York in the dog days of late July, 1970, a headline writer for the New York Daily News added a gratuitous editorial by topping the story with this headline: CON ED CUTS VOLTS WHILE WE GET MUGGED.

Yet in the longer run, this confrontation between those who are "for" and those "against" will be seen to be superficial: neither excessive pollution nor crippling power shortages will be acceptable as permanent conditions. Mayor Lindsay's decision to split the difference – by approving half the proposed expansion of the Astoria plant——is at best a stop-gap style for decision-making.

For the moment neither the Federal Government nor public opinion appears to be ready to face the range of hard choices, with their various levels and kinds of costs – and breaks with tradition – implicit in environmental management. Only when that happens will answers begin to emerge to the question: how much environmental quality at what price does the public want?

In the meantime, it is a good guess that general public opinion is, and likely will remain, somewhat ahead of Congressional opinion and that Congressional opinion is, and likely will remain, somewhat ahead of the Executive Branch in reaction to the environmental crisis. Straight political considerations will inspire each of the two major parties to try to talk a better environmental game than the other. Nor will either Congress or the Executive Branch wish to be seen dragging its feet. The net effect will be to raise the level of mutually reinforcing pressures for action.

Thus, the negative conclusion appears clear: the Federal Government is unlikely to be constrained in the near future through lack of public support for environmental action.

Policy

The National Environmental Policy Act of 1969 provides for the first time just what its title says it provides: a national policy with respect to the environment, voted by the Congress and signed by the President.

The language of the Act necessarily is general, its goals necessarily abstract. As broad policy, however, it is clear and comprehensive. It begins by recognizing "the profound impact of man's activity on the interrelations of all components of the natural environment..." and declares it national policy to "use all practical means and measures" to:

fulfill the responsibilities of each generation as trustee of the environment for succeeding generations;

assure for all Americans safe, healthful, productive, and esthetically and culturally pleasing surroundings;

attain the widest range of beneficial uses of the environment without degradation...;

preserve important historic, cultural, and natural aspects of our national heritage...;

achieve a balance between population and resource use...;

approach the maximum attainable recycling of depletable resources. (For complete text see Appendix A.)

As to how these goals can be pursued, the Act instructs all agencies of the Federal Government, among other things, to take "a systematic, interdisciplinary approach which will insure the integrated use of the natural and social sciences and environmental design arts... ." Moreover, the Act directs the Executive Branch to develop procedures "which will insure that presently unquantified environmental amenities and values may be given appropriate consideration in decision-making ... ."

All this is easier to say than do, but for overall policy and general approach it would be difficult to ask for more. This leaves it up to the Executive and the Congress to add flesh to the skeleton of broad national policy.

Four quite substantial pieces of policy flesh were recommended officially before 1970 had run its course.

The first is for the development of a comprehensive national energy policy. "Even now," says the Council on Environmental Quality in its first report to the President on the state of the environment, "the nation needs to use its fuel resources more effectively through development of a national energy policy."[1]

An ultimate need for rational allocation of roles to alternate sources of future power supply has been foreseen for many years, but has been opposed strongly by the major industries involved; and previous Administrations have been happy to look the other way and hope for the best. It seems unlikely that this Administration can do the same for long. It can expect increasing Congressional and public pressure to bring future power supply and demand into a manageable relationship reasonably consistent with environmental protection.

1. U.S., Council on Environmental Quality. "Environmental Quality," First Annual Report to Congress (Washington, D.C.: Government Printing Office, 1970). (See Appendix B for excerpted chapter on "Present and Future Environmental Needs.")

An August 1970 report by the Energy Policy Staff of the President's Office of Science and Technology proposed a four-part program for resolving the apparent conflict between power needs and environmental protection:

(1) long-range planning of utility expansions on a regional basis at least 10 years ahead of construction.

(2) participation in the planning by the environmental protection agencies and notice to the public of plant sites at least 5 years in advance of construction.

(3) pre-construction review and approval of all new large power facilities by a public agency at the state or regional level, or by the federal government if the states fail to act.

(4) an expanded program of research and development aimed at better pollution controls, underground high voltage power lines, improved generation techniques, and advanced siting approaches so as to minimize the environmental problems inherent in existing technology.[2]

On August 6, 1970 the White House announced that the President had asked the Domestic Council "...to study the national energy situation and to develop for his consideration new or revised policies." In addition to consideration of immediate near-term problems, the Council was requested to recommend Federal actions to ensure an adequate fuel supply for the next five years. The members of the Council committee include the Secretaries of State, of the Interior and of Health, Education and Welfare; the Director of the Office of Science and Technology; the Chairmen of the Council on Environmental Quality, the Federal Power Commission, the Atomic Energy Commission, and the Council of Economic Advisors (who will also chair this committee); the Director of the Office of Emergency Preparedness; the Special Assistant to the President for Consumer Affairs, and the Director of the Office of Management and Budget.

The second major area requiring national policy formulation, in the view of the CEQ, is land use. In the chapter on "The Status of the Land" in its report to the President, the Council concluded:

...the above summary does indicate the need for developing standards to evaluate what is happening to this basic resource [land] and to develop policies that will guarantee its continued integrity. In short, there is a need to begin shaping a national land use policy.[3]

2. U.S., Executive Office of the President, "Electric Power and the Environment," a report sponsored by the Energy Policy Staff, Office of Science and Technology (Washington, D.C.: Government Printing Office, August 1970), p. iii.

The Council stated that "the reforms in government activity needed to institute a national land use policy are undeveloped at this time" but indicated ten "aspects of a strategy" which it believes merit special attention. [4]

Nor was the CEQ the first body to note the need to allocate land to chosen uses – a favorite topic of some for years past. A few months before the CEQ report, a major study by the Public Land Law Review Commission made extensive proposals in the direction of comprehensive land use planning and policy. [5] The Commission was established by the Senate Committee on Interior and Insular Affairs and its proposals presumably have a future on Capitol Hill.

A third area in which the CEQ assumes the need for national planning is the field of transportation. No specific recommendations are made in its report. But again, the need has long been foreseen; and again, general concern for environmental quality is adding to the steam behind proposals for national planning in major sectors of the economy.

The fourth major policy proposal since passage of the Environmental Quality Policy Act is in the field of ocean pollution; it will be referred to at a later place.

Meanwhile the prickliest issue of all is getting increasing policy attention. In the spring of 1970, the President announced the membership of his Commission on Population Growth and the American Future to consider, among other things, "what steps the Nation should take to best meet the problems of excessive population density and too rapid growth."

On September 15, 1970, in his message to the Congress on Foreign Assistance for the Seventies, the President proposed "...that the United States place strong emphasis on ... the special problem of population."

> The initiative in this area rests with each individual country, and ultimately with each family. But the time has come for the international community to come to grips with the world population problem with a sense of urgency. I am gratified at the progress being made by the new United Nations

3. CEQ, op. cit., p. 191.

4. Ibid., p. 192.

5. U.S., Public Land Law Review Commission "One Third of the Nation's Land," A Report to the President and to the Congress (Washington, D.C.: Government Printing Office, June 1970).

Fund for Population Activities and propose that it undertake a study of world needs and possible steps to deal with them. In order to cooperate fully in support of this international effort, the proposed U.S. International Development Institute should focus the energy and expertise of this country on new and more effective measures for dealing with the problem of population.[6]

More generally on the policy front, President Nixon's brief letter in August 1970, transmitting to Congress the first annual report on the state of the environment, raised the decibel-rating of his Administration's official voice of concern about environmental degradation. He referred to "our environmental crisis," warned of "the prospect of ecological disaster," and spoke of the need for "effective environmental management." Presumably this strengthens the hands of those within his Administration who had been using similar language vis-a-vis those who have deplored "hysteria" and counseled a "more balanced"view of the environmental issue. (See Appendix C for full text of the President's message.)

The President's letter to Congress also reflected a sense that managing the environment has implications for society well beyond the technology of pollution abatement. Indeed he used the word "reform" in four places within less than two pages. And in one sentence he bit the bullet directly:

We must seek nothing less than a basic reform in the way our society looks at problems and makes decisions.

The thrust of that statement was not amplified; whether it will remain in the category of rhetoric cannot be known at this time. But the President said it to Congress and that makes it official Administration doctrine.

With an overall environmental policy on the books, with official support for comprehensive national policies on energy, land use, and transportation, with an official commission exploring the population issue, with the President calling for a "basic reform" in problem-solving and decision-making, a tentative conclusion can be reached that the Federal Government is acquiring the beginnings of a policy base for a sustained national effort to cope with the environmental crisis.

6. U.S., Congress, House, Congressional Record, 91st Congress, 2nd Session, 1970, Vol. 116 No. 160, p. H. 8698.

Priorities

President Nixon's special message to the Congress on problems of the environment transmitted on February 10, 1970, focused on four subjects:

(1) Water pollution
(2) Air pollution
(3) Solid waste disposal
(4) Accelerated acquisition of public parks and recreation areas.

These can thus be taken as the first list of national priorities for the Federal Government in tackling the environmental issue. (For full text of this message and for excerpts from the State of the Union address, January 22, 1970, see Apendixes D and E.)

The Council on Environmental Quality, however, hints in its first report that the priority problem is not solved by naming the major symptoms of environmental malaise: "In the future, the difficult task of deciding the Nation's environmental priorities must be faced."[7] The problem begins, the Council says, with the lack of current knowledge about environmental quality generally, and is compounded by great regional differences, one result being that Federal priorities will not always coincide with state priorities.

"Resources for combating environmental blight and decay are limited," the Council says, and "Choices will have to be made on which problems have first claim on these resources." Such choices will have to resolve "deep conflict over which problems are most important." For the time being, the best that the CEQ could do in its first report was to suggest four main criteria for determining priorities:

> The intrinsic importance of the problems – the harm caused by failing to solve them.
>
> The rate at which the problems are going to increase in magnitude and intensity over the next few years.
>
> The irreversibility of the damage if immediate action is not taken.
>
> The measure of the benefits to society compared to the cost of not taking action.[8]

Part of the reaction of the Federal Government, then, has been to

7. CEQ, op. cit., p. 237.
8. Ibid.

establish a first rough set of priorities, and to recognize that the task will become tougher and more sophisticated as the problem unfolds.

Programs

The Federal Government's action programs for coping with environmental issues generally reflect President Nixon's first identification of priority problems. Extensive and detailed material on the scope, status, funding, and legislative authority for these programs is available elsewhere and they need only the briefest mention here.

Water Pollution

The Federal Government's five-year, $10-billion program against water pollution within the United States is reasonably well defined and funded. One positive factor is that existing abatement technology is adequate for significant progress toward cleaner water resources.

At the same time, there is recent evidence that the scope of the problem may have been seriously underrated; e.g., the unsuspected discovery of mercury contamination in Silver Lake in a remote and almost inaccessible corner of Vermont.

And while the CEQ report stated that "The Nation is on the threshold of a major attack on water pollution," it also listed under "what needs to be done" in the water pollution field: more research, development, and demonstration; a significant increase in investment; management reforms; area planning; manpower training; and intensified attacks on such problems as agricultural pollution, eutrophication, recycling of wastes, and thermal pollution.[9]

In the long run, the report said, "control of water pollution will require institutional and management changes, possibly some changes in the products that people consume."[10]

Maritime pollution, of course, is another and more complicated matter: this raises technical, institutional, legal, and political problems on the global scale.

The Nixon Administration, however, has made three specific legislative proposals dealing with the pollution of international waters. Legislation was submitted to Congress in November 1969, to provide com-

9. Ibid., pp. 55-59.
10. Ibid.

prehensive management by the states of the land and waters of the coastal zone and in April 1970, to control dumping of dredge spoils in the Great Lakes. On October 7, 1970, the President transmitted the report of the Council on Environmental Quality entitled "Ocean Dumping: A National Policy" with a promise to submit specific legislative proposals to implement this report's recommendations to the next Congress. (See Appendixes F and G for message and report, "Findings and Recommendations.")

The Ocean Dumping report, recognizing that "...International cooperation is essential to preservation of the oceans...," recommends that "...the Federal Government develop proposals to control ocean dumping for consideration at international forums such as the 1972 UN Conference on the Human Environment at Stockholm... . Provision should be made for:

> Cooperative research on the marine environment and on the impacts of ocean dumping of materials;
>
> Development of a worldwide monitoring capability to provide continuing information on the state of the world's marine environment;
>
> Development of technological and economic data on alternatives to ocean disposal.
>
> Domestic and international action is necessary if ocean dumping is to be controlled. The United States must show its concern by strong domestic action through implementation of recommended policy. But unilateral action alone will not solve a global problem. International controls, supported by global monitoring and coordinated research, will be necessary to deal effectively and comprehensively with pollution caused by ocean dumping.[11]

Air Pollution

By late 1970, the Federal Government's program against air pollution in the United States was well on the way toward establishing air quality control regions covering more than half the population; the National Air Pollution Control Administration had its own network of more than 1,000 air sampling devices supplementing state and local monitoring facilities; and by the election recess of Congress, the Senate had proposed authority to establish national air quality standards with enforcement procedures and severe penalties for violation – a proposal which stirred a lively argument about whether such standards would operate as maximum or minimum curbs on pollution levels.

11. U.S., Council on Environmental Quality, "Ocean Dumping: A National Policy" (Washington, D.C.: Government Printing Office, October 1970), p. 37.

The cost of bringing the four major sources of air pollution in a hundred metropolitan areas under control within four years has been estimated at $2.6 billion – less than one percent of the value of the annual product of the industries involved and very probably well under direct financial damages from polluted air. In its own context, then, clean air is a bargain and, as in the case of water pollution, the necessary abatement technology is in hand or in sight.

But in the background of the seemingly manageable air quality problem are the issues of energy policy, the future of the internal combustion engine, mass public transport, Federal-State-local government relations in the enforcement of standards, and the foreign affairs implications of pollution transported in the atmosphere from nation to nation and continent to continent.

Solid Waste Disposal

The Solid Waste Disposal Act of 1965 limited the Federal Government's program to providing assistance in research, training, technology demonstrations, technical assistance, and grants for state and interstate planning. The Federal Government could do little about the tangled web of local jurisdictions, issues, and politics.

President Nixon said in his environmental message to Congress that he had ordered a "redirection" of research to place greater emphasis on recycling and the development of degradable materials, but he did not ask for additional funds. The CEQ report asserts that "The Federal government is heavily committed to the emerging technology of salvaging and recycling" and it refers to current work on a "recycle strategy."[1][2]

Here again, as in the case of water quality, Congress stepped ahead of the Executive Branch and in the Resource Recovery Act of 1970, signed by the President October 26, expanded the Federal Government's authority and greatly increased its financial muscle for dealing with solid waste management. The purposes of the 1965 Act were expanded to include:

> to promote the demonstration, construction, and application of solid waste management and resource recovery systems which preserve and enhance the quality of air, water, and land resources;
>
> to provide for the promulgation of guidelines for solid waste collection,

12. CEQ, First Annual Report, p. 119.

transport, separation, recovery, and disposal systems; and

to provide for training grants in occupations involving the design, operation, and maintenance of solid waste disposal systems. [13]

The 1969 fiscal year authorization of $32,500,000 for solid waste management activities was lifted to $50,250,000 for fiscal 1971 and increased to $238,500,000 by 1973. Included in these ceilings were authorizations for Federal grants to states and municipalities for up to 75 percent of costs for resource recovery systems and improved solid waste disposal systems – $80,000,000 authorized for fiscal 1972 and $140,000,000 for fiscal 1973.

The 1970 Act directs the Secretary of HEW to submit to the Congress within two years "...a comprehensive report and plan for the creation of a system of national disposal sites for the storage and disposal of hazardous wastes... ."

The Act also created the National Commission on Materials Policy to conduct studies leading to the development of a "...national materials policy to utilize present resources and technology more efficiently, to anticipate the future materials requirements of the Nation and the world, and to make recommendations on the supply, use, recovery and disposal of materials."

Parks and Public Recreation

In his message to the Congress on environmental affairs, President Nixon recommended "full funding in fiscal 1971 of the $327 million available through the Land and Water Conservation Fund for additional park and recreational facilities... ." Congress responded by appropriating for the 1971 fiscal year $357 million (the then accumulated amount in the Fund). Congress also, by separate legislation, raised the annual ceiling on the Fund from $200 to $300 million. (The Fund is fed by net receipts from the sale of surplus government real estate, charges for use of Federal recreation areas, the Federal excise tax on fuel for pleasure boats, and an allocation, to fill the balance in the authorized ceiling, from receipts of the outer continental shelf oil leases.)

The President also outlined a series of steps for possible conversion and transfer of Federal properties and idle cropland for use as public parks and recreation areas. What this will turn up remains to be seen.

13. Public Law 91-152, 91st Congress, H. R. 11833, October 26, 1970, Sec. 101.

Increasing interest has also been evidenced by the Administration recently in the development of marine and estuarine parks.

Environmental Education

In his message to Congress transmitting the first annual report of the Council on Environmental Quality, the President said, "Our educational system has a key role to play... . It is ... vital that our entire society develop a new understanding and a new awareness of man's relation to his environment – what might be called 'environmental literacy.' This will require the development and teaching of environmental concepts at every point in the educational process."[14]

On October 30, 1970, the President signed Public Law 91-516 authorizing a new program of education about the environment. The U.S. Office of Education is authorized to provide support for environmental education programs in elementary and secondary schools, development of curricula, teacher training, planning of outdoor ecological study centers, and preparation and dissemination of informational materials. The Act also establishes a program of small grants – under $10,000 annually – to civic groups and other public and private organizations to conduct courses or conferences for adults and community groups.

The new law authorizes a three-year $45 million program – $5 million in fiscal year 1971; $15 million in fiscal 1972, and $25 million in fiscal 1973. Actual availability of funds is subject, however, to annual appropriation within these ceilings.

All in all, the President's message in February outlined "a comprehensive, 37-point program" made up of 23 legislative proposals and 14 measures to be taken by Executive Order or Administrative action. They all dealt with the first four priority areas for national attention to the environmental crisis, plus Administrative actions. By Executive Order and policy direction, the President has undertaken to set examples of pollution abatement by Federally owned facilities. (See Appendixes H and I.)

Institutional Mechanisms

In July 1970, President Nixon sent to the Congress two reorganization plans for a far-reaching restructuring of Federal Government responsi-

14. CEQ, First Annual Report, p. vii.

bilities for dealing with the environment. Two new agencies were created – an Environmental Protection Agency (EPA), effective December 2, 1970 under Reorganization Plan 3 (see Appendixes J and K) and a National Oceanic and Atmospheric Administration (NOAA), effective October 3, 1970 under Reorganization Plan 4 (see Apendix L). Most if not quite all of the scattered agencies and units dealing with segments of the environmental problem throughout the Federal structure were combined in these institutions, the first of which has the major day-to-day operational responsibility, while the second would work on longer-range aspects of environmental modification with more emphasis on research on such matters as temperature and climatic effects. Budgets and staffs would be transferred from existing agencies; there would be no new funds for the present. (See Appendix M for Interim Organization of NOAA.)

Not the least of changes on the institutional front is the requirement laid down in the Environmental Policy Act for all Federal agencies contemplating projects with implications for environmental quality to prepare for CEQ a full statement and analysis of environmental consequences and alternatives prior to going forward with the project. The statements are to be available for inspection by the Congress and the general public. Guidelines to Federal agencies for the preparation of these statements, drawn up by CEQ, appear to interpret strictly the terms of the National Environmental Quality Act. (See Appendix N for the guidelines.)

This requirement is potentially a radical step toward reform of governmental procedures. Its practical impact on the Federal machinery remains to be seen, and the procedures for arbitrating conflict remain obscure.

The long and short of it is, however, that a major reorganization of the Federal structure is in the works in response to the environmental crisis. Administratively, the point is to end piecemeal responsibility, duplication, overlapping, and proliferation in favor of centralized control. But beyond that, the point is to place responsibility for bringing to bear an "environmental point of view" outside the functional Departments concerned with separate sectors of economic and social life.

The least that can be said is that a large amount of bureaucratic crockery is likely to be cracked in the process.

Money

Has the Federal Government allocated sufficient funds to finance a sustained national effort to cope with the problems of the environment? In August 1969, the National Citizens' Committee on Environmental Quality did not think so. In a report to the President at that time, the committee said: "The hard fact is that over the past few years a number of promising environmental programs have been authorized, but the money to fund them has simply not been forthcoming."[1][5]

Since then appropriations, especially for clean water, have picked up significantly. Estimated Federal funding for all pollution control and abatement programs for the last three fiscal years show the following totals:

1969:	$862 million
1970:	$1.5 billion
1971:	$4.8 billion

(See Appendix P for more detailed Federal Funding tables and Appendix Q for Report on Federal Expenditures on Research, Development, and Demonstration Related to Funding for FY 1969 and FY 1970)

If the question is whether funds have been made available to take the first steps in anti-pollution programs that seem feasible in the light of present knowledge and institutional capabilities, the answer might be a qualified yes.

If the question is whether financial resources are being mobilized, in the words of National Environmental Policy Act, "to assure all Americans safe, healthful, productive, and esthetically and culturally pleasing surroundings," the answer, of course, would be quite different.

Political Will

The degree of commitment of any government to deal with the crisis of the environment necessarily is a function of its total commitments: priorities assigned to environmental programs must fall within the overall scale of national priorities, whether these are established by long-term plan, pragmatic flexibility, or political opportunism.

15. Citizens' Advisory Committee on Environmental Quality, "Report to the President" (Washington, D.C.: The Committee, August 1969), p. 7. (See Appendix O for reprint of Committee's Table on Federal Funding.)

In the United States, the environmental crisis moved toward the center of the public stage at a time of lively and emotional ferment over national priorities. Environmental issues have contributed to the tension and complexity of that debate.

Behind this challenging of the order of national priorities lies a world caught up in multiple patterns of change. The post-war view of a bipolar world is becoming blurred; structures of cold war confrontation are cracking; thunder fades from the crises of the 1950's and 1960's; a national consensus on post-war foreign policy seems somehow overwhelmed by novel issues and accelerating change.

Yet old issues have an anachronistic and often expensive way of lingering on to compete for the attention of political leaders, to lay claims upon resources, to put constraints on action in other areas. And how far a major power can go by itself in disengaging from old but unresolved issues and their related commitments is a nice question for political science.

On balance, world affairs appear to be moving in a direction favorable to an increasing mobilization of will and resources for a larger-scale, sustained effort by the Federal Government to cope with environmental issues.[16]

Yet in looking at the "pressing needs for tomorrow," the Council on Environmental Quality report said that what is needed most of all is a conceptual framework as a point of departure for approaching environmental problems.[17]

When it comes to the environment, the Federal Government – like the natural and social sciences – has a long way to go merely to comprehend the arts of managing relations between Man and Nature.

---

16. As this book was going to press, a further measure of President Nixon's commitment to environmental action was provided in his February 8, 1971, message to the Congress. The full text of this message is included in Appendix DD.

17. CEQ, First Annual Report, pp. 231-232.

Part 3

The Environment and the World Community

A. An Overview

At the beginning of 1971, very little was known in a systematic way about the specific reactions of governments around the world to the emergent crisis of the environment. A few generalizations, however, could be put forward:

Concerns about environmental degradation had spread throughout the highly industrialized world.

National action programs were in various stages of formulation or execution; e.g., the United Kingdom already had made significant progress in the abatement of air and inland water pollution; Sweden was actively pushing environmental research; the Council of Europe proclaimed 1970 as "Conservation Year" and promoted public awareness of environmental issues; the Soviet Union showed increasing alarm about the integrity of its water, soil, and air resources; the current Indian five-year plan includes environmental policy guidelines; in Japan, a prolonged mid-summer photochemical smog over Tokyo put an end to political apathy about environmental conditions and led to the establishment of an emergency cabinet-level group, chaired by the Prime Minister, to develop a national program of action.

In the developing world, first reactions to the sudden concern about an environmental crisis ranged from indifference to deep suspicion.

By the latter part of 1970, however, a number of governments in the developing world had come to the conclusion that they, too, were in trouble with the natural system; e.g., Singapore, Indonesia, Malaysia, Yugoslavia, Mexico, and several governments in Central and South America.

Regardless of the perspectives and actions or inactions of national governments, the fact remains that the oceans which cover three-quarters of the planet and the atmosphere which surrounds all of it are the common resources of all nations and peoples; the interactions between sea and air influence climate and weather affecting everyone; and pollutants discharged into inland waters and domestic skies more often than not wind up in the international commons. These problems being world-wide by definition, resolution of them is inherently a matter for global cooperation.

Moreover, the near-universal drive for industrialization has created and will create increasingly analagous problems of resource conservation, urbanization, population pressures, and other issues that plague the more developed societies. And while action programs in such areas can and should be on national and subnational bases, the advantages of cooperative research and exchanges of information and experience are obvious.

If governments are to tackle seriously even the most pressing environmental problems, they are condemned, whether they like it or not, to a level of internationalism that will set precedents and ultimately alter the way in which sovereign nation-states traditionally have related to each other.

The present community of international organizations is even less prepared for the tasks of environmental management than are most national governments. Nonetheless, the United Nations and its system of agencies constitute the principal institutional foundations for international cooperation in the environmental field; their activities reflect the interests of the member nations which must finance their programs, and it is here that the levels and directions of agreed international concern will become manifest.

Nongovernmental international organizations, especially those of the scientific community, also have a present and future role in environmental affairs.

A review of public and private agencies on the multinational level leads to the following general conclusions:

1. International organizations, mainly but not exclusively represented by the United Nations and its agencies, have been engaged, in some cases for many years, with a large number of questions now subsumed under the rubric of environmental problems. (A summary description of these activities is provided in the following chapter.)

2. These activities, however, have been sublimated to the overriding goal of promoting economic growth, essentially along historical patterns of industrialization, in the less developed areas of the world.

3. As with national governments, the international agencies have pursued their interests on a specialized, functional basis with little or no coordination and without an integrative, environment-oriented point of view. They have approached research and problem-solving on the traditional linear basis.

4. In the recent past, international organizations, like national agencies in the United States, ostensibly have tended to abandon the previously prevailing "conservationist" point of view and to adopt an "ecological" approach toward matters within their purview.

5. Nongovernmental organizations, especially international scientific unions and foundations, are also moving toward adoption of an ecological approach, toward interdisciplinary research, and toward systems analysis.

6. In the international community of agencies there is no dissent from the view that environmental management will not be possible without major and novel extensions of international cooperation and action programs under international direction.

7. Proposals abound for treaties, conventions, and mechanisms to cope internationally with environmental problems, but there is no consensus on whether the emphasis should be on new institutions or on the adaptation, coordination, and reform of existing agencies. In either event, there are important implications for the future of the United Nations.

8. The UN decision to convene a Conference on the Human Environment in Stockholm in late June of 1972 has served to stimulate and to orient the current work of the UN agencies, and to some extent other international organizations, toward that event; and this has imposed a rough but discernible scenario of activities on the part of international agencies concerned with various aspects of environmental problems. Much the same may be inferred about the plans and activities of national governments as they relate to environmental problems with international implications.

A New Awareness

UNESCO's Biosphere Conference in 1968 might be identified as the first sign of an environmental point of view emerging within the community of trans-national organizations. It is more convenient, however, to think of the introduction of the Swedish Resolution in the General Assembly as the trigger of a new international awareness of an environmental crisis. That Resolution, authorizing the world conference, was passed unanimously by the General Assembly in 1969. (Text of the Resolution is found at Appendix S.)

Generally speaking, the work done within the UN agencies in the past is being reviewed for its potential contribution to the Stockholm conference, and the Specialized Agencies have been engaged in preparations for that event. The Economic Commission for Europe, a regional UN body, has scheduled for the spring of 1971 a conference on environmental problems common to industrially advanced countries; this can be considered as part of the preparatory process, as can, in some measure, environmental studies under way in the North Atlantic Treaty Organization and the Organization for Economic Cooperation and Development.

Nongovernmental organizations also are engaged in substantive preparations for the world conference – notably the International Council of Scientific Unions and the International Union for the Conservation of Nature and Natural Resources.

The agenda of the Stockholm conference itself is being planned around six major subject areas: human settlements; natural resource management; control of pollutants and nuisances; environmental education; development impact; and organizational implications of action proposals.

The UN Secretariat hopes to make available in advance of the conference a major paper on the state of the human environment and, in the process, to provide a conceptual framework for coming to grips with the issues of environmental management on the international level.

In the early planning stages, it is expected that much of the conference deliberations will be devoted to agreeing upon a work program for the years ahead on subjects which can be identified as requiring international action. The list could be an extensive one.

In addition to adopting this work program for future action, it is expected that definitive decisions can be taken at Stockholm on at least a few international steps toward environmental management.

One likely candidate for decision is agreement to proceed with the creation of a global network of environmental monitoring stations to collect the first comprehensive data on pollution of the world's commons and on selected environmental phenomena. Another candidate for action is an international convention against dumping wastes in the oceans. A third might be an agreement to manage the waters of the coastal zones, particularly around the environmentally crucial estuaries where fresh water, salt water, and their living organisms comingle.

If conventions or other international agreements are to be adopted at Stockholm, the terms will have to be well worked out in advance of a conference of more than a thousand delegates from more than a hundred countries – a poor forum for technical negotiations. Yet the technical details will count for far less than the political temperament of the Stockholm meeting.

The United Nations has no authority and no resources save the authority and resources which its members agree to transfer to it; its attainments and shortcomings are those of national governments acting, or failing to act, together. The world organization will be able to move toward management of the global environment only to the extent and only at the pace which reflects the lowest common denominator of the will of the member governments; and that is a political, not a technical question.

This has to be looked at in two major contexts – for shorthand, the East-West and North-South dimensions.

The East-West Context

The United States and the Soviet Union are the largest industrialized technical societies in the world and enough is known to conclude that there is not much to choose between a free enterprise economy and a socialist economy when it comes to burdening the environment – an observation that applies to "East" and "West" generally.

The post-war history of East-West relations shows that cooperation has been possible when both sides perceived it to be in their national interests to cooperate – and especially in matters that inherently cannot be pursued unilaterally: for example, international rules for aerial navigation and the international allocation of radio frequencies.

Soviet and American interests in the integrity of the global environment are fundamentally, if not in detail, identical. It is difficult to avoid the conclusion that the environmental crisis will lead to major cooperative action and to strengthening the world community in its East-West dimension; to what extent and how rapidly will depend upon shared political will to leave behind the outworn assumption that "national interests" are naturally conflicting – to shift attention from "power vacuums" to living systems – to discern that the fate of nation hinges upon the fate of man.

The North-South Context

The North-South dimension is quite another story. Here there is danger that a potentially unifying concern for the quality of Earth's environment could turn out to be politically divisive. It would be bitter irony indeed if a new awareness of the unity and fragility and finite character of the global life-support system were to provoke a confrontation between the rich and the poor nations of the planet. Yet this may be more than a distant danger.

The root of the issue lies in suspicions about the motivations behind sudden concern in the industrially developed countries for the quality of their environment. Such suspicions are quickened by the popular literature of the environmental movement in the United States. In articles, books, speeches, television shows, the impression is left, explicitly or implicitly, that concern for environmental quality and concern for better standards of living are on a head-on collision course – that economic development and environmental quality are mutually exclusive.

In too much of the environmental literature, man is simply left out of the picture: yet for many millions "the environment" means a squalid hut, a patch of poor ground, and a shallow well with dirty water – or the four walls of a room shared with rats in a city slum.

So – cast in ideological terms – the environmental movement becomes an imperialist plot to keep down the poor countries, restrict their economies to raw material production for factories elsewhere, and retain in the hands of the already-rich a monopoly on profitable world trade in manufactures. A less ideological and more specific fear is that a dollar spent on environmental improvement in the industrialized areas will be a dollar transferred from developmental assistance funds for the countries just beginning to industrialize.

It is demonstrably not true that the environmental issue is something for the rich alone to worry about. The greatest obstacle to improved living standards in most of the poor countries is the same population explosion which is at the root of most environmental problems almost everywhere. Some of the developing countries are facing urban futures that will make Harlem, by comparison, look like a pastoral scene. The three cities with the worst air pollution in the world are Seoul, Taipei, and Ankara; and "unspoiled Africa" already is a myth. Ocean pollution threatens the fishing activities of rich and poor country alike – and the diets of the poor more than the diets of the rich. The whole range of land, water, forest, and mineral conservation issues also exist in various combinations in the developing countries. So it goes.

In large measure, the presumed conflict is a semantic issue. People in more developed countries are likely to look upon, say, urban growth and off-shore oil drilling as "environmental" problems, while people in less developed countries look upon them as "development" problems. Yet both see them as problems. The perspective depends upon the point of departure; but the two perspectives must be synthesized in an acceptable fashion if a political collision is to be avoided. And this is one measure of the task before the Secretariat of the United Nations in working out a conceptual framework for the Conference on the Human Environment. The trick is to see man at the center of both environmental and developmental concerns.

In point of fact, a movement toward convergence of the two lines of thought already is taking place; some of the ecologists and economists are accommodating their doctrines to the other's perspective.

This process began, somewhat paradoxically, by documenting the fact that many completed development projects, including some of the more ambitious ones, have turned out to be disappointing and, in some cases, disastrous. Hydrological projects have had damaging physical and social side-effects; irrigation works have increased the incidence of water-borne diseases and created problems of salinity; dams have damaged crop yields by stopping sediment flow and had deleterious effects on coastlines; and clearing of tropical forests has turned soil into barren crusts.

The list of ecological boomerangs from development projects is now a long one, and it is not simply the result of heedless "exploitation." Nor do these horror stories prove that, in the interests of environmental health, the world must stop building dams or irrigating land or controlling pests. What they prove is that the environmental imperative is not just to begin to learn how to manage the environment but to begin to learn how to conceive, plan and manage economic development in a way that will not produce side-effects seriously damaging to the environment, to human health, or to the social fabric. The search is now on for environmentally sound guidelines for economic development planning and for improved methodologies of forecasting environmental side effects of economic activity.

Robert S. McNamara, in his report to the U.N. Economic and Social

Council on his second year as President of the World Bank Group, emphasized the importance of evaluating the environmental consequences of development projects:

> The problem facing development finance institutions, including the World Bank, is whether and how we can help the developing countries to avoid or mitigate some of the damage economic development can do to the environment, without at the same time slowing down the pace of economic progress. It is clear that the costs resulting from adverse environmental change can be tremendous. It is equally clear that, in many cases, a small investment in prevention would be worth many times over what would have to be expended later to repair the damage.
>
> In the Bank, therefore, we recently have established a small unit to foresee, to the extent possible, the environmental consequences of development projects proposed to us for financing. Even more important, we want to work toward concepts that will enable us and other development financing agencies to consider the environmental factors of development projects in some kind of cost-benefit framework. I am well aware of the complexities of the task. But I am equally convinced of its importance.[1]

The United Nations Development Program (UNDP) has helped finance institutions for conservation and resource management; has studied the environmental problems of man-made lakes; and is developing policy guidelines for shaping economic and social development along ecologically sound lines.

The (U.S.) Agency for International Development has contracted for environmental post-audits of completed development projects, especially in tropical zones, and is adapting project review and survey procedures to take earlier account of possible environmental side effects.

Yet however rational the case may be for universal interest in environmental quality, there is a tough psychological-political hurdle to clear: the more developed countries began worrying about the problem only after they had built their industries and attained affluence. Leaders of impoverished countries may be responsive to the notion that they should avoid making all the same mistakes made by the industrially advanced countries – provided this does not include the "mistake" of raising material standards of living.

---

1. Address to the U.N. Economic and Social Council by Robert S. McNamara, President of the World Bank, the International Finance Corporation, and the International Development Association, November 13, 1970, United Nations, New York. See also Michael L. Hoffman, "Development Finance and the Environment," *Finance and Development* (a publication of the International Monetary Fund and the World Bank Group), VII, 3 (September 1970) pp. 3-6.

Organizing the World Community
for Environmental Management

During the month of July 1970, a large group of scientists and other professionals gathered on the Williams College campus to focus on "environmental problems whose cumulative effect on ecological systems are so large and prevalent that they have worldwide significance."[2] The summer study, under the sponsorship of the Massachusetts Institute of Technology, had been in preparation for nearly a year; it had been conceived as a contribution to preparations for the Stockholm conference and the work may be carried another step by an international group before that conference convenes.

All in all, the several work groups made thirty-five recommendations. But the group found that data required for analysis and projections with respect to environmental problems was so fragmentary that its first recommendations were for the development of new methods for gathering and compiling global information, for studying the possibility of international measurement standards, and for immediate work on a global environmental monitoring system.

There can be little doubt, then, that the environmental crisis will stimulate a major program of international data exchange; coordinated, cooperative, and combined research efforts; and the emergence of international standards for such things as measurements and instrument calibration. This is likely to require world data processing centers and common computerized information storage systems, perhaps as part of a permanent global monitoring system.

Beyond this, and the likelihood of new conventions on ocean polluting and other matters, there is no consensus on how the international community needs to organize itself to watch the world.

Some see the environmental crisis as an opportunity to make the United Nations truly universal by bringing in China and "unrecognized regimes" resulting from the divisions of Germany, Korea, and Vietnam. Others see it as requiring the industrialized countries to form their own organization to do battle against the environmental degradation for which they are mainly responsible.

In the fall of 1970, the U.S. Senate passed a Resolution (S. Res. 339;

2. The study group's report of findings and recommendations was published by the MIT Press in the Fall of 1970 under the title "Man's Impact on the Global Environment."

see Appendix T) urging the establishment of a World Environmental Institute to act as "a global research center and to disseminate knowledge of environmental problems and their solution to all nations of the world upon their request... ."

Some in the international science community recommended a larger role in environmental affairs for nongovernmental groups, including regional associations of academies of science. The International Council of Scientific Unions has established a Scientific Committee on Problems of the Environment which may establish, in turn, a recommended International Center for the Environment.

There is no lack of suggestions for new world institutions – including some which would establish separate organizations for policy, operations, research, funding, and enforcement.

On the other side of the institutional coin, there was the question – with no agreed answers – of the impact of the requirement for environmental management on the United Nations system. Should there be an overall agency charged with dealing with global environmental problems? Could the existing Specialized Agencies and other organs of the United Nations somehow be infused with a broader and shared environmental way of looking at things? Could not the environmental concern be used as an instrument to induce reforms and the coordination which is lacking within the present system? Will the UN itself take a new lease on life and move more rapidly toward fulfillment of some of the high expectations inspired by its charter a quarter of a century ago?

The Environment and National Interest

Relations between sovereign nation-states still reflect nineteenth-century geopolitical concepts of power and national interests, including peace, which arms are intended to serve. If the option is open, one or more of the major powers traditionally chooses to pursue its goals – often competitively – on a national basis. Under such concepts, governments develop a large number of "secrets" which they protect in the interests of national security.

Protecting the environment has nothing to do with national security, where the interests of nations may collide, but with global security, where the interests of nations can only converge. In environmental affairs there are no secrets to protect from others; nor is there the option of competitive pursuit of environmental goals.

It may take governments a while to adjust their concepts and consequent attitudes to the radically different kind of international relations opened up by the perception of a global crisis of the environment. When they do, the relevant institutional forms for environmental management will suggest themselves. And they will be the institutions of a far more open world, a much more cooperative world, a world in which information increasingly represents the only useable form of power and the power is freely shared.

B. Summary of International Organization Activities in Environment–Related Fields

The United Nations

The United Nations Secretariat, the Specialized Agencies and the Regional Economic Commissions are all, in one way or another, concerned with questions which are now subsumed under the heading of "environmental problems," quite apart from the work of the UN Population Division and other international activities related to family planning. The following is a summary description of those activities:

The Secretariat

Environmental questions are handled within the UN Secretariat in the Department of Economic and Social Affairs and involve the following units:

The Office of Science and Technology. Among other things, it has an advisory committee on the development and rational utilization of natural resources.

The Social Development Division. Relevant work includes studies of the social aspects of industrialization and urbanization, research and training programs for regional planning, and development and utilization of human resources.

The Centre for Housing, Building and Planning. Its concerns include the development of measures designed to prevent deterioration of the human environment due to urban sprawl, over-crowding, noise, air and water pollution, traffic congestion, etc.

The Resources and Transport Division. Within its purview is the planning of integrated development of whole river basins involving the need for difficult trade-offs.

The Public Administration Division. This impinges on environmental questions through such activities as a comparative study of administrative aspects of urbanization.

The United Nations Development Program

The Development Program has helped to finance a large number of resources surveys, projects related to conservation such as afforestation and land reclamation, studies of ecological changes as a result of proposed creation of large man-made bodies of water, and training programs such as the Forestry and Watershed Management Training Institute in Argentina, similar institutes in Turkey and Chile and forestry training projects in the Philippines, Lebanon, and Jordan.

It is expected that the Development Program will be in a better position in the future to insist upon a more rigorous application of an environmental approach to economic development decision-making.

The United Nations Scientific Committee on the Effects of Atomic Radiation

The Committee was established in 1955 in response to concern about radioactive fallout from nuclear weapons testing. It has produced five technical reports on prevailing levels of natural and man-made radioactivity in the atmosphere, soil and oceans, in food chains, and in human tissues, and has estimated mean doses to populations and attendant health hazards. It seems probable, partly as a result of the work of this Committee over the past fifteen years, that more is known about radiation than any other pollutant. (Perhaps the more significant point is that the AEC financed the research by the Oak Ridge Laboratory which provided the hard data for internationally agreed conclusions on tolerable levels of radiation in the atmosphere.)

The Specialized and Affiliated Agencies

A capsule review of the relevant interests of the UN's Specialized and Affiliated Agencies follows:

The International Labor Organization. The Organization is concerned with occupational health and hazards and thus with such specifics as the prevention and suppression of dust in mining, tunneling, and quarrying, and in air pollution control in industrial establishments. It develops model safety codes and guides on such questions as atmospheric controls in foundries. Its International Occupational Safety and Health Information Center abstracts materials dealing with air pollution questions from more than thirty national centers.

The Food and Agricultural Organization. FAO is deeply involved in conservationist aspects of soil, forests, and terrestrial waters -- and, for example, with water quality criteria for fish, integrated pest control techniques, pulp and paper mill effluents, and the use of sewage effluents for agriculture, forestry, and fisheries. The Organization has been working with an inter-agency experts group on scientific aspects of marine pollution and in December 1970 sponsored in Rome a Technical Conference on Marine Pollution and Its Effects on Living Resources and Fishing. FAO also has been active in promoting the following international conventions and agreements:

Fisheries Councils in the Indian Pacific and Mediterranean Regions;

Commissions for Controlling the Desert Locust in the Near East and South-West Asia;

A Commission for the Control of Foot-and-Mouth Disease in Europe;

An Inter-Governmental Agreement for the Control of African Horse Sickness in the Near East Region;

The International Plant Protection Association; and

An International Commission for the Conservation of Atlantic Tunas.

United Nations Educational, Scientific, and Cultural Organization. UNESCO has been more deeply involved in more aspects of environmental problems than any of the intergovernmental organizations – and probably has come closer to adoption of an ecological point of view.

Beginning from its earliest years with research on natural resources and programs on such problems as Arid Zone Research and Humid Tropics Research, UNESCO established the Intergovernmental Oceanographic Commission and sponsored the International Hydrological Decade; it is now working with WMO on an Integrated Global Ocean Station System for monitoring the ocean environment.

By 1968 the organization started a long-term program on "Man and the Biosphere" to supplement a social science program on "Man and His Environment – Design for Living" begun in 1966.

In describing the work of UNESCO on environment-related questions, the Secretary-General's report includes this statement: "...UNESCO has particular obligations in these fields because *it is becoming increasingly clear that development programmes must be structured on the basis of sound ecological principles and that there is no rational use without conservation.* [1] Given the preoccupation of a majority of the members of the UN with development programs" this principle acquires potential significance for future consideration of environmental problems within the United Nations.

World Health Organization. WHO's concerns with the human environment have focused on three aspects.

1. The definition of environmental standards, including research designed to establish the limits of human adaptability to various stress factors.

2. The identification of environmental hazards – air, water, soil, and food pollution – the effects of pesticides, the ecology and biology of disease vectors, the abuse of drugs and noise. This has led to the establishment in 1967 of an international reference center for air pollution and a year later, the International Reference Center on Waste Disposal and Community Water Supply.

3. The study of the effect of induced changes in the environment, such as rapid population changes, massive migration, urbanization, rapid industrialization, and the construction of irrigation dams and man-made lakes.

World Meteorological Organization. WMO is engaged in the development of a World Weather Watch, based on an international monitoring

1. The UN's Economic and Social Council, "Problems of the Human Environment," Report of the Secretary-General (New York: E/4667, May 26, 1969) p. 57 Mimeographed.

system with world data processing centers in the United States, the Soviet Union, and New Zealand. The relevance of these facilities to proposed monitoring systems to keep watch on atmospheric and maritime pollution raises technical questions already under study at MIT, the U.S. National Committee for the International Biological Program, and elsewhere. The WMO is currently planning, in conjunction with the International Council of Scientific Unions, a Global Atmospheric Research Program. It has, among other things, worked on standardization of instruments and techniques for data collection and analysis; studied the relationship of air pollutants, meteorology, and plant damage; and worked with the International Atomic Energy Agency on the measurement of isotopes in precipitation.

International Maritime Consultative Organization. IMCO is the repository of the 1954 International Convention for the Prevention of Pollution of the Sea by Oil, strengthened by amendments adopted at an IMCO conference at Brussels in November 1969. It also studies new methods for the removal of oil from the sea, techniques for protecting coastal areas from pollution, and the detection and penalization of deliberate marine pollution.

International Atomic Energy Agency. The IAEA's environment-related functions turn around monitoring, studying, and providing technical assistance on radioactive pollution of all environments, and problems involving storage and disposal of radioactive wastes. It maintains research laboratories in Monaco and Seibersdorf in connection with this work.

International Civil Aviation Organization. ICAO's concern with the human environment centers on two subjects: aircraft noise in the vicinity of airports, including studies of human tolerance to noise; and the problem of the "sonic boom."

The UN Regional Economic Commissions

The Economic Commission for Asia and the Far East. Except for emphasis on prevention of slums in connection with urban and regional planning, ECAFE appears to have treated with questions of river pollution, soil erosion, and air pollution only in connection with specific development projects such as hydroelectric and thermal power stations.

The Economic Commission for Latin America. ECLA has been involved for a decade in analyses of Latin American water resources and their potential uses, including multi-purpose river valley projects. In connection with this work, such questions as pollution of rivers and streams and waste water disposal, for example, have been considered, though consistently within an economic development context.

The Economic Commission for Africa. ECA has been engaged almost exclusively in helping develop policy-making and planning machinery on a regional basis and in the development of resources, though it maintains that "appropriate account of the environmental implications" is observed.

The Economic Commission for Europe. ECE has been by far the most active of the regional commissions on environmental problems, especially in the fields of industrial pollution of water and air. Because the ECE includes the United States and the Soviet Union, and members from both Western and Eastern Europe as well as nonaligned states, its work can be seen as a testing ground for East-West cooperation in the environmental field and therefore merits special attention. A summary follows:

1. Water: The ECE first took an interest in water pollution in 1957 when it initiated a study identifying specific water pollution control problems. A committee on water problems and a subsidiary body to survey water resources and needs, each meeting annually, were created. The committee sponsored a seminar on oil pollution in December 1969 and one on river basin management in June 1970.

2. Air Pollution: In 1969 the ECE established a working party on air pollution control to meet once a year. It conducted a seminar on the desulfurization of fuels and combustion gases in November 1970 – the result of a suggestion by the USSR. A number of standing committees also have air pollution control programs including the Steel Committee, the Coal Committee, and the group of experts under the Inland Transport Committee who are considering various standards to govern the manufacture of motor vehicles.

3. Cities: The ECE's Committee on Housing, Building and Planning has been active in urban environment for over 20 years. This committee sponsored a Symposium on Urban Renewal in Budapest last April and May. Under the Committee is a working party on Urban Renewal and Planning, which has sponsored seminars and studies, including ones on

land use planning, development of recreational areas and urban transport.

It is evident from this brief survey that United Nations agencies – like national governments and private organizations – have followed a functional approach to problem-solving which has led to overlapping interests and sometimes to working at cross purposes.

Other Inter-Governmental Organizations

Outside the United Nations system, other inter-governmental organizations, originally established for collective defense or for promotion of economic growth, are in early stages of adjustment to an awareness of environmental problems. The following notes do more to suggest the range of institutional facilities available for international cooperation in this field than to describe their present activities and plans.

The World Bank

This institution will be involved importantly in any systematic effort to apply environmental criteria to major economic development projects and, indeed, to the evolution of development goals and strategies taking proper account of ecological considerations. For several years, the World Bank has recognized the critical relationship between development prospects and population growth as described earlier.

Mr. McNamara has taken the general policy position that no loans shall be made in the future without careful screening for possible environmental side effects. He announced in his November 1970 report to the UN Economic and Social Council that the Bank had established a unit to foresee, to the extent possible, the environmental consequences of proposed development projects. The unit is to include outstanding ecologists. The unit will consider the general problem of how to infuse an ecological point of view into procedures at key points, including the earliest stages of development programming.

The role of the World Bank in advising on national development plans, in organizing international lending consortia, and in helping to train economic planners and other officials from developing countries will draw this institution much more deeply into environmental issues related to economic and social development. Its considerable research capability may be similarly engaged.

The Organization for Economic
Cooperation and Development

The OECD Council, at a ministerial level meeting in May 1970, decided the Organization's program should emphasize the economic and trade implications of environmental policies and, in particular, the relation of those policies to quantitative and qualitative economic growth. The managerial aspects will be considered, with the stress on promoting concerted solutions to problems having substantial international implications.

The Secretariat is being reorganized and a new Environment Committee met for the first time in November to draw up a detailed work program. The *OECD Observer,* the Organization's official publication, states, "..the Committee's approach will be multidisciplinary, encompassing not only scientific and technical developments but also their economic, financial, and social consequences ... ."[2] Existing study groups have been working since 1968-69 on water management research, air management research, transportation research (including noise abatement), unintended occurrence of pesticides, and innovation in urban management.

The OECD offers advantages through its relatively broad international appeal; its membership includes the world's major non-Communist industrial powers.

The North Atlantic Treaty Organization

The newly organized Committee on the Challenges of Modern Society of the North Atlantic Council has undertaken eight cooperative study projects on which one or two members serve as "pilot countries" for open-ended groups of national participants. (A list of these projects with rapporteurs and participating countries is found at Appendix U). NATO's work is coordinated with the OECD, ECE, and the European Economic Community; it invites non-member countries, e.g., Japan and Sweden, to participate in its studies; and it already is engaged in the first international effort to identify criteria for the establishment of air and water quality standards. Its principal advantages are that its members represent a large segment of the industrially advanced world; it has a high level of expertise and a competent organizational frame-

2. The *OECD Observer* (published by the OECD, Paris, No. 48, October 1970), p. 14.

work; and it is experienced in the ways of international cooperation and in the search for a common viewpoint toward complex situations.

The Council of Europe

The Council has been involved actively for a number of years in conservation activities and in formulating and promoting international conventions and agreements such as the International Commission for the Protection of the River Rhine Against Pollution, the European Water Charter, and the International Plant Protection Convention, developed by FAO.

The Council proclaimed 1970 as Conservation Year, has sponsored regional research and study groups, and supported environmental education and publicity programs.

Other Organizations

Only fragmentary information is available currently on environment-related work of other inter-governmental organizations; e.g., in 1968 the Organization for African Unity adopted the African Convention on Conservation of Natural Resources, and the Organization of American States asserts that environmental factors are taken into account in its extensive surveys of water resources in Latin America. SEATO and the several regional organizations still taking form in Southeast Asia may touch peripherally on environmental questions as they consult on developmental and educational questions. New studies from the ecological point of view have been made recently of the Mekong Valley and Delta development project, supported by a large consortium of UN agencies and national governments, and some changes may be made in this ambitious plan. There is no available indication that CEMA (the Warsaw Pact organization) has been seized with environmental issues.

Non-Governmental International Programs

The most important international programs related to environmental problems now under way are the following:

The International Biological Program

The Program is a cooperative effort of scientists from more than fifty nations to engage in a global plan of research on environmental systems with the theme of "The Biological Basis of Productivity and Human Welfare." IBP sponsored initial studies on international monitoring systems and is conducting "biome" research projects. To help insure comparability of methods and measurements, IBP scientists from many countries have collaborated in the preparation of a series of IBP Handbooks.

The International Hydrological Decade

Proclaimed in January 1965, this is a major cooperative endeavor embracing half a dozen UN agencies and the relevant international scientific societies, including ICSU. UNESCO took the lead in developing and executing the program. The program consists essentially of action projects of the 104 participating countries, stimulated by existing intergovernmental agencies and international scientific organizations. The program is designed to advance scientific knowledge about water resources and the water cycle, to improve the education and training of water specialists, and to stimulate all countries to increase their ability to cope with their own water problems.

Some Non-Governmental Institutions And Organizations

The extensive network of international scientific professional societies and unions covers, in one way and to some degree, the spectrum of subjects now subsumed under the environmental or ecological rubrics.*

The International Council of Scientific Unions

ICSU established an Ad Hoc Committee to prepare a report on those characteristics of the environment being altered by human action. The report, completed late in 1969, recommended, among other things, the creation of a Scientific Committee on Problems of the Environment (SCOPE). This was subsequently approved by the Executive Committee of ICSU. Functions of SCOPE are:

* The Conservation Directory for 1970 (published by The National Wildlife Federation, Washington, D.C.) lists a dozen organizations with the word "international" in their titles. Some are commissions and others have highly limited interests e.g. The International Shade Tree Conference, Inc. Only a few organizations with broad international interests in the environmental field need to be noted here.

to promote and coordinate research on environmental quality control and rational use of natural resources;

to advise ICSU on policies concerning man's interaction with the environment;

to advise UN agencies and other international bodies;

to operate an International Center for the Environment; and

to promote public awareness of the importance of environmental problems.

Plans for the establishment of the proposed International Center for the Environment are still in process of formulation, but the functions recommended by the Ad Hoc Committee are:

1. A monitoring service.

2. A research and planning service "...to be responsible for reviewing specific environmental problems and for coordinating current research projects; to organize symposia."

3. An intelligence service "...to gather information and intelligence relevant to the environment from all sources; to keep abreast of inter-governmental activities and non-governmental activities. The Committee calls attention to the fact that no such office now exists... ."[3]

The National Academy of Sciences

As already indicated, the Academy provides advisory committees for both AID and the Department of State. In early May 1970 the President of the Academy visited Moscow to work out areas of future cooperation with the Soviet Academy of Sciences, including several aspects of environmental problems. The Academy is currently studying these proposals.

In the summer of 1969, an Environmental Study Group prepared, for the Academy's Environmental Studies Board, a report entitled *Institutions for Effective Management of the Environment* (see Appendix V) which proposed, among other things, the establishment of:

3. Report of the Ad Hoc Committee of ICSU on Problems of the Human Environment, 1969, pp. 9-10. Mimeographed.

A National Laboratory for the Environmental Sciences. A number of bills have been introduced in Congress calling for such a laboratory or laboratories, which would, of course, be Federally financed and require legislation.

An Institute for Environmental Studies, with a broad mandate, to be financed mainly by the private sector. A staff of approximately 200 professional researchers and analysts is foreseen in the recommendation.

A National Environmental Coalition. Since this suggestion has attracted less attention than the foregoing two proposals (and others which already have been dealt with by legislation and Executive action), it seems worthwhile to point out here that the proposed function of the National Coalition would be "to facilitate the process of public education" and to "encourage and support the formation of local environmental coalitions all over the country and provide all possible support and encouragement for the formation of similar groups abroad." With respect to publication, it was recommended that the coalition develop and carry out:

> displays and demonstrations in museums, schools, and similar public places about the environment
>
> semi-popular literature about the environment
>
> use of commercial and educational television and radio and means of creating "environmental consciousness"
>
> the development of curricula for adult education
>
> The encouragement of public discussion groups and organizations[4]

The International Union for the
Conservation of Nature and Natural Resources (IUCN)

This is a union of 30 governments or governmental departments (the U.S. Department of the Interior is a member) and 225 non political organizations in 70 countries.

The IUCN has broadened its scope of interests from traditional con-

4."Institutions for Effective Management of the Environment," (Report of the Environmental Study Group to the Environmental Studies Board, National Academy of Sciences – National Research Council, Washington, D.C., 1969).

servation to embrace the ecology, specifically including the promotion of conservation as a basic component of development programs. It also is planning to shift from basically internal communications to address itself to a broader public.

The IUCN recently has received a new infusion of foundation funds, has appointed new senior officials, and may move its headquarters from Morges, Switzerland, to Geneva, though the latter step is not definite. The organization has official standing with UNESCO and other UN agencies; it most likely will be involved in preparations for the Stockholm Conference.

The Conservation Foundation

This has a number of international projects; has shifted from "conservation" to "environmental" issues; and also has served in a consulting capacity to UN agencies, especially UNESCO.

The most relevant work of the Conservation Foundation to the priority tasks ahead is in connection with the environmental side effects of economic development. In late 1968, the Foundation sponsored, in connection with Washington University's Center for the Biology of Natural Systems, a conference on the ecological consequences of international development programs. This was the first known occasion on which environmental scientists attempted to take a systematic look at the ecological backlash of major development projects. The full proceedings have not yet been published. However, a summary has been prepared of the case histories studied and articles based on the conference have appeared in *Natural History, Science,* and the *International Development Review.* The full proceedings are planned for publication in early 1971.

The Woodrow Wilson International Center for Scholars

The Center at the Smithsonian Institution has decided that environmental problems will be one of its two major fields of inquiry as its program becomes operative. This institution is included here because of its international focus, its interest in environmental problems, its possible relevance to stimulating ecological perceptions among leaders in developing countries, its extensive physical facilities, and its distinguished board of trustees.

The Smithsonian Institution Office of Ecology Program

This office is likely to undertake several projects directly relevant to preparations for the Stockholm Conference.

Finally, it should be noted that a number of international and internationally oriented non-governmental organizations almost surely will be drawn into the issue of adapting development strategy to ecological imperatives — for example, the International Union for the Conservation of Nature and the International Institute for Environmental Affairs.

Part 4

The Environmental Crisis and Selected Sectors of U.S. Society

Introduction: Fad or Fixed Interest

Below the Federal level of government, any effort to get a fix on the impact of environmental awareness on social institutions confronts a landscape of ignorance and a collection of moving targets.

In due course, reporting systems doubtless will be developed for systematic collection and analysis of information about regional, state, city, and rural agency activities related to environmental problems. During the first year of high awareness of the environment, they simply did not exist. Nor were central repositories yet in operation to collate data from industrial, business, agricultural, professional or other areas.

But by selecting a few key sectors of American society, and looking at a few targets of opportunity, one can get enough rough impressions to answer the question: will "the crisis of the environment" turn out to be a spring fad for a fickle public?

A good place to start appeared to be with the organizations which have been active over the years in the field of conservation. Hence the following report, "Conservation Groups: The New Approach."

This is followed by a collection of fragmentary information on the reactions of industry and business.

As an example of the impact on a state and a big-city administration – whether it is typical or not is an open question – a report is then made on the State of Maryland and the city of Baltimore.

Because environmental concerns already have led to new legislation and undoubtedly will lead to more, and because new legal concepts are in the air, a look was taken at the reactions so far to environmental issues in the courts and in the legal profession. The results are found in the study, "Impact of Environment on the Law and Vice-Versa," followed by notes on significant test cases.

One conclusion that can be drawn from this range of inquiries is that the country so far sees the priorities in the environmental realm pretty much as the President does: water pollution, air pollution, solid waste disposal, parks and recreation areas.

Another conclusion is that the environmental side effects of "progress" – long accepted as facts of life – are now held to be "problems" and "issues" that demand attention and action.

From what has happened and not happened so far in the sectors examined, one can also conclude that the glass is half full or half empty, depending upon the mind-set of the observer.

But if the trends examined are difficult to characterize, much less to quantify, there can be little doubt that American society is seized with the environmental issue for the indefinite future. Particular issues no doubt will intrigue the public interest for fleeting periods of time; one-issue organizations will come and go; the highly impatient will become frustrated with the discovery that the problem cannot be dealt with quickly or ever be "solved." But that is because the problem is real and society is obliged to cope with it whether the mass media drop it or not. The unavoidable need to make decisions that involve trade-offs among conflicting interests guarantee that the issues will be alive, and lively, for a long time to come.

Conservation Groups: The New Approach

In the past few years, literally hundreds of conservation groups have sprung up in the United States, and many civic organizations such as the League of Women Voters have begun to turn their considerable influence and large memberships toward environmental action.

More established conservation groups, whose concerns formerly centered on wilderness and wildlife, have changed considerably toward a broader ecological approach.

The Conservation Foundation is a good case in point. Set up in 1948, its focus of interest has changed from a general concern for soils, forest, water, and species to what F. Fraser Darling, its vice president, calls "the care of the human habitat, which is the whole planet... ." It has launched with the help of the Ford Foundation a demonstration study at Rookery Bay in Florida to show how development can occur in the context of environmental values. Similar demonstration projects have been started in the Tincium Marsh south of Philadelphia, on the Maine Coast, on the shoreline of Marin County near San Francisco, and on the lower James River in Virginia.

The National Wildlife Federation has moved to total resource protection and has published its first annual Index of Environmental Quality which attempts to gauge gain and loss in the protection of air, water, soil, forests, wildlife, and minerals.

The National Audubon Society has been particularly active in the Florida Everglades jetport fight; and one has only to compare the Society's brochure for 1970 to the one issued in 1960 to see how far its mission has developed.

The Wilderness Society, long concerned with creation and protection of National Parks, has turned its 60,000 members toward assuring that the Alaska pipeline does not proceed without thorough study of its side effects on the environment.

The Sierra Club is now involved in more than fifty lawsuits on behalf of environmental protection.

The Izaak Walton League also is involved in a number of lawsuits and was the organizing catalyst in the Citizen's Crusade for Clean Water, one of the most effective lobby operations of recent years. The Crusade was sponsored by the Natural Resources Council, itself a coalition of such conservation groups as the National Wildlife Federation, the Izaak Walton Leagues, the Sierra Club, and others. What happened is that for fiscal 1970 the Nixon Administration originally asked for only $214 million for water grants, the same amount appropriated in fiscal 1969, although the Clean Waters Restoration Act of 1966 had authorized $1 billion for fiscal 1970 grants. A House Appropriations subcommittee raised the amount to $450 million and the full committee recommended $600 million. Secretary of the Interior Hickel said that no more than $600 million could be handled by his Department, even if the billion was appropriated. Yet Congress voted for the full amount.*

* When the $1 billion figure reached the House floor, the coalition included: the AFL-CIO, the American Fisheries Society, the American Forestry Association, the American Association of University Women, the American Institute of Architects, the American Institute of Planners, the American Society of Landscape Architects, the Association of State and Interstate Water Pollution Control Administrators, the Citizens Committee on Natural Resources, the Conservation Foundation, the Consumer Federation of America, the Garden Club of America, the League of Women Voters, the National Association of Counties, the National

The large Foundations, now becoming more involved, have not previously played a major role in the conservation movement, although they have given considerable funds to the study of the problem. The Rockefeller Foundation, which has a long and heavy involvement in agriculture, genetics, and biology, recently announced almost two million dollars in grants to scientists and scholars working on the quality of the environment, including $500,000 to Resources for the Future.* The Battelle Memorial Institute has conducted major research on water problems, especially in the Great Lakes area.

There are other important organizations such as the Environmental Sciences Institute, which groups several hundred leading scientists, educators, businessmen, etc., as well as institutional members, including industries, government agencies, and universities.

There are presently more than 150 national organizations and thousands of local groups. The young, the militant, the disenchanted have set up a host of small groups which approach the ecological problem as an instrument to change the goals, the direction, the style, and the mores of society. Their philosophy was expressed by 32-year-old Cliff Humphrey, of Ecology Action, a militant new group in Berkeley, California: "The President is talking about cleaning up some smoke and dirty water, but that's not what we are concerned with. We're concerned with a whole way of life."

Recreation and Parks Association, the National Audubon Society, the National League of Cities, the Sport Fishing Institute, the United Auto Workers, the U.S. Conference of City Health Officers, the U.S. Conference of Mayors, the United Steelworkers of America, and the Wilderness Society.

Support also was expressed by organizations that did not formally join the coalition, such as the National Fisheries Institute, the Edison Electric Institute, the Waterworks Manufacturers Association and the Water Pollution Control Federation – the latter two groups representing, among others, manufacturers of pollution-control equipment. The Consulting Engineers Council, whose members design pollution-control systems, also indicated its interest in the coalition's goal. Individual firms like the Washington, D.C. Gas Light Co., and the Consolidated Edison Co. of New York, which has had many confrontations with conservation groups, also expressed support.

* Resources for the Future received an $8 million grant for general support for five years from the Ford Foundation in October 1968. Its projects include studies of distribution aspects of environmental quality - Time and space aspects - A regional management model - An air quality management model - Residuals management in industries - Air pollution and health - Systems of presentation for making choices - Governmental decision processes - Power structure and decisions - Institutional aspects of managing lakes and bays - Wetland management for San Francisco Bay - Litigating environmental quality - Impact of technology on natural areas - Environmental perceptions - The Pacific flyway - Outdoor recreation.

Ecology Action believes society must move away from the ideals of growth, consumption, and progress. It asserts that Western Society is having a cumulative impact which will run the life-support system of the planet down to zero.

The group practices the lifestyle it preaches, from the rejection of containers from markets to the conversion of their trucks to propane gas, minimum use of heat and water, reconversion of old pieces of machinery to new uses, growing their vegetables without pesticides and baking their bread without additives.

Other organizations, like Planned Parenthood, Zero Population Growth, or the National Association for Repeal of Abortion Laws have identified their continuing efforts as part of the environmental surge. Still others have sprung up around the country to deal with specific crises such as GOO (Get Oil Out) formed by the aroused burghers of Santa Barbara. Some go for acronyms like GASP, Inc. (Greater Birmingham Alliance to Stop Pollution), Chicago's CRAP (Citizens' Revolt Against Pollution), and PISST (Passengers Informed on the SST).

Some of the local organizations set up to prepare for Earth Day already have disappeared and no doubt many of the ad hoc and faddist groups will follow them.

But to take this as evidence of a loss of interest in environmental issues would ignore all the important evidence, including the role of the young. Apart from campus activities, the national organizers of Earth Day events are establishing both a political action group and an annual summer research project for graduate students.

Some of the glamor may well wear off for commercial news shows on television; but their place will be taken by more serious films and programs produced for noncommercial stations.

There may have been faddist reactions to the sudden awareness of the environmental crisis, but the crisis will not yield to frivolous or even short-term attention.

Business and the Environment

The response of American industry to the environmental crisis is widespread and growing, but was principally limited in the earliest stage to what might be called technical repair – improvement in incinerators, development of cleaner fuels, better after-burners, new water treatment plants, compacting of garbage, etc. A whole new and profitable set of industries has grown up to sell pollution control equipment and know-how.

Scores of 1969 corporate annual reports illustrate a pattern of rising percentage of costs devoted to environmental management measures. The outlays are, like built-in safety features in autos, considered a normal cost of production. Aesthetics are no longer considered irrelevant or even unmanly. And corporate decisions, particularly in the area of siting of new plants, traditionally made in private board rooms, are more often brought into the public arena before they are irreversible.

One may wonder whether industry has quite got the point when full-page advertisements by paper companies promote the "disposable seventies" in which everything from diapers to dresses, towels, sheets, and curtains can be "thrown away."

But while growth is still treated as a measure of progress, many American businessmen agree that some present production methods cause unacceptable damage to the environment, that the cost of industrial pollution is borne by the general public, and that the air and water should no longer be treated as "free" commodities. A *Fortune* poll revealed that a majority of executives favor national pollution standards and strict compliance laws in order that environmental reforms are not penalized by allowing the polluter a competitive advantage over his clean competitor. The same poll revealed that few businessmen thought that industry had done enough to date.[1]

A Union Carbide spokesman, quoted in *Business Week,* says, "In our processing work with chemicals and plastics, we used to concern ourselves with minimum investment and efficiences of raw materials. Now we have a third ingredient, pollution costs. So we reassess the process. We trade off the original reactants for more expensive ones if the process results in fewer pollution control costs."[2]

More broadly, the United States Chamber of Commerce, in a policy statement on environmental pollution, said:

> Industry should acknowledge a sense of stewardship for the natural resources upon which our environment depends -- air, land, and water. This involves sharing the mounting national concern for the quality of these resources as well as assisting to restore to acceptable levels those whose quality has suffered.

1. Robert S. Diamond, "What Business Thinks About Its Environment," in "The Environment, A National Mission for the Seventies," by the Editors of *Fortune* (New York, Evanston, and London: Harper and Row, Publishers, Perennial Library No. P-189, 1970) pp. 55-64.

2. Leon Shechter, quoted in *Business Week*, April 11, 1970, p. 66.

Industry has an obligation to recognize the impact of a growing population and its concentration. Acceptable resource management procedures of past years are no longer adequate and will be even less adequate in the years ahead...[3]

Factual evidence of industry's reaction was available only in fragments in 1970:

The Iron and Steel Institute estimated that its members already had spent some $25 million on anti-pollution measures.

The Manufacturing Chemists Association projected expenditures in that industry, between 1966 and 1971, at $400 million.

The auto industry was working on radical adjustment of engines to meet emission standards expected to be imposed by 1975.

The oil industry was removing or reducing lead in gasoline.*

The paper companies were spending millions to reduce radically the pollution caused by new paper mills.**

Two major textile companies were developing dyeing methods which utilize a completely closed system and another company had figured out how to get by with one-thirtieth of the previous volumes of water used in processing.

3. Chamber of Commerce of the United States, "Improving Environmental Quality" (Washington, D.C.: The Chamber, 1970) p. 9.

* According to a November 17, 1970 news release by the American Petroleum Institute, the U.S. petroleum industry spent more than $2.036 billion during the period 1966-70 for air and water conservation. This was derived from a Petroleum Institute survey of forty-five U.S. companies representing 98 percent of the nation's crude oil processing capacity. The release noted that the oil industry's yearly anti-pollution expenditures more than doubled in the past five years, rising from $271.4 million in 1966 to an estimated $559.5 million in 1970. More than $1.5 million is now being spent each day on pollution control equipment and environmental research.

** An American Paper Institute environmental statement issued in December 1970 reported expenditures approaching $500 million have already been made for water quality protection, and projected capital outlays by the paper industry for water pollution control in 1970 are $113 million, in 1971, $146 million, and in 1972, $177 million. The statement recognizes that even these expenditures may need to be further increased. Reported are sharp reductions in the solids content of paper mill effluents and increasing reuse of water in pulp and paper production, thus reducing the amount of water needed per ton of paper produced by well over a third. The industry's outlay for air quality are also reported as growing rapidly with $167 million spent to date and $90 million earmarked for additional air-treatment facilities in 1970-72. Pulp and paper mills are reported to have reduced particulates in their emissions by 90 percent.

Systematic collection of data on industry's response to the environmental crisis is one of the duties assigned to the National Industrial Pollution Control Council, established by President Nixon's Executive Order 11523 of April 9, 1970. (See Appendixes W,X,Y, and Z.) According to its charter, the primary mission of the NIPCC is to advise the President and the Chairman of the Council on Environmental Quality, through the Secretary of Commerce, on programs of industry relating to the quality of the environment. In particular, it is to:

Survey and evaluate the plans and actions of industry in the field of environmental quality.

Identify and examine problems of the effects on the environment of industrial practices and the needs of industry for improvements in the quality of the environment, and recommend solutions to those problems.

Provide liaison among members of the business and industrial community on environmental quality matters.

Encourage the business and industrial community to improve the quality of the environment.

Advise on plans and actions of Federal, state, and local agencies involving environmental quality policies affecting industry which are referred to it by the Secretary, or by the Chairman of the Council on Environmental Quality through the Secretary.

Within a few months, the Industrial Council had organized thirty-seven subgroups on an industry-by-industry basis.

Skeptics were quick to point out that many members of the Council are board chairmen or principal executive officers of some of the world's champion polluters. But Russell Train, chairman of the Council on Environmental Quality, said, "It is terribly important to engage the energy and the enthusiastic cooperation of the business and industry community in this job of providing a high quality environment." (See Appendix Y, p.2.)

Some felt that energy and cooperation in pollution abatement would not be enough.

Athelstan Spilhaus, as President of the American Association for the Advancement of Science, talked about the "next industrial revolution" which must develop "a loop from the user to the factory which industry must close."

The "crisis of the environment" has shifted ground rules for industry, for highway engineers, even for real estate developers. More and more the advantages of growth have to be measured against the quality of life. We need to decide where we want to go.

Impact of Environment on the Law and Vice-Versa*

Traditionally, the three branches of government in the United States are supposed to function as an effective system of checks and balances. In the environmental field, conservationists found the Executive Branch, through its specialized agencies, unlikely to respond to environmental responsibilities primarily because the original mandates were narrowly focused on functional goals such as highways, power, etc. The Legislative Branch was often busy with many matters, governed by a rigid committee system, and in general slow to respond to new imperatives. It was inevitable, therefore, that conservationists would turn to the courts.

A whole series of legal actions over environmental issues have been initiated, and are being fought out in the courts. The courts have responded in a significant way and forced previously unresponsive groups to take environmental factors increasingly into account. A court decision to hold up the Alaska pipeline brought at least a temporary halt to a project involving $900 million in oil leases, a tacit agreement from the Department of the Interior to proceed with the pipeline, a $40 million investment in construction camps and supplies and strong political support within Alaska for the economic shot in the arm that petroleum development would provide.

Recourse to the courts is often a quicker process than waiting until an "appropriate" official takes action or until new laws make their way through the legislative mills. As of mid-1970, twenty-nine states allowed any citizen to file suit to contest official conduct.

Environmental law is not new. There have been suits for many years, but they have usually revolved around damage to an individual or his property, and seldom have dealt with such intangibles as the desecration of a community or a region.

*This section was prepared after interviews with Malcolm Baldwin, Legal Associate, The Conservation Foundation, and Joseph L. Sax, Professor of Law, University of Michigan.

During the 19th century and the early 20th century, the courts became, in a real sense, the instruments of laissez-faire economics. In one classic case, decided by a Tennessee court in 1904, two copper smelting companies were allowed to continue their practice of reducing copper ore by cooking it over open-air wood fires, a process that produced billowing clouds of sulfur dioxide smoke which made a wasteland of the surrounding valley.

Farmers who had complained were told by the court that they were not entitled to injunctive relief because "the law must make the best arrangement it can between the contending parties, with a view to preserving to each one the largest measure of liberty possible under the circumstances." A Cornell law professor observes that "'liberty' here meant that the companies were free to create a wasteland if they paid for it (some damages were awarded), whereas the farmers were free to take jobs with the industry and continue to reside in a valley totally polluted with chemicals."

Proprietary rights have been at the base of our substantive and procedural law. Environmental law is now moving toward protection of public rather than private interest, environmental rather than economic interest.

The new approach to law was preceded by the phenomenon of increasing public concern and awareness. The Sierra Club was the first of the traditional conservation organizations to challenge legal tradition. It dramatized the Redwoods issue, and the attempt by the Corps of Engineers to flood the Grand Canyon. Out of the resultant public concern, young lawyers, often previously active in civil rights, but defining their role as defenders of public rather than private interests, began to combine with ad hoc citizens groups and some of the conservation groups, and to question the alliance of public bodies and private interests in specific environmental cases. With little money, they took on the unassailable giants. Victor J. Yannacone, Jr., a volatile trial lawyer, said "sue the bastards."

It is, says Yannacone, "the law" which zones the housing patterns which lead to building too many highways for too many autos; "the law" which appropriates public property for private promoters; "the law" which permits environmental degradation; "the law" which asserts equal protection of "the law" for the corporation and denies it to the poor, the black, the inarticulate, the politically weak.

Young lawyers such as Yannacone characterize the changes in the profession which have led more and more of them into such social concerns as defense of the poor, civil rights, and now the environment. They have had to operate on a shoestring, and their biggest problem has been money, despite the fact that the Environmental Defense Fund has removed one obstacle by mobilizing free scientific expert opinion to testify against well-financed government and corporate defendants.

Many large law firms are giving their young lawyers requested time off for public service suits, some dealing with the environment and, for a fee, corporate law firms are taking environmental cases. For example, Wilmer, Cutler and Pickering, which law students had picketed for representing the automotive industry, represented citizens in Memphis against a planned road through Overton Park and joined the case against a highway through the central city and historic Vieux Carre in New Orleans. In Washington, D.C., Covington and Burling provided legal support to a group protesting a planned highway and bridge across the Potomac which would detract from the beauty of areas bordering the river and displace houses and schools in poor sections of the city.

Some firms, like Arnold and Porter, have a strong public service adjunct. Its lawyers represent the Indians in Alaska and conservationists in Maryland opposing the Calvert Cliffs power development. Scores of other firms are participating in other environment suits. There are new and sometimes struggling law firms which are now specializing in environmental actions.

The American Bar Association has a committee on environmental quality. The American Trial Lawyers Association runs an educational seminar program to train lawyers in environmental defense. An environmental law reporting service has come into being.

A landmark Conference on Law and the Environment was held in Warrenton, Virginia, at Airlie House in September 1969. Sponsored by the Conservation Foundation and the Conservation and Research Foundation (New London, Conn.), the conference drew together some 65 lawyers, conservationists, and law professors to discuss what they could do to protect the environment and to define the problems and opportunities facing the emerging new breed of attorneys who specialize in environmental law.

Participants included Ralph Nader; Raymond A. Haik, president of the Izaak Walton League; Philip Berry, president of the Sierra Club; Representative Paul N. McCloskey, Jr.; and former Vermont Governor Phillip H. Hoff, as well as Yannacone and other conservation lawyers.

For two days they discussed theory, tactics, and doctrine, examined what law schools were doing in the field, and concluded with a variety of recommendations.

One of the practical follow-ups to this gathering was the establishment on December 22, 1969 of an Environmental Law Institute in Washington, D.C. as a joint project of the Public Law Education Institute and the Conservation Foundation.

Its announced objectives are:

1. to conduct and sponsor research into problems of conservation and utilization of the environment and the application of the law thereto;

2. to institute and maintain a clearinghouse for information regarding the law of the environment, including but not limited to the statute and regulatory law of the United States, the several states and other political jurisdictions; the cases and decisions of courts and other judicial and quasi-judicial bodies; the briefs, memoranda, treatises, commentaries, and similar works by members of the legal profession and others;

3. to publish and disseminate these and related materials;

4. to engage in such educational activities as classes, workshops, panels, lectures, etc.[4]

The Natural Resources Defense Council was formed in early 1970 after a meeting in Princeton, organized by the Conservation Foundation and attended by some sixty lawyers. The Council proposes to serve as a watchdog on violations of the environment on behalf of private citizens. The group is headed by Stephen Duggan, a partner in the New York law firm of Simpson, Thacher and Bartlett, and founder of the Scenic Hudson Preservation Conference which, in a case opposing Consolidated Edison's plans to build a power plant at Storm King, won a historic Federal Court ruling acknowledging the legal standing to sue on environmental issues. In addition to individuals, sponsors of the Natural Resources Defense Council include the National Audubon Society and the Beinecke Foundation of New York.

Participation of the states in environmental lawsuits is increasing, as indicated by the announcement of the National Association of Attorneys General that it would act as a nationwide law firm "with fifty senior partners working together" to mount a drive against pollution.

4. As stated in prospectus issued by the Environmental Law Institute, 1346 Connecticut Avenue, N.W., Washington, D.C., March 1970.

Its president, Minnesota Attorney General Douglas M. Head, calls this a "whole new concept of revitalizing state government." (Minnesota mounted a suit against the Atomic Energy Commission in which twelve other states became associated, asserting a state's right to set stricter protection standards than does the Federal Government.)

In February 1970, at its meeting in Washington, the Association appointed a nine-member Environmental Committee under the chairmanship of Illinois Attorney General William Scott, whose crackdowns on corporate polluters gained national attention.

The Association envisages the following activities:

A clearinghouse of the names of legal and environmental experts.

Joint litigation against polluters, where appropriate.

Development and distribution to state legislators of model pollution enforcement legislation which would empower an Attorney General to take prompt and effective action.

Distribution of relevant state legislation and litigation undertaken to all Attorneys General.

The law schools of the nation have been deeply affected by the impact of the new environmental awareness. The curricula are changing, and about 100 seminars in environmental law are being offered. Environmental law books are being written and published and the students are, in many cases, helping in litigation.

The Law and Environment conference at Airlie recommended expansion of these programs, compulsory environmental courses with particular reference to natural resource decision-making, credit for participation in legal action, and more interdisciplinary programs.

Among the universities which have placed new emphasis on the environment in their law programs are the Universities of Michigan, Chicago, Colorado, and Wisconsin and also Rutgers, Harvard, and Stanford.

The lawyers and the judiciary already have effected changes in the direction of new principles of responsibility in the use of resources. The whole question of property rights and regulations governing the use of public and private property is in flux.

These are not the only social changes that are in the air as a result of concerns for the integrity of the natural system. For example, Paul McCloskey, Jr., Republican Congressman from California, has said:

> I think perhaps the true enemy of preservation of our environment is our own system of government, and by that I mean that the local government and the county government which is entirely dependent upon the property tax and the increase of its payroll structure is the true enemy of conservation today. It may be that we must revise the entire structure of the United States as to taxes, that conservation can never be accomplished so long as a local government ... must as a means of its financial survival get a new tax base, new development, new payrolls into its boundaries.[5]

The future of public-interest law firms appears to be assured. In the second week of October 1970, the Internal Revenue Service let it be known that it was undertaking a sixty-day study of whether contributions to such firms – their main source of support – would continue to be tax deductible. Senator Gaylord Nelson announced hearings on the subject would begin during the third week of November, the Council on Environmental Quality spoke out on behalf of the public-interest law; so did the President's consumer advisor and the just-appointed head of the Environmental Protection Agency.

In the second week of November, the IRS announced it had developed "guidelines" which probably would protect the tax status of existing public interest law firms and that the issuance of exemptions for such firms would be resumed. According to the *Wall Street Journal,* a Treasury Department official said: "Sure, we backed down. With the kind of pressure we got, what else did you expect?"[6]

Maryland and the Environment

Maryland, small in area and population,* nevertheless has a fairly typical gamut of environmental problems, most caused by runaway growth and technology.

Public concern about resources historically has centered on the Chesapeake Bay, probably the most valuable and vulnerable large estuary in the world, which is linked to a six-state water system, the Susquehanna, Delaware, and Potomac Rivers. Washington, Norfolk and Baltimore were founded to take advantage of the Bay; and it consti-

5. From remarks made by Congressman McCloskey during the course of a conference on Law and the Environment at Airlie House, Warrenton, Virginia, September 1969.

6. *Wall Street Journal,* November 13, 1970, p. 14, col. 2.

*3,922,399 according to 1970 census.

tutes 22 percent of the area of the State of Maryland, whose citizens refer to it as a "way of life."

In addition, Maryland is attempting to cope with the familiar crises of air and water pollution; solid waste disposal; persistent biocides; acid mine drainage; the disappearance of wetlands; the loss of shoreline and open space; field and farm losses to highways, factories, and developers; and the deterioration of cities.

The state of Maryland has a characteristic maze of municipal, county,* state, regional, and national jurisdictions, and a love-hate relationship with the nearby Federal Government on which it depends for money, services, and sometimes excuses. It has a slice of Appalachia, a rural "south," racial and poverty problems, progressive and backward businessmen, universities paying increasing attention to the environment, conservationist movements, and a younger generation very much aware that it is they, after all, who will inherit whatever earth is preserved or fashioned for them.

Until the 1964 reapportionment of Maryland, the rural conservative interests typified by the "Eastern Shore" delegates partly controlled policy through over-representation in the legislature. Since 1966, the rural block has lost power, the urban representatives have gained some, but the really significant growth in influence has gone to the suburbs.** Original fears that Baltimore City would dominate the whole state have been quelled by this essentially middle-class and cautious suburban bloc.

Marvin Mandel, the first governor in Maryland's history to have come out of the state legislature, was elected into office by that legislature when Spiro Agnew assumed the Vice-Presidency. Far from being a caretaker of the office, he has used his knowledge of the legislative art, with the help of a capable staff, to manage passage of some fifty bills

---

* Of Maryland's 23 counties, five have home rule (Montgomery, Howard, Baltimore, Ann Arundel and Wicomico) which permits them to pass their own ordinances. The city of Baltimore also operates under home rule charter. Other counties must go through the assembly for approval of county ordinances. State law, of course, applies to all equally.

** Before 1966 there were 29 Senators, of which 6 came from Baltimore City, 9 from the rural Eastern Shore. After reapportionment there are now 43 Senators, of which 12 are from Baltimore City and 4 from the Eastern Shore. Baltimore County, wealthy and suburban, has 7. The suburban areas clearly hold the levers of power, over Eastern Shore, Southern Maryland and Western Maryland rural areas.

through the legislature during the session which ended March 31, 1970. In these, environmental matters played an important part. Like President Nixon on the national level, Governor Mandel had spoken of environment in his State of the State Message and two weeks later delivered a second message exclusively on the environment.

In the session which ended on March 31, the Maryland legislature passed a set of environmental bills* which Governor Mandel claims are "probably the strongest environmental protection laws in the country." Behind this achievement was a whole set of related factors: the earlier reapportionment, a politically acute governor, public awareness, a few key conservationist legislators, and the first steps in a reorganization of an unwieldy government structure which the Governor had pushed through the legislature.

The reorganization is the key to the workability of the program. It has vastly increased Maryland's ability to deal with the environment. Until it took place, there were some 250 separate agencies, responsible only to the governor's office. Now there will be eleven cabinet-level departments. The Department of Natural Resources, under the nominal leadership of former Governor Millard Tawes, but actively headed by James Coulter, brings together water resources, fish, and game and other agencies which had been involved piecemeal in aspects of environmental control.

In the State House, the legislators acted to preserve privately owned wetlands and to provide some safeguards against the transfer of state-owned wetlands. They tightened the procedures and penalties in state action against air polluters and gave stronger powers to the State Department of Natural Resources in its efforts to control industrial waste water.

The most controversial measure in the package was the bill creating a state environmental service empowered to acquire, construct and operate sewage treatment plants throughout Maryland. The Governor origi-

---

* Maryland Environmental Service. Abandoned Mine Drainage Control Act, strengthening of enforcement powers of Department of Water Resources, amendment of Sanitary Districts Law to provide for solid waste facilities, permission for Sanitary Facilities Fund to be used for planning of solid waste disposal systems and acceptance facilities, regulation of operators of sanitary landfills, requirement for County plans for solid waste acceptance facilities and disposal systems, erosion control, strengthening of Air Quality Control Act, revision of Water Quality Loan Act of 1968; revision of Department of Natural Resources Reorganization Bill, dredging of Back River for sludge removal.

nally had proposed that county and municipal governments be given only a consulting role in the preparation of five-year sewage treatment and solid waste disposal plans and in their implementation by the state agencies. But when strong opposition from local governments developed, the bill was amended to give the counties an absolute veto over solid waste disposal projects and a partial veto over preparation of five-year liquid waste disposal plans.

The legislature also stood behind the administration proposal for a $5,000,000 fund to reclaim abandoned mines, long a source of acid water pollution in Western Maryland, and passed two other bills dealing with the planning and financing of solid waste disposal.

The first state controls over sedimentation and erosion around construction and road projects were imposed, and the legislature made it mandatory for landfill operators to post performance bonds as guarantees that their dumps will be closed and covered.

Against the background of these legislative improvements, a look at the status of water and resources management and at reactions in the educational community, plus a series of brief case studies will indicate something of the impact of the environmental crisis and reactions to it in the state of Maryland.

Water Resources

The impact of environmental awareness in Maryland is reflected in a comparison of state expenditures over a three-year period for water pollution control. Of $7.5 million authorized in 1966, Maryland allocated $3.5 million. In 1969, $11.8 was authorized, but only $3.6 million allocated. In fiscal 1970, $17 million was authorized and $13.6 million allocated. This jump was paralled in other states, sometimes even more dramatically as in Ohio, Illinois, and Texas.*

The State Department of Water Resources has been heavily criticized by conservationists who pointed out that fewer than 100 actions against polluters were filed in the first twenty-two years of its existence. More than that number of actions were brought in the first few months of 1970. The department now has an assistant attorney-general on its staff, and ten engineers in six districts to identify sources of industrial pollution in the waterways.

* Source: Federal Water Pollution Control Administration.

The procedure of the department is admittedly slow, but is designed to elicit compliance and only in extreme situations to undertake legal action. The offending industry is given 90 days to come up with a plan of corrective action. If this is not satisfactory, subsequent negotiations are undertaken which may take additional months. Only ten polluters had been brought to court by mid-1970. The new law, however, allows the Department of Natural Resources to review action taken by the Department. And the strengthened Department of Natural Resources now requires new industries to get permits for water use before breaking ground.

Maryland can be said to have turned the corner on primary and secondary water treatment facilities, although many of the latter remain to be built. But a tertiary stage of treatment to remove nutrients such as phosphates and nitrogen, which cause the growth of algae and speed up eutrophication, is far from guaranteed.

There is considerable room for improved technology in the treatment of wastes or in the manufacturing process, in improved recycling of materials, and, on the political level, in such measures as an effluent tax* (which might need a federal basis to avoid the flight of industry from a strictly controlled to a more permissive location). In fact, until money and staff are made available, the state cannot fully utilize presently available technology.

On the water resources development side, Maryland, like other jurisdictions, is concerned about unanticipated side effects of previous decisions. The Chesapeake and Delaware Canal widening and deepening project, a 10-year $100 million development considered to be of critical importance to the port of Baltimore as it competes for containership traffic, is about 80 percent complete. Its target date is 1972. But such conservationists as Congressman Gilbert Gude of Maryland have warned that the Corps of Engineers may not have paid sufficient attention to the effects of diverting 800 million gallons of fresh water a day from the Chesapeake Bay to the Delaware River, thus increasing the salinity of the upper bay with unknown consequences on fish and marine life. Because a proposed hydraulic model of the Chesapeake Bay is unlikely to be completed before 1976, at best, the Corps of Engineers has ad-

---

* Senator Gaylord Nelson has proposed Federal legislation setting up such an effluent tax, which would automatically reduce the burden of the states in treating waste by providing an incentive for all companies to institute technical changes which would considerably reduce the volume of their waste.

mitted that all the effects of the canal widening cannot be foreseen.

In the larger sense, the time for trade-offs has come; for Maryland will have to place comparative values on commercial fishing, shellfish cultivation, recreation, access to the Bay, navigation and industry, wildlife, and a host of related problems. The wrong choices would destroy the possibility of an ecologically balanced, multi-use pattern of development for future generations.

Air Resources

Some of the legislation proposed but not passed by the legislature in 1970 is a measure of the magnitude of the task ahead; e.g., measures to control pollution by automobile exhausts. In fact, the State of Maryland will have to depend on Federal initiatives in this field. Because Maryland is above all a water-conscious state, public awareness of the smog problem has developed more slowly than in the case of water pollution.

Industry, in turn, has moved more slowly to develop and install control devices on its own initiative; and until recently little pressure had been exerted on the state level to control bus, car, and truck pollution. The expressway controversy has been fought out more on aesthetic, social, racial, and even historical grounds (one section of the Baltimore system is very much in dispute because of its possible encroachment on Fort McHenry) than on the effect of automobiles on the ambient air.

Baltimore, which spews some 3,225 tons of pollutants daily into the air, is the nation's thirteenth dirtiest city. Official concern with air pollution dates back to 1905. Twenty years ago the then Governor appointed a Commission on Noxious Fumes which concluded that Maryland did indeed have problems; subsequent legislation calling for $100,000 per year for study and control of air pollution passed, but the money was not appropriated. The city of Baltimore, on its part, has had a modest program of its own since 1931, but it has not been an effective bar to increasing pollution.

Although a law was passed in 1958, no real regulations were adopted until the presently operative Air Quality Control Act was signed by Governor Agnew in 1967. Specific responsibility for implementation has been assigned to the State Department of Health, whose program of monitoring and enforcement has been given new impetus this year.

A list of 44 major Baltimore Area polluters is topped by far by the Baltimore Gas and Electric Company which emits more than the next nine worst polluters combined. It was, however, the first company to sign an abatement agreement with the State and is in the process of shifting from burning coal to burning oil. (Gas would be cleaner, but would raise costs much higher and the company says there is insufficient supply.) The second largest polluter is Bethlehem Steel, which has also negotiated with the State and will install some $19 million worth of air pollution control equipment in its Sparrows Point and other plants.

The Better Air Coalition, a grouping of a number of Baltimore civic organizations, has been formed to support more effective regulations and implementation of existing laws. A second generation of air pollution laws are likely, according to Health Official Jean Schueneman, to cover:

1. More restrictive controls on pollution by industry.

2. Lower limits on the sulfur content of heating oil for homes, as well as those already imposed for industry.

3. Prohibition of coal burning.

4. Total banning of use of small incinerators, now used in stores and apartment houses.

5. Stronger laws on automobile emissions.

The complexity of the problem is illustrated by the fact that the city of Baltimore itself is a major polluter (two large incinerators), and fifty public schools still burn coal. Four state hospitals, Fort Meade, and the U.S. Naval Academy are also on the state's list of serious polluters.

An effective solution will require higher taxes and a rearrangement of the use of cars in the Maryland transportation system. As in other places, public attitudes toward mounting costs of control measures and such other factors as willingness to alter patterns of car use can well be the key to just how effective the campaign will be.

Education

The environmental crisis has had an important effect on the role of the university in society, according to Dr. Donald Pritchard of Johns Hopkins University. It has given new impetus to the multi-disciplinary approach,* long recognized in principle but thwarted by departmental specialization and the PhD system which encourages concentration on fragmented areas of knowledge rather than greater understanding of larger relationships. Pritchard feels that many university professors thought "that contact with the real world was sort of immoral ... only for engineers and people like that." Now, he says, they are coming around to the view that, at least in social and environmental matters, they do have a part to play in the "real world" despite the traditional view that the university's role is not to take positions on social issues but to produce scholars of excellence.

L. Eugene Cronin of the Natural Resources Institute** at the University of Maryland feels that the university's role has been increased, but stresses the need for non-traditional inputs designed to solve problems as distinguished from analysis of problems to be endured. As in other universities, a good deal of money has been poured in for environmental research, money which had not been available when the scientists were among the few concerned that the world's resources were in danger.

This is steering the university to a reappraisal of its organization and its mission. The students themselves are very much aware of environmental issues, but are split on the methods needed to attack the problem. Students are pessimistic, emotional, and often convinced that

* One interesting development in the academic structure at Hopkins is the reorganization of the departments of geography, geology, environmental science, and engineering, and oceanography, meteorology, and geophysical fluid mechanics into what is called an Earth Sciences Group, with a committee of five at its head and two departments: 1) Earth and Planetary Sciences and 2) Geography and Environmental Engineering. In the merger, which took place two years ago, the group added several social scientists (particularly economists) to its staff. The new department has set out to provide a completely flexible, broad training for doctoral candidates who have a professional interest in seeking solutions to the problems of environmental deterioration. Students work on a wide range of problems – management of air, human geography, urban systems, thermal effects, environmental health engineering – but the primary emphasis is technological and most of the students have a biology or engineering background. The program has been financed largely by grants from the Public Health Service and the Ford Foundation. (See also Appendix AA.)

** The Natural Resources Institute describes as its function the carrying-out of an interwoven program of research, education, and training in the field of natural resources. It works under the direction of the University's Board of Regents and in cooperation with other public and private agencies and institutions. The Institute strives – through greater knowledge – to advance the best uses of Maryland's forests, fish, wildlife, and surface waters for the benefit of people, now and in the future. (See Appendix BB.)

the "system" doesn't work. There is, however, a deep schism between the militant, fairly johnny-come-latelies to the environmental scene who want to tie their action to Vietnam and other potentially divisive issues, and what might be called the environmental pragmatists who want to mobilize a wide spectrum of opinion and ameliorate actual situations.

A graduate student at the University of Maryland's zoology department has founded a group called North American Habitat Preservation Society, Inc. Their initial impulse was to go on the attack, and they requested a "raft of information" which could be used against polluters from Dr. Cronin and his institute. They were upset when refused (it would have taken six months of staff time to fulfill the request), but Cronin cites this as an example of the gap between the hard and onerous pursuit of knowledge and the desire on the part of some students to have it handed to them without the pain of acquiring it.

On the secondary and primary school level, the State has just begun to pay attention to environmental education. The legislature passed a resolution requesting the Governor to set up a task force to design a statewide system of environmental education. The State Board of Education in January 1970 passed its own resolution urging the establishment of "a program of environmental studies as a planned part of the curriculum in all elementary and secondary schools in Maryland." (See Appendix CC.) A Committee on Environmental Education, under the chairmanship of Dr. James Latham, is to develop the short-term and long-term measures which can be introduced into all schools in the state.

At present, the schools, depending on the degree of interest of individual educators, are increasing their emphasis on environmental studies. Many were spurred by the preparations for Earth Day.

Even at the lower levels, the implications of the environment are causing new looks at the traditional separation of science from social studies. The new methods of teaching biology, chemistry, and physics will be extended to yet another dimension, according to Dr. Latham. The National Science Foundation program of Summer Institutes for Science Teachers is, for the first time, bringing environmental education into the training program. The teacher colleges in Maryland, for the moment, confine their work in this field to "outdoor education," an important but far from inclusive approach to the total environment.

Some textbooks are beginning to reflect the national concern, but the pattern is still quite spotty.*

Transit and Baltimore City

The Greater Baltimore Committee (GBC) is made up of representatives of the most influential businessmen in the area, whose concept of development includes education, housing, balanced transportation, and an imaginative approach to the checking of urban rot and the construction of huge new pedestrian complexes in the city center and harbor which can rejuvenate community life.

Their involvement in improving the environment of the city is an exercise in civic responsibility and a recognition that profits are related to the quality of the urban centers in which they work. (Wearing other hats, representatives of the same companies may have mixed records in connection with air and water pollution which they are now making some efforts to correct through technical repair. The Greater Baltimore Committee, in fact, is only peripherally involved in air pollution at all, considering that problem the business of the Chamber of Commerce.)

The rejuvenation of Charles Center and the Inner Harbor, for which the GBC marshalled funds and public support, is almost a prototype of progressive business action to reverse the death throes of a cancerous city center. The total design concept conviction has led to its current interest in planning for a transportation system rather than for highways alone.

The future of Baltimore is tied to the success or failure of a balanced transportation system as much as it is to education, housing, and jobs. By 1985, the Committee feels that an additional million people will have been born or moved to Baltimore, if the projected rates of population growth and immigration are valid. (Planning for that number must also include the creation of new towns or satellite cities outside of Baltimore.)

With GBC support, Baltimore became the first city to adopt a highway plan which took into account social, economic, and aesthetic needs, as well as coordination with other forms of transportation. In tandem with an engineering firm, state highway officials had proposed to run an expressway through the heart of the city without regard to

* Rand-McNally has a Grade 7 textbook on ecology.

the havoc it would cause. A single architect and planner, Archibald Rogers, mobilizing the local chapter of the American Institute of Architects, fought this single-minded approach; and the Federal Government later provided funds to hire Skidmore, Owings & Merrill and a team of architects, traffic consultants, and experts in landscape design, sociology, acoustics, community relations, and other disciplines. An alternate plan, which bypasses the center and harbor bridge and better serves the city's needs, has since been adopted despite its greater cost. Through marshalling of public support, a $4.8 million Federal grant, and the involvement of the State Roads Commission and the City Commissioner of Public Works, a practical plan was evolved and was approved by Mayor Alessandro.

The Regional Planning Council, whose role is to provide information rather than to carry out programs, influenced the decision by providing scientific backup for a broader approach than that of the highway engineers. Twenty-four years of studies, however, have consumed some $50,000,000 in public funds, and it has only been since recent public awareness of expressway damage to the people it displaces and the neighborhoods it degrades that more intelligent plans have been selected.

William Boucher, the executive director of GBC, is looking beyond highways to the role of all transportation in what he calls "Design Year for Center City, 1990." The Governor's Task Force on Transportation and the Legislature have erected a single Department of Transportation at the cabinet level, combining the previously separate State Roads Commission and the Motor Vehicles, Transit Authority, Ports, and Aviation agencies. Most important, it set up a single trust fund which does away with special funds, issuing bonds for all projects. The exclusive use for highways of the sacrosanct gasoline tax, still a sacred cow in many states, will be altered to benefit mass transit as well.

Maryland has, because of its delay in choosing routes for highways, been behind most states in the use of Federal funds. As it turns out, this may be a blessing in disguise.

Boucher is optimistic, feeling that Baltimore is still a manageable proposition. He feels that the city is aware, the state cooperative, and the private sector progressive, forward-looking, and conscious of the need for planning. The GBC has been able to persuade its own members to make such temporary sacrifices as to tear down 160 acres in downtown Baltimore, including buildings of recent construction, in order to fit in with the master plan – a feat probably quite beyond the persua-sive powers of the regional planning council.

The fate of mass transit, however, on which a number of other issues eventually will depend, including perhaps a solution to air pollution, is still uncertain. Planning is going ahead by a strengthened Metropolitan Transit Authority for a 71-mile, 63-station rapid transit system, and it is now authorized to acquire the Baltimore Transit Company in order to integrate it into a regional plan for bus and rail traffic in the region.

Austin E. Penn, who is also the chairman of the board of Baltimore Electric and Power Co., is chairman of the new MTA. The GBC is putting its weight behind a swift completion of planning and local financing, the latter in some doubt, in order not to lose Federal assis-tance in funding the proposed system.

Thus, the environmental activities of this prestigious Greater Balti-more Committee are predicated upon an optimistic prediction that the city can absorb and keep up with a very large anticipated growth in both population and the production of goods and services to support that population.

Case Study -- Calvert Cliffs

In many instances involving environmental degradation, Maryland, like other states, will still have to pay the piper on decisions made a decade and more ago. The Calvert Cliffs atomic energy project is a good ex-ample of site selections being made before environmental factors were understood to be as important a consideration as they are today. (Throughout the country, public protests have delayed construction of 28 nuclear power plants with 22,000 megawatt capacity – half the total capacity of the United States 30 years ago.)

A publication, *Nuclear Power Plants in Maryland,*[7] outlines the tech-nical considerations studied in connection with granting the Baltimore Gas and Electric Company permission to construct a nuclear facility at Calvert Cliffs. Despite some reservations on the part of L. Eugene Cronin of the University of Maryland's Natural Resources Institute, who believes that the environmental effects are not sufficiently pre-dictable to permit a go-ahead without further study, most observers

7. State of Maryland, Governor:s Task Force on Nuclear Power Plants, *Nuclear Power Plants in Maryland* (Annapolis, Maryland: The Task Force, State Office Building, December 1969).

believe that this plant will be constructed and will constitute an important source of needed power in the seventies.

The Maryland dilemma is shared by many if not all states. AEC Chairman Glenn Seaborg has testified in hearings before the Joint Atomic Energy Committee that U.S. power needs by the end of the century will be 800 percent greater than at present, with atomic power expected to replace fossil fuel at a rapidly increasing rate. Maryland officials confirm this estimate for their own state, and point out that however the long-range increase may be looked at, the short-term needs will double within the next decade, and are more or less irrevocable.

In the words of Federal Power Commissioner Carl Bagge, "In the past, utilities were prone to plan their growth covertly, to acquire land without deliberate disclosure, and to exhibit confidence, perhaps even arrogance, fostered by the endemic power of eminent domain." Now Maryland, like other states, has given its public service commission a specific mandate to license siting of plants and transmission facilities.

Baltimore Gas and Electric hopes to build an additional six nuclear power plants. The next proposed nuclear plant, slated for the Bush River in Harford County, is expected to run into much greater opposition than the Calvert Cliffs plant, unless considerably better technology to avoid thermal pollution is perfected.

Maryland conservationists contend that decision-making has not yet changed in depth, and that the government agencies do not yet represent the public interest. They point out that in the hearings on the Calvert Cliffs atomic energy plant, the State Department of Water Resources did no investigations on its own and questioned no witnesses. The Baltimore Gas and Electric Company brought in twelve paid expert witnesses; the lawyers representing conservationist interests had to make do without fees and lacked the money to buy transcripts of the hearings in order to make their appeal.

At the end of 1970, Maryland conservation groups had not yet given up their efforts to prevent the Calvert Cliffs plant from coming into operation and the outcome could not be predicted definitely.

Case Study -- Piney Point

Maryland conservationists claim that, however negative their position appears, it is a necessary counterbalance to the reluctance of traditional interests to mend their ways except under extreme pressure. The state agencies, they say, tend to accommodate industry as a first reaction and then take measures to limit the pollution which a narrowly-based decision too often produces. For example, when the Steuart Oil Company made application to construct a topping plant at Piney Point in St. Mary's County, conservationists claimed that the location was obviously undesirable. It is near valuable residential and resort areas, and the Potomac waters produce large quantities of shell fish. Virginia, which had not had a voice in the decision, is across the river and vulnerable; and naturalists tell us that 70 percent of the waterfowl population of the Atlantic flyway use the Potomac during their migratory life.

And yet, say the conservationists, the first reaction of the state agencies is to approve the application on condition that the company not pollute and this enjoinder is an impossible restraint on any refinery, because it is not able to guarantee, even with improved technology, that there will be no odors, no spills, no fires.

The company, which is the principal supplier of fuel for the Washington area, has for twenty years had a storage facility at Piney Point, a deep water facility, into which it has imported refined oil for transhipment to Washington. It claims that with modern technology it can guarantee a pollution-free processing cycle. The conservationists mobilized strong public support, a general outcry, and even a meeting in Secretary Hickel's office with groups from both Virginia and Maryland. In the end, pressure on the county commissioners caused their appointed committee narrowly (5-4) to deny the application. In the meantime, the matter had become academic in that the import license for the oil from abroad on which the topping plant would have depended was denied by the Federal Government.

Since that time, company plans to build a $6 million pipeline from Piney Point to the PEPCO generating plant in Morgantown, Md. have been frustrated by conservationist property owners in Charles and St. Mary's counties who are afraid that the pipeline will bring new industry and accompanying pollution. The company now plans to use barges and trucks to transport the oil, a method which on the surface appears to carry more risks to the environment than a pipeline below ground.

The State, say the conservationists, played a passive role, only reacting to original pressure on the part of industry and later in reaction to public pressure.

Industry, despite the pressure it exerts on the State to permit profit-making expansion, professes itself anxious to have overall guidelines as to the extent and manner in which the area is to grow, what kind of total power needs should be met, and the exact requirements for its operations. Both sides have complained that their own initiatives have occurred because the State follows rather than leads.

Case Study—Green Springs and Worthington Valleys

An article in *Fortune* by Max Ways describes an innovative effort to protect the environment and save open space.[8] Just north of Baltimore, the Green Spring and Worthington Valleys spread for 45,000 acres and constitute one of America's most beautiful landscapes. Occupants are wealthy landowners who breed horses and cattle, and who do not want to see this spacious beauty defiled by growth. But building of new highways has made the area more accessible to Baltimore and real estate developers are circling the area, waiting for the chance to buy and subdivide.

Recognizing the inevitability of change, the landowners sought assistance from David A. Wallace, the planner of Charles Center in Baltimore, and Ian L. McHarg, a landscape architect who has achieved national attention. The planners worked out a scheme to preserve the beautiful valley floor, and at the same time generate roughly the $33,500,000 in profits that they estimated the subdivision would have brought in. Building would be prohibited on the valley floor, while clusters of development would be permitted on the area's plateaus. A way will have to be found to channel some of the profits from the sale of plateau land to owners in the valley who would agree not to sell to developers. Within thirty years, the population of the area might rise six times from its present level of 17,000 without ruining the valley. *Fortune* has described the essential elements of the plan as 1) the wishes of the private owners; 2) a recognition that the pressure for housing from outside would require change in the area; 3) a combination of ecological and socio-economic planning principles; and 4) support of the plan by government.[9]

8. Max Ways, "How to Think About the Environment," in "The Environment, a National Mission for the Seventies," by the Editors of *Fortune* (New York, Evanston, and London: Harper and Row, Publishers, Perennial Library No. P-189, 1970), pp. 213-214. The "Plan for the Valleys" is described in a chapter of Ian L. McHarg, "Design With Nature" (Garden City, New York: Published by the National History Press for The American Museum of Natural History, 1969), pp. 79-93.

9. Ibid.

Case Study – Ocean City

Ocean City, in Worcester County, has long been a leisurely Atlantic City type of beach resort; but growth and consequent crowding have made it an example of the ability of man to foul his own nest. Its spectacular frontage on the Atlantic Ocean and its fertile marshlands, in which a chain of fish and shellfish life is nourished, made it a pleasurable place on the ocean.

But real estate developers, with the help of compliant officials, have allowed it to grow without tolerable limits in the name of "broadening the tax base." Much of its marshland has been filled in, paved over or otherwise altered, and there are now too many people, too many cracker-box houses, fewer animals, plants, and fish. The cycle is almost complete: people have been attracted to Ocean City by its natural qualities and like hordes of locusts they are degrading the environment which attracted them there in the first place.

Passage of the Wetlands Bill* may slow the degradation of Ocean City, but it is by no means certain that the local government has a full understanding of the cancerous nature of the growth which already has taken place.

Ironically, many of the developers who have prospered through the exploitation of Ocean City have moved to a desirable nearby community called Captain's Hills, where the marshlands have been preserved and rational planning observed.

Case Study -- Scenic Rivers

A two-year-old state law has led Maryland's conservation and planning agencies to recommend geographical limits on the use and development of the lands, parks, forests, and wetlands surrounding the Patuxtent, Pocomoke, Severn, Wicomico, and Youghiogheny Rivers.

An eight-man commission headed by Spencer P. Ellis, the director of Forests and Parks, was drawn from the relevant State agencies and

---

* Sale of 122 acres of Ocean City wetlands for $100 an acre to a developer who promptly turned a huge profit by dividing and selling lots to the public caused tremendous adverse publicity in late 1968 when the transaction occurred. The event was a major factor influencing the decision of the legislature to pass two bills which give the State strict control over the uses of all wetlands and guidelines for disposal of any by the State.

provided an example of the ability of a number of agencies to cooperate and agree on recommended solutions. They recommended that the five rivers be regulated by State law under a "scenic rivers" system which would permit the Secretary of Natural Resources to prohibit the construction of dams or channels in the rivers. This would require new legislation and the cooperation of local governments since the most power which State officials expect is merely a veto power over county plans.

As with the Wetlands Bill, local developers and county officials are likely to fight down the line any attempt to limit development or industrialization, with their concomitant water pollution and ecological disorder.

Development and the Maryland Environment

The impact of the environmental crisis, with much of the confusion and mixed reactions which it generates, is nowhere better reflected than in the sometimes beleaguered office of Director William Pate of the Department of Economic Development. Originally this office, as in other states, was set up in a government-business boosterism climate to attract new industry and "sell" the state as an ideal place to locate. Competition among states for new industry has long been in vogue, with some states boasting of cheap and docile labor; others, like Maryland, of ample water resources on which so much U.S. industry depends. Power is the handmaiden of this growth, and power companies attempt to expand in time to meet estimated and multiplying demands of industry as well as that of the population which new industry attracts.

Pate says that environmental awareness has led the State to what he calls a new goal of quality for economic development, but insists that practical action requires "trade-offs" in the process. Baltimore Harbor, for instance, is responsible for more than 11 percent of the economy of the entire state. If it is not to lose business to the other deep-water ports, it will need to handle the larger cargos involved in the containerization revolution which is changing traditional shipping practices. The controversial widening of the Chesapeake and Delaware Canal which conservationists fear will change the salinity and ecology of the bay is necessary if the larger containerization ships are to come in. Oysters account for less than one percent of the economy. If such a move takes out oyster beds, this must be measured in juxtaposition with the 11 percent represented by the harbor.

Pate speaks of the new industry which Maryland has lost, principally because the "environmental lobby" prevented the Department from offering them suitable sites. One, Steuart's topping plant, was an obvious polluter, but the other two in his judgment represented more important economic gains than they did environmental loss (a plastics factory and a chemical plant).

Pate deplores "blind dedication" to conservation and believes that as long as we have our present economic and political system, our total environment has to accommodate some disadvantages. He believes it is technically possible to "whip" water pollution, but that in some cases compromises with aesthetic principles must be made, as in building an access road to a factory, pipelines for fuel and power, etc.

The negative approach of the conservationists, he feels, is unrealistic, because it concentrates on what people don't want, rather than on what they want. He feels that a comprehensive state development plan is needed, which could be drawn up, not by the formal planning agencies, but by an ad hoc group in which all interested parties could participate. Their frame of reference would at first be established by agreement, and specific policies might evolve. Only through this kind of total approach could all aspects of Maryland's needs – social, economic, cultural, and environmental – be included. Where local government policy impinges on these agreed goals, the State would then have much more leverage to exert needed pressure on purely local interests.

This is, he says, a transitional period in our civilization. Our democratic-capitalistic system has been based on a blind faith in growth. (Stock prices, for instance, are predicated on accelerated growth in the future rather than on present measurable value.) He feels that the era of the car is drawing to an end and that, despite the need for crash development of technology to meet power demands, a cutback in per capita power is inevitable. But basically, he says, no long-range solution is possible without redistribution of population, which can only be accomplished by redistribution of industry.

Mr. Pate's reflections illustrate the impact of environmental concern when it reaches officials with a hitherto straightforward mission. In Maryland the time for trade-offs has arrived; decision-making no longer can be made in the relatively simple frameworks of highways, or urban housing, or schools, or fishing; and the values formerly attached to industrial growth have been rejected in isolated, local cases.

Hard Choices Ahead

From the case studies presented in this survey of Maryland institutions, it is clear that the effect on the Governor, on the legislature, on the State agencies, business, and the conservationist groups has been profound and wide-reaching. Legislation has passed which formerly was buried in committees. Funds have been provided. The State has gathered significant power, as in the sewage treatment plants legislation, to overcome local obstruction to needed technological measures. The State agencies dealing with the environment have been reorganized and strengthened. The conservation groups have begun to act in concert.* Young lawyers have switched from civil rights to the environment as a primary cause. The universities have begun to look at the relationships between disciplines in a creative way which may ultimately affect the structure of higher education. Business is investing considerably more money in anti-pollution devices, which it once felt it could not afford.

And yet with all the brouhaha, only a few legislators are beginning to look at the larger dimensions of the problem, to wonder if technical repair and anti-pollution legislation is going to be sufficient to stem the tide. New industry in Maryland attracts many new citizens from Pennsylvania and West Virginia. It is the question of future economic growth for the state as a whole which is not being faced. For thinking Marylanders the dilemma is that even better sewage systems can be overloaded, and the state must run fast to stand still in this and other areas. There is a kind of inexorable force about growth, built upon the very American optimism that technical solutions can be found to everything, that the system can always work. The language of the environment is confusing to the working man, the small entrepreneur, the merchant, the "silent majority," and the urban poor or the ethnic minorities. The intellectuals have already developed special jargon which they repeat to each other as careers are made and exclusive rights are staked out to the preserve of environmental issues. But for the general public there are mainly over-simplified media presentations on television and in the

---

* In Maryland's historic and cozy State house, special interest lobbyists actually used to sit in the empty chairs of Senators and delegates during the legislative sessions, drafting notes to solons, chatting with the speaker. Legislation was often drafted by representatives of the industries or interest which it was supposed to control. Now these lobbyists are barred from the floor, and the environment has provided a focus for citizens' groups to participate in a meaningful way in the legislative process, helping to draw up legislation, and gaining experience in the lively horsetrading which goes on in the halls during the session.

press, villains to rage against, and horror stories to titillate, but little light on the real dilemma.

An interview with a Maryland labor leader was illuminating. He said that he expected 94 percent of the available open space and farmland in the state of Maryland to be covered by housing and industry in the next twenty to thirty years, but that American know-how would come up with processed foods to amply feed everyone. Cities, he said, might very well have to be built under glass, but he had faith that this could be done. In response to a question on what the labor unions were doing about environment, he said that they were trying to prepare for the 35-hour work week. Although local labor serves on air and water pollution commissions set up by the governor, they have not yet created their own research committees to give them the kind of knowledge needed for meaningful participation.

The general concern is real, even though the rhetoric may eventually deescalate. The important thing is to institutionalize that concern so that environmental factors can be built into all future decisions. The State, for instance, has not really come to grips with the dynamics of land use. An example is instructive:

Only three of the eleven counties that front directly on the Chesapeake Bay are in the Baltimore region, but when compared to the other "on bay" jurisdictions they represent 79 percent of the 1960 population and 83 percent of the estimated 1980 population.

The three jurisdictions on the bay of the Baltimore region contain the bulk of the present bay population and have the highest growth rates. The shorefront, however, is a finite commodity and becoming more attractive to development because of its scarcity in the metropolitan area and the extension of utilities, such as public water, sewers, and new or improved roads.

This development pressure is stronger along the Baltimore regional shoreline than it is along any other portion of the bay, and this trend is expected to continue with subsequent increases in land values. If present trends continue, the Regional Planning Council anticipates that the entire shoreline will be urbanized in the next twenty years – already, there are fewer than 50 large, undeveloped parcels on the upper western shore.

The choice is clear: If policies relating to desired development objectives are not formulated now, the entire shoreline may become developed without regard for the needs of future generations or optimal use of the land-water resource.

At this stage of land management, the new laws do not really affect the damaging siting decisions which are being made even now. (Instead of preventing builders from constructing on a hill or grade, they merely require him to provide safeguards against sedimentation.) The future should see an extension of zoning, perhaps a siting bill based on the Maine prototype, and the creation of a shoreline commission.* But the ultimate question is whether the state can continue to be carved up and "developed" indefinitely.

The state will have to face the problem of growth in other ways. Another bill which was buried in legislative council dealt with the power question. Resources are not presently available to establish regulatory safeguards in terms of monitoring and staffing of the agencies. The bill would have created a mechanism by a tiny surcharge on electric power generated to pay for the physical model of the Chesapeake Bay, which has languished for lack of funds, a comprehensive research program, monitoring equipment, and the staffing of regulatory agencies. The bill was opposed by the Baltimore Gas and Electric Company, but it will surely return in another legislative session.

Pesticides, a major concern in other parts of the country, has not been as big an issue in Maryland. Anti-pesticide legislation failed during the last session because its sponsors had not adequately prepared the data needed for a meaningful bill and because the agricultural interests accepted the Wetlands Bill with the tacit understanding that a ban on pesticides would not be pushed that session. Because wetlands were a major public issue,** this compromise was accepted.

It is likely that in coming years, the great water compacts—the Potomac Basin, the Susquehanna, and the Chesapeake Bay—will take on more importance as realization of the need for regional solutions increases. Hopefully, taxing policy and its influence on land use, both in urban and rural areas, will be reviewed and gradually reformed.

In the field of transportation, which so vitally affects both land use and the air we breathe, there is still insufficient public awareness of the need for new attitudes. For such matters as the nature of car engines,

---

* A bill to provide state controls on shoreline: i.e., property 100 yards inland from the water, failed in the 1970 legislative session.

** Passage of the Wetlands Bill was aided by three conservationist groups, whose representatives can take a great deal of credit for public awareness and the lobbying effort which influenced the legislature. Jim Glazier, president of the Izaak Walton League, Armin Behr, of the Wilderness Society, and Ruth Mathes, of the Sierra Club, were particularly effective in the fight to preserve the ecologically valuable marshes and submerged tidal wetlands.

the pattern of interstate transportation, the kinds of subsidies given for mass transit, railroads, airplanes, and their associated facilities, the State must depend largely on Federal action. Yet it can influence national policy by its own attitude toward highways or water and air. The States, in the courts, are testing their right to set higher standards in controls on pollution, but Federal policies and Federal funds are key catalysts to State activity.

On balance, the undoubted steps forward taken by the State of Maryland have bought time, and may even arrest the spread of or even temporarily turn back some of its pollution problems. But hard questions hang over the state, and the shape of its future may lie in the answers to such questions as whether or not private developers can continue to purchase, level and subdivide, how much industrial expansion of water-based industries is feasible, whether power needs can be met without damage to the environment. Behind these questions are more serious ones which bear on life styles: Can per capita power consumption be curtailed? Are present definitions of property rights destructive to the environment? Will citizens accept restrictions on the use and size of their cars? Will they accept new taxes, higher prices if that proves necessary? Can home be brought nearer to factory? And to carry it one step further, do we really know how much of our growth is inexorable?

Do we know what really *are* the choices ahead?

Part 5

Some Closing Thoughts

General Conclusions

Analysis of the facts, opinions, and trends examined in the course of the survey lead to a number of general conclusions:

1. Scientific data are not available for an accurate description of the nature, gravity, or imminence of the "environmental crisis."

2. There is, however, a general consensus to the effect that

    a. An urgent need exists for extensive and intensive programs of research and data-gathering on local, regional, and global levels of pollution, on the biological effects of air, water, and land pollutants; on the possibility of meteorological effects from environmental degradation; and on ecosystems generally – their nature, processes, and inter-relationships.

    b. Whatever the level of the current "crisis," the time has arrived when men and nations can continue to treat natural resources as though they were infinite only at the risk of some sort of disaster in the very near future, historically speaking.

3. The political world is beginning, tentatively, to take up the task of planned environmental management at many levels of organization, and this will lead ultimately to permanent management of critical elements of the global environment – a task which cannot easily be defined yet, but can easily be identified as one ultimately involving a quantum jump in international cooperation.

4. Planned environmental management will require unpredictable but

profound and pervasive changes in national and international attitudes, traditions, values, and organizations – which is to say that the "environmental crisis" is at the same time a crisis in beliefs and institutions.

5. Effective concern for the quality of the global life-support system will serve as an agent for, and lend legitimacy to, societal reform not otherwise acceptable – and will nourish the emergence and imposition of an "ecological point of view" with important implications for international political life.

6. Federal, regional, local and trans-national organizations, public and private, are in no more than a very preliminary stage of approaching the problem of environmental management in terms of policy, organization, research, and development, or allocation of financial resources. Their initial focus tends strongly to be on the symptoms of the problem; e.g., pollution.

7. Pressures from the general public, from legislatures, and from specific segments of the population such as the legal profession, predictably will force or reinforce internal governmental initiatives to move more generally and more rapidly toward planned environmental management – creating in the process changes in political climates and possibly new alignments of political power and influence.

8. Environmental issues have broad implications for formal education, from pre-kindergarten to post-graduate levels, and might become the activating agent for pervasive reform of the educational system.

9. Professional and other private organizations have an important, conceivably critical, role to play in the evolution of a global environmental management system, especially in helping to overcome the obstacles to cooperation imposed by conflicting political interests, official ideology and bureaucratic inertia.

10. The initial and continuing costs of environmental management at the various levels of political organization are not yet foreseeable but certainly will reach orders of magnitude that will raise major questions of budgetary, financial, and tax policies – and may well require drastic changes in national defense policies and programs.

11. The outstanding immediate issue requiring urgent attention is an essentially doctrinal problem: the successful assimilation, on both the national and international scenes, of undeniable concerns for the quality of the environment with undeniable concerns for improved material standards of living for people everywhere still existing at and below the level of poverty. Unless the two concerns can be seen and understood as mutually supporting forces with compatible if not identical goals, the net political effect of the "environmental crisis" could well be more divisive than unifying.

Postscript: The Blessings of Complexity

The present state of environmental affairs is unique for at least two reasons: first, because it is global in the immutable sense that it involves ultimately the relationship of the whole human race with the finite life-support system of Earth; and second, because it is a problem that cannot be solved but only managed on a permanent basis.

There is no way back to a prior condition, real or imagined. And it would be socially disastrous if not suicidal to multiply, on extrapolated scales, past trends of environmental damage. What's the point of surviving in a world growing steadily less livable in an accelerating slide toward physical degradation, unmanageable social chaos, and political and moral stagnation?

So there is no choice but to start mastering the process of planned environmental management. Somehow we obviously must learn how:

To produce more efficiently with less waste and contamination – which may involve another "industrial revolution" in the technologies of recycling and reusing resources.

To consume with more restraint and less littering – which will involve not just technology, but the purposes for which technology is used, with reflections in research, product design, marketing policy, pricing, and advertising.

To weigh, for decision-making purposes, such social factors as educational, health, and recreational facilities, such elements as landscape and cityscape design, and such resources as scenic beauty and architectural harmony – which will induce a more quality-oriented concept of "growth" and the goals it serves.

To recast our institutions, public and private, for the new, more complex, and more sophisticated tasks of decision-making, which will impinge upon traditional notions of "individual rights" in relation to private property and the "public interest," and upon prevailing notions of democratic practices in relation to allocation and control of resources.

To make cities somehow more satisfying and less stressful places in which to live – injecting aesthetic and even psychic factors into urban planning.

To start putting behind us nineteenth-century concepts of national interests and the role of power in international life in favor of a much more cooperative and open world community.

Above all, perhaps, we must learn how to think and talk about the shape of the predicament in its whole dimension, searching the while for viable concepts of "optimal" population sizes and distribution patterns and optimal levels of production, consumption, and productivity.

The fact of the matter is that we do not yet know how to do the things that we know we must do. In practice, we can get only the faintest glimpse of what effective environmental management planning is going to mean. Theoretical work is being done on systems analysis; academic research is moving in the direction of interdisciplinary study and problem-orientation; and some urbanologists are groping toward what they call a "total design concept."

But the public discourse about environmental problems has been dominated so far by a monkish penitence about past "greed," a futile search for the devil of the piece, a hopeless yearning for an imaginary past, a waspish demand to destroy "the system" in favor of a spectral Utopia – plus calls for action to clean up past pollution and estop new projects with undesirable environmental or social side effects.

Something much more comprehensive, expansive, positive, and dynamic is needed, which implies an evolved concept of economic-social evolution measured by more humane criteria than statistical averages.

It is necessary to note that powerful traditions, stubborn conflicts, human obstinacy, inexperience and plain ignorance all serve as brakes on such an evolution – and that growing communities have their own built-in potentials for stress and alienation.

It is necessary to know, too, that the agencies of government at various levels are only in the most preliminary stages of attempting to adapt to or even perceive the shape of the whole predicament – and are a long way from having the knowledge, the institutional forms, the administrative techniques, or the philosophical insights which ultimately will be needed for effective management of the life-support system of a lonely spaceship known as Earth and its crew called Man.

Yet what makes all this complexity tolerable is that a view of the whole can liberate the mind from benighted tunnels of specialized knowledge and thought. It can free decision-makers from functionalism and from a linear approach to problem-solving. Thus the ultimate effect of consciousness of the predicament in toto can be illuminating and potentially ennobling.

Elements of great new insights undoubtedly are in the air, ready to be seized, synthesized, and formulated– ready to reveal pathways from physical crisis to human inventiveness and social creativity. In the end the crisis is in the mind.

Part 6

Appendixes

APPENDIX A:

Public Law 91-190, National Environmental Improvement Policy Act of 1969

An Act to establish a national policy for the environment, to provide for the establishment of a Council on Environmental Quality, and for other purposes.

Be it enacted by the Senate and House of Representatives of the United States of America in Congress assembled, That this Act may be cited as the "National Environmental Policy Act of 1969".

PURPOSE

Sec. 2. The purposes of this Act are: To declare a national policy which will encourage productive and enjoyable harmony between man and his environment; to promote efforts which will prevent or eliminate damage to the environment and biosphere and stimulate the health and welfare of man; to enrich the understanding of the ecological systems and natural resources important to the Nation; and to establish a Council on Environmental Quality.

TITLE I

DECLARATION OF NATIONAL ENVIRONMENTAL POLICY

Sec. 101. (a) The Congress, recognizing the profound impact of man's activity on the interrelations of all components of the natural environment, particularly the profound influences of population growth, high-density urbanization, industrial expansion, resource exploitation, and new and expanding technological advances and recognizing further the critical importance of restoring and maintaining environmental quality to the overall welfare and development of man, declares that it is the continuing policy of the Federal Government, in cooperation with State and local governments, and other concerned public and private organizations, to use all practicable means and measures, including financial and technical assistance, in a manner calculated to foster and promote the general welfare, to create and maintain conditions under which man and nature can exist in productive harmony, and fulfill the social, economic, and other requirements of present and future generations of Americans.

(b) In order to carry out the policy set forth in this Act, it is the continuing responsibility of the Federal Government to use all practicable means, consistent with other essential considerations of national policy, to improve and coordinate Federal plans, functions, programs, and resources to the end that the Nation may—

1. fulfill the responsibilities of each generation as trustee of the environment for succeeding generations;
2. assure for all Americans safe, healthful, productive, and esthetically and culturally pleasing surroundings;
3. attain the widest range of beneficial uses of the environment without degradation, risk to health or safety, or other undesirable and unintended consequences;
4. preserve important historic, cultural, and natural aspects of our national heritage, and maintain, wherever possible, an environment which supports diversity and variety of individual choice;
5. achieve a balance between population and resource use which will permit high standards of living and a wide sharing of life's amenities; and
6. enhance the quality of renewable resources and approach the maximum attainable recycling of depletable resources.

(c) The Congress recognizes that each person should enjoy a healthful environment and that each person has a responsibility to contribute to the preservation and enhancement of the environment.

Sec. 102. The Congress authorizes and directs that, to the fullest extent possible: (1) the policies, regulations, and public laws of the United States shall be interpreted and administered in accordance with the policies set forth in this Act, and (2) all agencies of the Federal Government shall—

A. utilize a systematic, interdisciplinary approach which will insure the integrated use of the natural and social sciences and the environmental design arts in planning and in decisionmaking which may have an impact on man's environment;

B. identify and develop methods and procedures, in consultation with the Council on Environmental Quality established by title II of this Act, which will insure that presently unquantified environmental amenities and values may be given appropriate consideration in decisionmaking along with economic and technical considerations;

C. include in every recommendation or report on proposals for legislation and other major Federal actions significantly affecting the quality of the human environment, a detailed statement by the responsible official on—

    i. the environmental impact of the proposed action,

    ii. any adverse environmental effects which cannot be avoided should the proposal be implemented,

    iii. alternatives to the proposed action,

    iv. the relationship between local short-term uses of man's environment and the maintenance and enhancement of long-term productivity, and

    v. any irreversible and irretrievable commitments of resources which would be involved in the proposed action should it be implemented.

Prior to making any detailed statement, the responsible Federal official shall consult with and obtain the comments of any Federal agency which has jurisdiction by law or special expertise with respect to any environmental impact involved. Copies of such statement and the comments and views of the appropriate Federal, State, and local agencies, which are authorized to develop and enforce environmental standards, shall be made available to the President, the Council on Environmental Quality and to the public as provided by section 552 of title 5. United States Code, and shall accompany the proposal through the existing agency review processes;

D. study, develop, and describe appropriate alternatives to recommended courses of action in any proposal which involves unresolved conflicts concerning alternative uses of available resources;

E. recognize the worldwide and long-range character of environmental problems and, where consistent with the foreign policy of the United States, lend appropriate support to initiatives, resolutions, and programs designed to maximize international cooperation in anticipating and preventing a decline in the quality of mankind's world environment;

F. make available to States, counties, municipalities, institutions, and individuals, advice and information useful in restoring; maintaining, and enhancing the quality of the environment;

G. initiate and utilize ecological information in the planning and development of resource-oriented projects; and

H. assist the Council on Environmental Quality established by title II of this Act.

Sec. 103. All agencies of the Federal Government shall review their present statutory authority, administrative regulations, and current policies and procedures for the purpose of determining whether there are any deficiencies or inconsistencies therein which prohibit full compliance with the purposes and provisions of this Act and shall propose to the President not later than July 1, 1971, such measures as may be necessary to bring their authority and policies into conformity with the intent, purposes, and procedures set forth in this Act.

Sec. 104. Nothing in Section 102 or 103 shall in any way affect the specific statutory obligations of any Federal agency (1) to comply with criteria or standards of environmental quality, (2) to coordinate or consult with any other Federal or State agency, or (3) to act, or refrain from acting contingent upon the recommendations or certification of any other Federal or State agency.

Sec. 105. The policies and goals set forth in this Act are supplementary to those set forth in existing authorizations of Federal agencies.

TITLE II

COUNCIL ON ENVIRONMENTAL QUALITY

Sec. 201. The President shall transmit to the Congress annually beginning July 1, 1970, an Environmental Quality Report (hereinafter referred to as the "report") which shall set forth (1) the status and condition of the major natural, manmade, or altered environmental classes of the Nation, including, but not limited to, the air, the aquatic, including marine, estuarine, and fresh water, and the terrestrial environment, including, but not limited to, the forest, dryland, wetland, range, urban, suburban, and rural environment; (2) current and foreseeable trends in the quality, management and utilization of such environments and the effects of those trends on the social, economic, and other requirements of the Nation; (3) the adequacy of available natural resources for fulfilling human and economic requirements of the Nation in the light of expected population pressures; (4) a review of the programs and activities (including regulatory activities) of the Federal Government, the State and local governments, and nongovernmental entities or individuals, with particular reference to their effect on the environment and on the conservation, development and utilization of natural resources; and (5) a program for remedying the deficiencies of existing programs and activities, together with recommendations for legislation.

Sec. 202. There is created in the Executive Office of the President a Council on Environmental Quality (hereinafter referred to as the "Council"). The Council shall be composed of three members who shall be appointed by the President to serve at his pleasure, by and with the advice and consent of the Senate. The President shall designate one of the members of the Council to serve as Chairman. Each member shall be a person who, as a result of his training, experience, and attainments, is exceptionally well qualified to analyze and interpret environmental trends and information of all kinds; to appraise programs and activities of the Federal Government in the light of the policy set forth in title I of this Act; to be conscious of and responsive to the scientific, economic, social, esthetic, and cultural needs and interests of the Nation; and to formulate and recommend national policies to promote the improvement of the quality of the environment.

Sec. 203. The Council may employ such officers and employees as may be necessary to carry out its functions under this Act. In addition, the Council may employ and fix the compensation of such experts and consultants as may be necessary for the carrying out of its functions under this Act, in accordance with section 3109 of title 5, United States Code (but without regard to the last sentence thereof).

Sec. 204. It shall be the duty and function of the Council—

1. to assist and advise the President in the preparation of the Environmental Quality Report required by section 201;

2. to gather timely and authoritative information concerning the conditions and trends in the quality of the environment both current and prospective, to analyze and interpret such information for the purpose of determining whether such conditions and trends are interfering, or are likely to interfere, with the achievement of the policy set forth in title I of this Act, and to compile and submit to the President studies relating to such conditions and trends;

3. to review and appraise the various programs and activities of the Federal Government in the light of the policy set forth in title I of this Act for the purpose of determining the extent to which such programs and activities are contributing to the achievement of such policy, and to make recommendations to the President with respect thereto;

4. to develop and recommend to the President national policies to foster and promote the improvement of environmental quality to meet the conservation, social, economic, health, and other require-

ments and goals of the Nation;

5. to conduct investigations, studies, surveys, research, and analyses relating to ecological systems and environmental quality;

6. to document and define changes in the natural environment, including the plant and animal systems, and to accumulate necessary data and other information for a continuing analysis of these changes or trends and an interpretation of their underlying causes;

7. to report at least once each year to the President on the state and condition of the environment; and

8. to make and furnish such studies, reports thereon, and recommendations with respect to matters of policy and legislation as the President may request.

Sec. 205. In exercising its powers, functions, and duties under this Act, the Council shall—

1. consult with the Citizens' Advisory Committee on Environmental Quality established by Executive Order numbered 11472, dated May 29, 1969, and with such representatives of science, industry, agriculture, labor, conservation organizations, State and local governments and other groups, as it deems advisable; and

2. utilize, to the fullest extent possible, the services, facilities, and information (including statistical information) of public and private agencies and organizations, and individuals, in order that duplication of effort and expense may be avoided, thus assuring that the Council's activities will not unnecessarily overlap or conflict with similar activities authorized by law and performed by established agencies.

Sec. 206. Members of the Council shall serve full time and the Chairman of the Council shall be compensated at the rate provided for Level II of the Executive Schedule Pay Rates (5 U.S.C. 5313). The other members of the Council shall be compensated at the rate provided for Level IV or the Executive Schedule Pay Rates (5 U.S.C.5315).

Sec. 207. There are authorized to be appropriated to carry out the provisions of this Act not to exceed $300,000 for fiscal year 1970, $700,000 for fiscal year 1971, and $1,000,000 for each fiscal year thereafter.

Approved January 1, 1970.

APPENDIX B:

Excerpt from First Annual Report of the Council on Environmental Quality, August 1970

Chapter XIII: Present and Future Environmental Needs

This report has looked closely at particular environmental problems. It has looked at what is being done now to combat them. And it has looked at what might be done in the days, months, and years ahead. The agenda for urgent action is long. Much has already been done, but much more must still be done with current management tools wielded by existing institutions. Moreover, the pace of change in programs underway promises, over the next few years, to brake even further what has seemed a headlong careening toward environmental decay.

The pressing need for tomorrow is to know much more than we do today. We lack scientific data about how natural forces work on our environment and how pollutants alter our natural world. We lack experience in innovating solutions. We lack tools to tell us whether our environment is improving or deteriorating. And most of all, we lack an agreed upon basic concept from which to look at environmental problems and then to solve them.

Needed—A Conceptual Framework

A problem is said to exist when our view of what conditions are does not square with our view of what they should be. Problems, in short, are products of our values. People agree—for example, that a river should not be polluted. And when they see that it is, water pollution becomes a problem. But some of the values dealt with in this report are not unanimously agreed upon. The chapter on land use is critical of urban sprawl; yet many Americans choose to live in dwellings which abet such sprawl. This uncertainty about what values are relevant to environmental questions and how widely or strongly they are held throws up a major obstacle to conceiving environmental problems. How much value do Americans place on the natural environment as against the man-made environment of cities? How much do people value esthetics? Do they agree about what is esthetically desirable? These and a host of similar questions must be raised when trying to align priorities for coping with environmental decline.

Our ignorance of the interrelationship of separate pollution problems is a handicap in devising control strategies. Is pollution directly related to population or to land use or to resources? Is so, how? Indeed, does it do any good to talk about pollution in general, or must we deal with a series of particular pollution problems radiation, pesticides, solid waste? A systems approach is needed, but what kind of system? The pollution system, the materials and resources use system, the land use system, the water resources or atmospheric system? In this report the Council has suggested tentative answers to some of these questions. But much more thought is necessary before we can be confident that we have the intellectual tools necessary to delineate accurately the problems and long-range strategies for action.

Experience will help resolve some of the conceptual problems. We already know what problems are most pressing. Clearly we need stronger institutions and financing. We need to examine alternative approaches to pollution control. We need better monitoring and research. And we need to establish priorities and comprehensive policies.

Needed—Stronger Institutions

Most of the burden for dealing with environmental problems falls to governments at all levels. And the Nation's ability to strengthen these institutions is central to the struggle for environmental quality. To make them stronger, fundamental changes are necessary at Federal, State, and local levels of government. Chapter II of this report treats in detail the President's proposed improvements in the Federal Government for better environmental policy development and management. Although these changes will not be the final answer, they do lay the base for a comprehensive and coordinated Federal attack on environmental problems.

States play a key role in environmental management because of their geographic scope and broad legal powers. Many have reorganized to focus comprehensively on environmental problems. Many are helping municipalities build sewage treatment plants; some are planning statewide treatment authorities to construct and operate plants. And California has led the Nation in trying to curb automobile air pollution since the 1950's. In land use control many States are carving out larger responsibilities for land use decisions of regional scope.

In many respects local government, of all the levels, most needs institutional improvement. It has suffered from fragmentation, from skyrocketing demands and costs for public services, and from generally inelastic tax sources. The financial burden of environmental improvement staggers local governments. Most of the costs of water pollution control, both capital and operating expenses, come from their budgets. In some cities, efforts to deal with combined sewer overflows raise almost insuperable financial and technical hardships. Solid waste disposal is a major expense for most local governments, and the costs grow as disposal techniques are upgraded, as land grows scarcer, and as wages spiral. On top of its financial headaches, local government is caught in a tangled web of overlapping and conflicting jurisdictions that hamstring solutions to land use and air pollution.

Existing institutions must be made better and, in some cases, new institutions created to deal with the environment. Occasionally more funds, personnel, and public support are all that is necessary. Other cases call for a more fundamental restructuring. This may mean extending geographic coverage and operational capabilities. Air and water pollution, for example, do not respect political boundaries, so institutions covering entire watersheds or airsheds may be necessary to cope with them. Important aspects of land use planning, review, and control may need to be shifted to regional or State levels as the only way to tie land use needs together over wide areas. And new forms of land use criteria may be necessary to reverse the current myopia of local government zoning.

Many environmental problems cross not only local, state, and regional boundaries, but international boundaries as well. Control of pollution of the seas and the atmosphere requires new forms of international cooperation—for monitoring, research, and regulation.

Needed—Financial Reform

Financing for environmental quality is in need of dramatic overhaul. Liquid and solid waste collection and disposal by local governments represent an indispensible service—not unlike electricity and water. Yet rarely do the users of these services, industry and homeowners, bear the full costs of operation and amortization. Rather, financially beleaguered local governments subsidize these services. The current method of financing, therefore, is not only inequitable; it encourages a greater accumulation of waste by industries because they do not bear the full costs of disposal. It deprives local governments of needed funds to operate and maintain waste disposal facilities properly. In short, it contributes to the sorry performance of facilities in the United States in treating sewage and disposing of solid wastes. If future demands for environmental improvement are to be funded adequately, better methods of financing must be developed.

Needed—Pollution Control Curbs.

This report discusses many tools for curbing pollution. Most have been regulatory. For centuries authority to regulate has been wielded to a limited extent—more broadly by the middle of the 20th century. But there is considerable debate whether regulation represents the best course of action. Economic incentives have won increasing support as a pollution control weapon. Charges or taxes on the volume of pollutants—say, 10 cents a pound on oxygen-demanding material—are another lever that might spur industry to reduce wastes. The charge system, some say, would not only be more economic but also more effective compared to the traditionally cumbersome enforcement process.

In this report the Council urges stricter and more systematic enforcement of air and water standards. That cannot be done, however, without better monitoring and data—as well as clear-cut, enforcement policies that will leave no doubt of responsibilities on the part of the private sector.

The Council believes that economic incentives offer promise, especially if backed up by regulatory power. It believes that they should be selectively demonstrated. And it believes that effluent or emission charges should be evaluated as a supplementary method of stimulating abatement measures.

Needed—Monitoring and Research

Effective strategy for national environmental quality requires a foundation of information on the current status of the environment, on changes and trends in its condition, and on what these changes mean to man. Without such information, we can only react to environmental problems after they become serious enough for us to see. But we cannot develop a long-term strategy to prevent them, to anticipate them, and to deal with them before they become serious. For example, we became aware of the mercury problem only after it had become critical in some areas and had probably done environmental damage. Yet we still do not know the extent or significance of that damage. Our attack on the problem can now be but a cure or a cleanup. It has already happened. However, if we had possessed an adequate environmental early warning system, we would have been able to anticipate mercury pollution and take early action to stop it at its sources.

We do not know what low-level exposure to most pollutants does to man's health over the long term. Nor do we know how people react to changes in their environment. The challenge to the social sciences is to develop entirely new gauges to measure environmental stress. What do crowding, urban noise, and automation do to man? These are critical questions. We do not understand enough about the interactions of different environmental forces such as urbanization, land use, and pollution. We do not even understand many of the natural processes that play critical roles in environmental well being—such as changes in world climate.

To obtain such information, a comprehensive program is required. It involves nationwide environmental monitoring, collection, analysis, and—finally—effective use of the information. In the case of some pollution, such monitoring should be international.

The first step is to identify the environmental parameters—things in the environment which are or should be measured. These range from substances such as DDT, sulfur dioxide, and lead to percentages of open space in the cities, visitor use of parks, and survival of species. Once identified, the parameters must be monitored—measured on a regular, repeated, continuing basis. In this way, baselines of the present status can be determined and changes from that base detected.

Environmental indices can be developed from these data. Indices are data aggregated to provide a picture of some aspect of environmental quality—for example, the quality of air as it affects human health. They are not unlike the cost of living index by which economists measure the status of the economy and by which housewives measure their budgets. Some environmental indices—and the parameters on which they are based—are easily identified and measured. For example, conditions that clearly affect human health in air or drinking water can be easily detected. Other indices and parameters are based on value judgments and are much more difficult to deal with. The quality of National Parks and scenic beauty are examples. To develop indices, the information from monitoring must be collected, translated into a usable form, and analyzed. Good indices do two important things. They inform the general public of the quality of the environment, and they inform the government and other decision-makers who can take action. Good indices show the current environmental quality on a national or local scale and whether this condition is improving or degrading.

At present no nationwide environmental monitoring and information system exists. Federal, State, and local agencies now collect a variety of data. Many of these data, however, are obtained for limited program purposes or for scientific understanding. They are fragmentary and not comparable on a nationwide basis. Although it may be possible to use some of these in the comprehensive system which is needed, at present they do not provide the type of information or coverage necessary to evaluate the condition of the Nation's environment or to chart changes in its quality and trace their causes.

Therefore, a major national objective must be to develop a comprehensive nationwide system of environmental monitoring, information, and analysis. The Council has initiated a study of the nature and requirements for the early development of such a system. However, even after we have developed a system, we must then have additional knowledge to enable us to understand and interpret the data we get. We are not yet in a position to understand the significance of the monitoring results to man and to natural systems. More research is needed on how the environmental systems operate and on the impact of man on the environment and its impact on him. Consequently, augmenting such research must take a high national priority.

Needed—A System for Priorities

It is difficult, given the current state of environmental knowledge, to set long-term priorities for the future. Relevant measures of environmental quality are often not available or, if available, are inadequate. These difficulties are compounded by great regional differences. For the present we can use our limited current data to identify pressing problems for immediate attention. In the future, the difficult task of deciding the Nation's environmental priorities, however, must be faced. Resources for combating environmental blight and decay are limited. Choices will have to be made on which problems have first claim on these resources. Four main criteria should determine this priority:

The intrinsic importance of the problems—the harm caused by failing to solve them.

The rate at which the problems are going to increase in magnitude and intensity over the next few years.

The irreversibility of the damage of immediate action is not taken.

The measure of the benefits to society compared to the cost of taking action.

The process of setting priorities is difficult. There is deep conflict over which problems are most important. And the inertia of on-going activities is a major obstacle. There are conflicts between the needs of industry and the needs of the environment. And the public yearning for more conveniences clashes often with the best interests of the ecology. Nor will the priorities of the Federal Government always coincide with those of State and local governments. The Federal priorities will be broad and national. States and localities, however, will often give higher priority to other aspects of environmental quality. As long as these other levels of government at least meet national standards, the imposition of higher standards in some areas is welcome. Whatever the divergences, diligent application of priorities will be necessary to make any real progress toward a high quality environment.

Needed—Comprehensive Policies

As priorities are developed, policies must be devised to translate them into action. These policies may consist of a mix of activities aimed at a particular goal. Dealing with many environmental problems will require a battery of economic incentives, regulations, research, and assistance programs. In some areas, policies cannot be developed until more information is available. In other areas, they can and should be developed now.

For example, the need for a national energy policy is clear. As the demand for power increases rapidly, new power facilities have to be built. Power plants will pollute the air with oxides of sulfur and nitrogen, the water with heat, and the landscape with mammoth towers and obtrusive power lines.

This environmental harm cannot be wholly averted now, but it can be limited. For the short term, the design and siting of power generating facilities and transmission lines must be better planned and controlled. But for the longer run, a national energy policy should be developed. It would require a comprehensive analysis of energy resources and actual needs. It would provide for wise use of fuels, both conserving them for the future and lessening environmental damage. For example, wider use of nuclear fuel, natural gas, or low sulfur coal and oil would lower sulfur oxide levels in critical areas.

As national transportation policies are shaped, air pollution is one among several critical environmental factors that must be considered. Although air pollution can be abated by enforcing emission standards, control devices for individual vehicles and other technological solutions may not be enough in the long run to keep air pollution from worsening as population and the number of automobiles continue to increase in the cities. One part of a transportation policy should be the continued examination of alternative means of curbing auto emissions, such as the development and use of systems combining the flexibility of the individual automobile with the speed of modern mass transportation.

Control over land use, a critical need of the seventies, is lodged for the most part in local governments. And often local solutions are piecemeal and haphazard. The local property tax favors the single-family residence on a large lot over types of housing less wasteful of land. Planning often fails to take into account the impact of development on the natural surroundings and often is not heeded by local governments. All these factors together lead to a series of local zoning decisions and regulatory action that perpetuate urban sprawl.

The State role in land use control has traditionally been small because most of the authority has been delegated to local governments. And direct Federal control over local land use is smaller still. However, the Federal Government can influence how land is used through planning and capital grants. Under existing programs the Federal Government, by its actions, could spur more modern land use methods. It could encourage cluster zoning and timed development. It could identify natural areas for preservation and encourage channeling of future growth in more rational patterns.

The problems of land use are complicated and diffuse. And the challenge is to center all the capabilities of all levels of government in a coordinated attack on them. The problems and the challenge together argue for a national land use policy.

Population growth and economic growth are potential wellsprings of environmental decay. They increase the demands upon limited natural resources. The U.S. population will continue to grow for the next few decades. But environmental quality is difficult to achieve if population growth continues. The President has appointed a commission on Population Growth and the American Future, headed by John D. Rockefeller III, which will explore the policy implications of future population growth.

The development of knowledge will doubtless indicate many new areas in which national policies are appropriate. And as these policies are developed, specific programs for implementation must then be formulated.

Conclusions

The year 1970 represents a pivotal year in our battle for a clean environment. The Nation is committing resources at all levels of government and in the private sector. Public support is at an all-time high. And the President's proposal for consolidation of anti-pollution programs, coupled with the Council's policy advisory and coordinating role, provide an opportunity to look at environmental quality in new ways.

This report emphasizes the need to move aggressively now to deal with problems that can be dealt with within existing knowledge and by existing institutions. For the long term, we need much more knowledge of values; the scope and nature of environmental problems; status and trends in the environment; the workings of natural processes; and the effects of pollutants on man, animals, vegetation, and materials. As we gain this knowledge, we will need to develop the institutions and financing mechanisms, the priorities, the policies, and finally, the programs for implementation. Without such a systematic approach, the current piecemeal, unrelated efforts will achieve only partial and unsatisfactory progress in meeting environmental problems of tomorrow.

This report emphasizes that changes in one part of the environment inevitably trigger changes in other parts. These complex interactions of environmental processes must be looked at as a whole. While keeping in mind the indivisibility of the environment and its intricate interrelationships, it is also necessary that some segments be treated separately when attacking environmental decay. Water pollution caused by a specific source may affect an entire ecosystem. But enforcement action must be taken against the particular source, not against the ecosystem. The major portion of this report has dealt separately with interrelated environmental problems, but only because of the inadequacy of our current framework for considering the environment and the need to focus attention on particular problem areas.

The National Environmental Policy Act of 1969 clearly stresses the necessity of approaching environmental problems as a totality. The act requires that Federal decision making incorporate environmental values along with technical and economic values; that both short- and long-term effects be given careful consideration; and that irreversible actions and commitments be carefully weighed.

National environmental goals must be developed and pursued in the realization that the human environment is global in nature, and that international cooperation must be a principal ingredient to effective environmental management.

All levels of government should function in two distinct ways: Within their geographic scope and needs, they must consider and plan for the environment as an interrelated system. But at the same time they must make specific decisions and take specific actions to remedy environmental problems. These two levels apply to action by individual citizens and private institutions as well. Our view of the environment and its value is changing and will continue to change. But these changes have effect only as they relate to specific choices by local communities, by particular industries, and by individuals. People in the end shape the environment. If a better environment is passed down to future generations, it will be because of the values and actions of people—all of us—today.

APPENDIX C:

The President's Message of August 1970, Transmitting First Annual Report of the Council on Environmental Quality to the Congress

To the Congress of the United States:

This first report to the Congress on the state of the Nation's environment is an historic milestone. It represents the first time in the history of nations that a people has paused, consciously and systematically, to take comprehensive stock of the quality of its surroundings.

It comes not a moment too soon; The recent upsurge of public concern over environmental questions reflects a belated recognition that man has been too cavalier in his relations with nature. Unless we arrest the depredations that have been inflicted so carelessly on our natural systems—which exist in an intricate set of balance—we face the prospect of ecological disaster.

The hopeful side is that such a prospect *can* be avoided. Although recognition of the danger has come late, it has come forcefully. There still are large gaps in our environmental knowledge, but a great deal of what needs to be done can be identified. Much of this has already been begun, and much more can be started quickly if we act now.

Scope of the Council's Report

The accompanying report by the Council on Environmental Quality seeks to describe the conditions of our environment, and to identify major trends, problems, actions under way and opportunities for the future. This first report by the Council is necessarily incomplete in some respects, especially in the identification of trends. The National Environmental Policy Act, which created the Council, became law only at the beginning of this year. Existing systems for measuring and monitoring environmental conditions and trends, and for developing indicators of environmental quality, are still inadequate. There also is a great deal yet to be learned about the significance of these facts for the human condition.

However, the report will, I think, be of great value to the Congress (and also to the Executive Branch) by assembling in one comprehensive document a wealth of facts, analyses and recommendations concerning a wide range of our most pressing environmental challenges. It should also serve a major educational purpose, by clarifying for a broad public what those challenges are and where the principal dangers and opportunities lie.

Substantively as well as historically, this first report is an important document. No one can read it and remain complacent about the environmental threats we confront, or about the need both to do more and to learn more about those threats.

Getting at the Roots

"Environment" is not an abstract concern, or simply a matter of esthetics, or of personal taste—although it can and should involve these as well. Man is shaped to a great extent by his surroundings. Our physical nature, our mental health, our culture and institutions, our opportunities for challenge and fulfillment, our very survival—all of these are directly related to and affected by the environment in which we live. They depend upon the continued healthy functioning of the natural systems of the Earth.

Environmental deterioration is not a new phenomenon. But both the rate of deterioration and its critical impact have risen sharply in the years since the Second World War. Rapid population increases here and abroad, urbanization, the technology explosion and the patterns of economic growth have all contributed to our environmental crisis. While growth has brought extraordinary benefits, it has not been accompanied by sufficiently foresighted efforts to guide its development.

At the same time, in many localities determined action has brought positive improvements in the quality of air or water—demonstrating that, if we have the will and make the effort, we can meet environmental goals. We also have made important beginnings in developing the institutions and processes upon which any fundamental, long-range environmental improvement must be based.

The basic causes of our environmental troubles are complex and deeply imbedded. They include: our past tendency to emphasize quantitative growth at the expense of qualitative growth; the failure of our economy to provide full accounting for the social costs of environmental pollution; the failure to take environmental factors into account as a normal and necessary part of our planning and decision-making; the inadequacy of our institutions for dealing with problems that cut across traditional political boundaries; our dependence on conveniences, without regard for their impact on the environment; and more fundamentally, our failure to perceive the environment as a totality and to understand and to recognize the fundamental interdependence of all its parts, including man himself. It should be obvious that we cannot correct such deep-rooted causes overnight. Nor can we simply legislate them away. We need new knowledge, new perceptions, new attitudes—and these must extend to all levels of government and throughout the private sector as well: to industry; to the professions; to each individual citizen in his job and in his home. We must seek nothing less than a basic reform in the way our society looks at problems and makes decisions.

Our educational system has a key role to play in bringing about this reform. We must train professional environmental managers to deal with pollution, land planning, and all the other technical requirements of a high quality environment. It is also vital that our entire society develop a new understanding and a new awareness of man's relation to his environment—what might be called "environmental literacy." This will require the development and teaching of environmental concepts at every point in the educational process.

While education may provide ultimate answers to long-range environmental problems, however, we cannot afford to defer reforms which are needed now. We have already begun to provide the institutional framework for effective environmental improvement.

Organizing for Improvement

As my first official act of the decade, on January first I signed into law the National Environmental Policy Act. That Act established the Council on Environmental Quality. I have charged the Council with coordinating all environmental quality programs and with making a thorough review of all other Federal programs which affect the environment.

Federal agencies are now required to file with the Council and the public a statement setting out in detail the environmental implications of all proposals for legislation and for other major activities with a significant environmental impact. With the help of this provision, I intend to ensure that environmental considerations are taken into account at the earliest possible stage of the decision-making process.

On July 9 I sent to the Congress a reorganization plan which would establish an Environmental Protection Agency, consolidating the major environmental pollution responsibilities of the Federal Government.

This reform is long overdue.

Responsibility for anti-pollution and related programs is now fragmented among several Departments and agencies, thus weakening our overall Federal effort. Air pollution, water pollution and solid wastes are different forms of a single problem, and it becomes increasingly evident that broad systems approaches are going to be needed to bring our pollution problems under control. The reorganization would give unified direction to our war on pollution and provide a stronger organizational base for our stepped-up effort.

The Council on Environmental Quality has begun the vital task of identifying indicators of environmental quality and determining the requirements for monitoring systems in order to enable us to assess environmental trends. These systems are needed to give early warning of environmental problems. They will provide data for determining environmental needs and establishing priorities, and for assessing the effectiveness of programs to improve the environment. The development of such monitoring systems is essential to effective environmental management.

There is also a need to develop new knowledge through research. We need to know far more, for example, about the effects of specific pollutants, about ecological relationships, and about human behavior in relation to environmental factors. The Environmental Protection Agency should develop an integrated research program aimed at pollution control. The Council on Environmental Quality will continue, in cooperation with the Office of Science and Technology, to review and coordinate our overall environmental research effort, as well as to undertake its own environmental studies and research.

These actions represent important additions to the institutional, procedural, and informational base for effective environmental management. They hold the promise of a real leap forward in the years to come. At the same time, we must move ahead now in those areas in which we already possess the knowledge and capability for effective action.

Recent Actions and Recommendations

On February 10 of this year, I sent to the Congress a special message on the environment. This presented a 37-point action program, with special emphasis on strengthening our fight against water and air pollution.

In the field of water pollution, my major legislative recommendations included:

Authorization of $4 billion to cover the Federal share of a $10 billion program to provide treatment facilities.

Establishment of an Environmental Financing Authority to help finance the State and local share of treatment plants.

Reform of the method by which funds are allocated under the treatment grant programs.

Greatly strengthened enforcement authority, including provisions for fines of up to $10,000 a day for violations.

Among my major legislative recommendations for the control of air pollution were:

More stringent procedures for reducing pollution from motor vehicles.

Establishment of national air quality standards.

Establishment of national emissions standards for extremely hazardous pollutants.

A major strengthening of enforcement procedures, including extension of Federal air pollution control authority to both inter- and intra-state situations and provision for fines of up to $10,000 a day for violators.

Other legislative actions recommended in my February 10 message included:

Appropriation in 1971 of the full $327 million authorized under the Land and Water Conservation Fund to provide additional parks and recreation areas, with increased emphasis on locating new recreation facilities in crowded urban areas.

Establishment of new procedures to encourage and finance the relocation of Federal facilities now occupying land that could better be turned to public recreational use.

Authorizing the transfer of surplus real property to State and local governments for park and recreational purposes at public benefit discounts of up to 100 percent.

In addition, the message spelled out 14 separate measures I was taking by administrative action or Executive Order. These included such wide-ranging initiatives as launching an extensive Federal research and development program in unconventionally-powered, low-pollution vehicles, requiring the development of comprehensive river basin plans for water pollution control, re-directing research on solid waste management to place greater emphasis on re-cycling and re-use, and the establishment of a Property Review Board to recommend specific Federal properties for conversion to recreational use.

I again urge the Congress to act soon and favorably on the legislative proposals contained in that message. They are vital to our growing effort to protect and improve our environment.

I consider the recommendations in my February 10 message only a beginning—although an important one. I said at the time that we must do much more and that we would do more as we gained experience and knowledge. Our Administration is living up to that commitment.

Previously, on February 4, I had issued an Executive Order directing a prompt clean-up of air and water pollution caused by Federal agencies. This task is well underway. As I said then, the Federal Government should set an example for the rest of the country. We are doing so.

On April 15, I sent legislation to the Congress that will, if enacted, bring to an end the dumping of dredged spoils into the Great Lakes as soon as disposal sites are available. At the same time, I directed the Council on Environmental Quality to make a study of ocean disposal of wastes and report to me by September 1.

On May 19, I proposed enactment of a special tax on lead additives in gasoline, to encourage industry to provide low or nonleaded gasoline.

On May 20, I sent to the Congress a special message dealing with oil pollution caused by marine transportation of oil. The comprehensive, 10-point program set out in the message included legislative proposals, the announcement of administrative actions, and the forwarding to the Senate of two international conventions and amendments to a third for ratification. The nations of the world must take aggressive action to end the growing pollution of the oceans.

On May 23, I announced that the United States would propose a new treaty placing the natural resources of the deep sea bed beyond the 200 meter depth under international regulation.

On June 4, a revised National Contingency Plan for dealing with oil spills was announced at my direction by the Chairman of the Council on Environmental Quality.

On June 11, I sent a message to the Congress requesting the enactment of legislation cancelling twenty Federal oil leases for off-shore drilling which had been granted in 1968 in the Santa Barbara Channel and creating a Marine Sanctuary.

As I mentioned above, on July 9 I sent to the Congress a reorganization plan to create a new Environmental Protection Agency. On the same date, I sent another reorganization plan to consolidate Federal marine resource management functions in a National Oceanic and Atmospheric Administration, within the Department of Commerce. This would provide better coordination and direction of our vital ocean resource programs.

Toward a Land Use Policy

Lately, our attention as a people has repeatedly and insistently been seized by urgent concerns and immediate crises: by the sudden blanketing of cities or even whole regions with dense clouds of smog, for example, or the discovery of mercury pollution in rivers. But as we take the longer view, we find another challenge looming large: the mounting pressures of population. Both the size and the distribution of our population have critical relevance to the quality of our environment and thus to the quality of our lives.

Population growth poses an urgent problem of global dimensions. If the United States is to have an effective voice in world population policies, it must demonstrate willingness to face its own population problems at home.

The particular impact of any given level of population growth depends in large measure on patterns of land use. Three quarters of our people now live in urban areas, and if present trends continue most of them in the future will live in a few mammoth urban concentrations. These concentrations put enormous pressure on transportation, sanitation and other public services. They sometimes create demands that exceed the resource capacity of the region, as in the case of water supply. They can aggravate pollution, overcrowd recreation facilities, limit open space, and make the restorative world of nature ever more remote from everyday life. Yet we would be blind not to recognize that for the most part the movement of people to the cities has been the result neither of perversity nor of happenstance, but rather of natural human aspirations for the better jobs, schools, medical services, cultural opportunities and excitement that have traditionally been associated with urban life.

If the aspirations which have drawn Americans to the city in the first instance and subsequently from the city core to the suburbs are often proving illusory, the solution does not lie in seeking escape from urban life. Our challenge is to find ways to promote the amenities of life in the midst of urban development: in short, to make urban life fulfilling rather than frustrating. Along with the essentials of jobs and housing, we must also provide open spaces and outdoor recreation opportunities, maintain acceptable levels of air and water quality, reduce noise and litter, and develop cityscapes that delight the eye and uplift the spirit.

By the same token, it is essential that we also make rural life itself more attractive, thus encouraging orderly growth in rural areas. The creation of greater economic, social, cultural, and recreational opportunities in rural parts of the country will lead to the strengthening of small cities and towns, contributing to the establishment of new growth centers in the nation's heartland region.

Throughout the nation there is a critical need for more effective land use planning, and for better controls over use of the land and the living systems that depend on it. Throughout our history, our greatest resource has been our land—forests and plains, mountains and marshlands, rivers and lakes. Our land has sustained us. It has given us a love of freedom, a sense of security, and courage to test the unknown.

We have treated our land as if it were a limitless resource. Traditionally, Americans have felt that what they do with their own land is their own business. This attitude has been a natural outgrowth of the pioneer spirit. Today, we are coming to realize that our land is finite, while our population is growing. The uses to which our generation puts the land can either expand or severely limit the choices our children will have. The time has come when we must accept the idea that none of us has a right to abuse the land, and that on the contrary society as a whole has a legitimate interest in proper land use. There is a national interest in effective land use planning all across the nation.

I believe that the problems of urbanization which I have described, of resource management, and of land and water use generally can only be met by comprehensive approaches which take into account the widest range of social, economic, and ecological concerns. I believe we must work toward development of a National Land Use Policy to be carried out by an effective partnership of Federal, State and local governments together, and, where appropriate, with new regional institutional arrangements.

Recycling of Wastes

The prospect of increasing population density adds urgency to the need for greater emphasis on recycling of "waste" products. More people means greater consumption—and thus more rapid depletion—of scarce natural resources; greater consumption means more "waste" to dispose of—whether in the form of solid wastes, or of the pollutants that foul our air and water.

Yet much of this waste is unnecessary. Essentially, waste is a human invention: Natural systems are generally "closed" systems. Energy is transformed into vegetation, vegetation into animal life, and the latter returns to the air and soil to be recycled once again. Man, on the other hand, has developed "open" systems—ending all too often in an open sewer or an open dump.

We can no longer afford the indiscriminate waste of our natural resources; neither should we accept as inevitable the mounting costs of waste removal. We must move increasingly toward closed systems that recycle what now are considered wastes back into useful and productive purposes. This poses a major challenge—and a major opportunity—for private industry. The Council on Environmental Quality is working to foster development of such systems. Establishment of the proposed Environmental Protection Agency would greatly increase our ability to address this need systematically and creatively.

Everyone's Task

As our government has moved ahead to improve our environmental management, it has been greatly heartening to me to see the extent and effectiveness of citizen concern and activity, and especially the commitment of young people to the task. The job of building a better environment is not one for government alone. It must engage the enthusiasm and commitment of our entire society. Citizen organizations have been in the forefront of action to support strengthened environmental programs. The Citizens Advisory Committee on Environmental Quality, under the chairmanship of Laurance S. Rockefeller, has provided an important link between the Federal Government's effort and this broad-ranging citizen activity.

Similarly, the active participation of the business community is essential. The government's regulation and enforcement activities will continue to be strengthened. Performance standards must be upgraded as rapidly as feasible. But regulation cannot do the whole job. Forward-looking initiatives by business itself are also vital—in research, in the development of new products and processes, in continuing and increased investment in pollution abatement equipment.

On the international front, the level of environmental concern and action has been rapidly rising. Many of our most pressing environmental problems know no political boundaries. Environmental monitoring and pollution of the seas are examples of major needs that require international cooperation, and that also provide an opportunity for the world's nations to work together for their common benefit.

In dealing with the environment we must learn not how to master nature but how to master ourselves, our institutions, and our technology. We must achieve a new awareness of our dependence on our surroundings and on the natural systems which support all life, but awareness must be coupled with a full realization of our enormous capability to alter these surroundings. Nowhere is this capability greater than in the United States, and this country must lead the way in showing that our human and technological resources can be devoted to a better life and an improved environment for ourselves and our inheritors on this planet.

Our environmental problems are very serious, indeed urgent, but they do not justify either panic or hysteria. The problems are highly complex, and their resolution will require rational, systematic approaches, hard work and patience. There must be a *national* commitment and a *rational* commitment.

The accompanying report by the Council describes the principal problems we face now and can expect to face in the future, and it provides us with perceptive guidelines for meeting them. These deserve the most careful consideration. They point the directions in which we must move as rapidly as circumstances permit.

The newly aroused concern with our natural environment embraces old and young alike, in all walks of life. For the young, it has a special urgency. They know that it involves not only our own lives now but the future of mankind. For their parents, it has a special poignancy— because ours is the first generation to feel the pangs of concern for the environmental legacy we leave to our children.

At the heart of this concern for the environment lies our concern for the human condition: for the welfare of man himself, now and in the future. As we look ahead to the end of this new decade of heightened environmental awareness, therefore, we should set ourselves a higher goal than merely remedying the damage wrought in decades past. We should strive for an environment that not only sustains life but enriches life, harmonizing the works of man and nature for the greater good of all.

Richard Nixon   The White House, *August 1970.*

APPENDIX D:

**The President's Message on the Environment,
February 10, 1970**

To The Congress of the United States:

Like those in the last century who tilled a plot of land to exhaustion and then moved on to another, we in this century have too casually and too long abused our natural environment. The time has come when we can wait no longer to repair the damage already done, and to establish new criteria to guide us in the future.

The fight against pollution, however, is not a search for villains. For the most part, the damage done to our environment has not been the work of evil men, nor has it been the inevitable by-product either of advancing technology or of growing population. It results not so much from choices made, as from choices neglected: not from malign intention, but from failure to take into account the full consequences of our actions.

Quite inadvertently, by ignoring environmental costs we have given an economic advantage to the careless polluter over his more conscientious rival. While adopting laws prohibiting injury to person or property, we have freely allowed injury to our shared surroundings. Conditioned by an expanding frontier, we came only late to a recognition of how precious and how vulnerable our resources of land, water and air really are.

The tasks that need doing require money, resolve and ingenuity—and they are too big to be done by government alone. They call for fundamentally new philosophies of land, air and water use, for stricter regulation, for expanded government action, for greater citizen involvement, and for new programs to ensure that government, industry and individuals all are called on to do their share of the job and to pay their share of the cost.

Because the many aspects of environmental quality are closely interwoven, to consider each in isolation would be unwise. Therefore, I am today outlining a comprehensive, 37-point program, embracing 23 major legislative proposals and 14 new measures being taken by administrative action or Executive Order in five major categories:
Water pollution control.
Air pollution control.

Solid waste management.

Parklands and public recreation.

Organizing for action.

As we deepen our understanding of complex ecological processes, as we improve our technologies and institutions and learn from experience, much more will be possible. But these 37 measures represent actions we can take *now,* and that can move us dramatically forward toward what has become an urgent common goal of all Americans: the rescue of our natural habitat as a place both habitable and hospitable to man.

Water Pollution

Water pollution has three principal sources: municipal, industrial and agricultural wastes. All three must eventually be controlled if we are to restore the purity of our lakes and rivers.

Of these three, the most troublesome to control are those from agricultural sources: animal wastes, eroded soil, fertilizers and pesticides. Some of these are nature's own pollutions. The Missouri River was known as "Big Muddy" long before towns and industries were built on its banks. But many of the same techniques of pest control, livestock feeding, irrigation and soil fertilization that have made American agriculture so abundantly productive have also caused serious water pollution.

Effective control will take time, and will require action on many fronts: modified agricultural practices, greater care in the disposal of animal wastes, better soil conservation methods, new kinds of fertilizers, new chemical pesticides and more widespread use of natural pest control techniques. A number of such actions are already underway. We have taken action to phase out the use of DDT and other hard pesticides. We have begun to place controls on wastes from concentrated animal feed-lots. We need programs of intensified research, both public and private, to develop new methods of reducing agricultural pollution while maintaining productivity. I have asked The Council on Environmental Quality to press forward in this area. Meanwhile, however, we have the technology and the resources to proceed *now* on a program of swift clean-up of pollution from the most acutely damaging sources: municipal and industrial waste.

Municipal Wastes

As long as we have the means to do something about it, there is no good reason why municipal pollution of our waters should be allowed to persist unchecked.

In the four years since the Clean Waters Restoration Act of 1966 was passed, we have failed to keep our promises to ourselves: Federal appropriations for constructing municipal treatment plants have totaled only about one-third of authorizations. Municipalities themselves have faced increasing difficulty in selling bonds to finance their share of the construction costs. Given the saturated condition of today's municipal bond markets, if a clean-up program is to work it has to provide the means by which municipalities can finance their share of the cost even as we increase Federal expenditures.

The best current estimate is that it will take a total capital investment of about $10 billion over a five-year period to provide the municipal waste treatment plants and interceptor lines needed to meet our national water quality standards. This figure is based on a recently-completed nationwide survey of the deficiencies of present facilities, plus projections of additional needs that will have developed by then— to accommodate the normal annual increase in the volume of wastes, and to replace equipment that can be expected to wear out or become obsolete in the interim.

This will provide every community that needs it with secondary waste treatment, and also special, additional treatment in areas of special need, including communities on the Great Lakes. We have the industrial capacity to do the job in five years if we begin now.

To meet this construction schedule, I propose a two-part program of Federal assistance:

I propose a Clean Waters Act with $4 billion to be authorized immediately, for Fiscal 1971, to cover the full Federal share of the total $10 billion cost on a matching fund basis. This would be allocated at a rate of $1 billion a year for the next four years, with a reassessment in 1973 of needs for 1975 and subsequent years.

By thus assuring communities of full Federal support, we can enable planning to begin *now* for all needed facilities and construction to proceed at an accelerated rate.

I propose creation of a new Environmental Financing Authority, to ensure that every municipality in the country has an opportunity to sell its waste treatment plant construction bonds.

The condition of the municipal bond market is such that, in 1969, 509 issues totaling $2.9 billion proved unsalable. If a municipality cannot sell waste treatment plant construction bonds, EFA will buy them and will sell its own bonds on the taxable market. Thus, construction of pollution control facilities will depend not on a community's credit rating, but on its waste disposal needs.

Providing money is important, but equally important is where and how the money is spent. A river cannot be polluted on its left bank and clean on its right. In a given waterway, abating *some* of the pollution is often litle better than doing nothing at all, and money spent on such partial efforts is often largely wasted. Present grant allocation formulas—those in the 1966 Act—have prevented the spending of funds where they could produce the greatest results in terms of clean water. Too little attention has been given to seeing that investments in specific waste treatment plants have been matched by other municipalities and industries on the same waterway. Many plants have been poorly designed and inefficiently operated. Some municipalities have offered free treatment to local industries, then not treated their wastes sufficiently to prevent pollution.

To ensure that the new funds are well invested, five major reforms are needed. One requires legislation: the other four will be achieved by administrative action.

I propose that the present, rigid allocation formula be revised, so that special emphasis can be given to areas where facilities are most needed and where the greatest improvements in water quality will result.

Under existing authority, the Secretary of the Interior will institute four major reforms:

Federally assisted treatment plants will be required to meet prescribed design, operation and maintenance standards, and to be operated only State-certified operators.

Municipalities receiving Federal assistance in construction plants will be required to impose reasonable users' fees on industrial users sufficient to meet the costs of treating industrial wastes.

Development of comprehensive river basin plans will be required at an early date, to ensure that Federally assisted treatment plants will in fact contribute to effective clean-up of entire river basin systems.

Collection of existing data on pollution sources and development of effluent inventories will permit systems approaches to pollution control.

Wherever feasible, communities will be strongly encouraged to cooperate in the construction of large regional treatment facilities, which provide economies of scale and give more efficient and more thorough waste treatment.

Industrial Pollution

Some industries discharge their wastes into municipal systems; others discharge them directly into lakes and rivers. Obviously unless we curb industrial as well as municipal pollution our waters will never be clean.

Industry itself has recognized the problem, and many industrial firms are making vigorous efforts to control their water-borne wastes. But strict standards and strict enforcement are nevertheless necessary—not only to ensure compliance, but also in fairness to those who have voluntarily assumed the often costly burden while their competitors have not. Good neighbors should not be placed at a competitive disadvantage because of their good neighborliness.

Under existing law, standards for water pollution control often are established in only the most general and insufficient terms: for example, by requiring all affected industries to install secondary treatment facilities. This approach takes little account of such crucial variables as the volume and toxicity of the wastes actually being discharged, or the capacity of a particular body of water to absorb wastes without becoming polluted. Even more important, it provides a poor basis for enforcement: with no effluent standard by which to measure, it is difficult to prove in court that standards are being violated.

The present fragmenting of jurisdictions also has hindered comprehensive efforts. At present, Federal jurisdiction generally extends only to interstate waters. One result has been that as stricter State-Federal standards have been imposed, pollution has actually increased in some other waters—in underground aquifers and the oceans. As controls over interstate waters are tightened, polluting industries will be increasingly tempted to locate on intrastate lakes and rivers—with a consequently increased threat to those waterways—unless they too are brought under the same strictures.

I propose that we take an entirely new approach: one which concerts Federal, State and private efforts, which provides for effective nationwide enforcement, and which rests on a simple but profoundly significant principle: that the nation's waterways belong to us all, and that neither a municipality nor an industry should be allowed to discharge wastes into those waterways beyond their capacity to absorb the wastes without becoming polluted.

Specifically, I propose a seven-point program of measures we should adopt *now* to enforce control of water pollution from industrial and municipal wastes, and to give the States more effective backing in their own efforts.

I propose that State-Federal water quality standards be amended to impose precise effluent requirements on all industrial and municipal sources. These should be imposed on an expeditious timetable, with the limit for each based on a fair allocation of the total capacity of the waterway to absorb the user's particular kind of waste without becoming polluted.

I propose that violation of established effluent requirements be considered sufficient cause for court action.

I propose that the Secretary of the Interior be allowed to proceed more swiftly in his enforcement actions, and that he be given new legal weapons including subpoena and discovery power.

I propose that failure to meet established water quality standards or implementation schedules be made subject to court-imposed fines of up to $10,000 per day.

I propose that the Secretary of the Interior be authorized to seek immediate injunctive relief in emergency situations in which severe water pollution constitutes an imminent danger to health, or threatens irreversible damage to water quality.

I propose that the Federal pollution-control program be extended to include all navigable waters, both inter- and intrastate, all interstate ground waters, the United States' portion of boundary waters, and waters of the Contiguous Zone.

I propose that Federal operating grants to State pollution control enforcement agencies be tripled over the next five years—from $10 million now to $30 million in fiscal year 1975—to assist them in meeting the new responsibilities that stricted and expanded enforcement will place upon them.

Air Pollution Control

Air is our most vital resource, and its pollution is our most serious environmental problem. Existing technology for the control of air pollution is less advanced than that for controlling water pollution, but there is a great deal we can do within the limits of existing technology—and more we can do to spur technological advance.

Most air pollution is produced by the burning of fuels. About half is produced by motor vehicles.

Motor Vehicles

The Federal Government began regulating automobile emissions of carbon monoxide and hydrocarbons with the 1968 model year. Standards for 1970 model cars have been made significantly tighter. This year, for the first time, emissions from new buses and heavy-duty trucks have also been brought under Federal regulation.

In future years, emission levels can and must be brought much lower. *The Secretary of Health, Education and Welfare is today publishing a notice of new, considerably more stringent motor vehicle emission standards he intends to issue for 1973 and 1975 models including control of nitrogen oxides by 1973 and of particulate emissions by 1975.*

These new standards represent our best present estimate of the lowest emission levels attainable by those years.

Effective control requires new legislation to correct two key deficiencies in the present law:

a. Testing procedures.— Under present law, only manufacturers' prototype vehicles are tested for compliance with emission standards, and even this is voluntary rather than mandatory.

I propose legislation requiring that representative samples of actual production vehicles be tested throughout the model year.

b. Fuel composition and additives.— What goes into a car's fuel has a major effect on what comes out of its exhaust, and also on what kind of pollution-control devices can effectively be employed. Federal standards for what comes out of a car's engine should be accompanied by standards for what goes into it.

I propose legislation authorizing the Secretary of Health, Education and Welfare to regulate fuel composition and additives.

With these changes, we can drastically reduce pollution from motor vehicles in the years just ahead. But in making and keeping our peace with nature, to plan only one year ahead or even five is hardly to plan at all. Our responsibility now is also to look beyond the Seventies, and the prospects then are uncertain. Based on present trends, it is quite possible that by 1980 the increase in the sheer number of cars in densely populated areas will begin outrunning the technological limits of our capacity to reduce pollution from the internal combustion engine. I hope this will not happen. I hope the automobile industry's presently determined effort to make the internal combustion engine sufficiently pollution-free succeeds. But if it does not, then unless motor vehicles with an alternative, low-pollution power source are available, vehicle-caused pollution will once again begin an inexorable increase.

Therefore, prudence dictates that we move now to ensure that such a vehicle will be available if needed.

I am inaugurating a program to marshal both government and private research with the goal of producing an unconventionally powered virtually pollution-free automobile within five years.

I have ordered the start of an extensive Federal research and development program in unconventional vehicles, to be conducted under the general direction of the Council on Environmental Quality.

As an incentive to private developers, I have ordered that the Federal Government should undertake the purchase of privately produced unconventional vehicles for testing and evaluation.

A proposal currently before the Congress would provide a further incentive to private developers by authorizing the Federal government to offer premium prices for purchasing low-pollution cars for its own use. This could be a highly productive program once such automobiles are approaching development, although current estimates are that, initially, prices offered would have to be up to 200% of the cost of equivalent conventional vehicles rather than the 125% contemplated in the proposal legislation. The immediate task, however, is to see that an intensified program of research and development begins at once.

One encouraging aspect of the effort to curb motor vehicle pollution is the extent to which industry itself is taking the initiative. For example, the nation's principal automobile manufacturers are not only developing devices now to meet present and future Federal emission standards, but are also, on their own initiative, preparing to put on the market by 1972 automobiles which will not require and, indeed, must not use leaded gasoline. Such cars will not only discharge no lead into the atmosphere, but will also be equipped with still more effective devices for controlling emissions—devices made possible by the use of lead-free gasoline.

This is a great forward step taken by the manufacturers before any Federal regulation of lead additives or emissions has been imposed. I am confident that the petroleum industry will see to it that suitable non-leaded gasoline is made widely available for these new cars when they come on the market.

Stationary-Source Pollution

Industries, power plants, furnaces, incinerators—these and other so-called "stationary sources" add enormously to the pollution of the air. In highly industrialized areas, such pollution can quite literally make breathing hazardous to health, and can cause unforeseen atmospheric and meteorological problems as well.

Increasingly, industry itself has been adopting ambitious pollution-control programs, and state and local authorities have been setting and enforcing stricter anti-pollution standards. But they have not gone far enough or fast enough, nor, to be realistic about it, will they be able to without the strongest possible Federal backing. Without effective government standards, industrial firms that spend the necessary money for pollution control may find themselves at a serious economic disadvantage as against their less conscientious competitors. And without effective Federal standards, states and communities that require such controls find themselves at a similar disadvantage in attracting industry, against more permissive rivals. Air is no respecter of political boundaries: a community that sets and enforces strict standards may still find its air polluted from sources in another community or another state.

Under the Clean Air Act of 1967, the Federal government is establishing air quality control regions around the nation's major industrial and metropolitan areas. Within these regions, states are setting air quality standards—permissible levels of pollutants in the air—and developing plans for pollution abatement to achieve those air quality standards. All state air quality standards and implementation plans require Federal approval.

This program has been the first major Federal effort to control air pollution. It has been a useful beginning. But we have learned in the past two years that it has shortcomings. Federal designation of air quality control regions, while necessary in areas where emissions from one state are polluting the air in another, has been a time-consuming process. Adjoining states within the same region often have proposed inconsistent air quality standards, causing further delays for compromise and revision. There are no provisions for controlling pollution *outside* of established air quality control regions. This means that even with the designation of hundreds of such regions, some areas of the country with serious air pollution problems would remain outside of the program. This is unfair not only to the public but to many industries as well, since those within regions with strict requirements could be unfairly disadvantaged with respect to competitors that are not within regions. Finally, insufficient Federal enforcement powers have circumscribed the Federal government's ability to support the states in establishing and enforcing effective abatement programs.

It is time to build on what we have learned, and to begin a more ambitious national effort. I recommend that the Clean Air Act be revised to expand the scope of strict pollution abatement, to simplify the task of industry in pollution abatement through more nearly uniform standards, and to provide special controls against particularly dangerous pollutants.

I propose that the Federal government establish nationwide air quality standards, with the states to prepare within one year abatement plans for meeting those standards.

This will provide a minimum standard for air quality for all areas of the nation, while permitting states to set more stringent standards for any or all sections within the state. National air quality standards will relieve the states of the lengthy process of standard-setting under Federal supervision, and allow them to concentrate on the immediate business of developing and implementing abatement plans.

These abatement plans would cover areas both inside and outside of Federally designated air quality control regions, and could be designed to achieve any higher levels of air quality which the states might choose to establish. They would include emission standards for stationary sources of air pollution.

I propose that designation of interstate air quality control regions continue at an accelerated rate, to provide a framework for establishing compatible abatement plans in interstate areas.

I propose that the Federal government establish national emissions standards for facilities that emit pollutants extremely hazardouz to health, and for selected classes of new facilities which could be major contributors to air pollution.

In the first instance, national standards are needed to guarantee the earliest possible elimination of certain air pollutants which are clear health hazards even in minute quantities. In the second instance, national standards will ensure that advanced abatement technology is used in constructing the new facilities, and that levels of air quality are maintained in the face of industrial expansion. Before any emissions standards were established, public hearings would be required involving all interested parties. The States would be responsible for enforcing these standards in conjunction with their own programs.

I propose that Federal authority to seek court action be extended to include both inter- and intrastate air pollution situations in which, because of local non-enforcement, air quality is below national standards, or in which emissions standards or implementation time-tables are being violated.

I propose that failure to meet established air quality standards or implementation schedules be made subject to court-imposed fines of up to $10,000 per day.

Solid Waste Management

"Solid wastes" are the discarded left-overs of our advanced consumer society. Increasing in volume, they litter the landscape and strain the facilities of municipal governments.

New packaging methods, using materials which do not degrade and cannot easily be burned, create difficult new disposal problems. Though many wastes are potentially re-usable, we often discard today what a generation ago we saved. Most bottles, for example, now are "non-returnable." We re-process used paper less than we used to, not only adding to the burden on municipal sanitation services but also making wasteful use of scarce timberlands. Often the least expensive way to dispose of an old automobile is to abandon it—and millions of people do precisely that, creating eyesores for millions of others.

One way to meet the problem of solid wastes is simply to surrender to it: to continue pouring more and more public money into collection and disposal of whatever happens to be privately produced and discarded. This is the old way; it amounts to a public subsidy of waste pollution. If we are ever truly to gain control of the problem, our goal must be broader: to reduce the volume of wastes and the difficulty of their disposal, and to encourage their constructive re-use instead.

To accomplish this, we need incentives, regulations and research directed especially at two major goals: a) making products more easily disposable—especially containers, which are designed for disposal; and b) re-using and recycling a far greater proportion of waste materials.

As we look toward the long-range future—to 1980, 2000 and beyond—recycling of materials will become increasingly necessary not only for waste disposal but also to conserve resources. While our population grows, each one of us keeps using more of the earth's resources. In the case of many common minerals, more than half those extracted from the earth since time began have been extracted since 1910.

A great deal of our space research has been directed toward creating self-sustaining environments, in which people can live for long periods of time by re-processing, re-cycling and re-using the same materials. We need to apply this kind of thinking more consciously and more broadly to our patterns of use and disposal of materials here on earth.

Many currently used techniques of solid waste disposal remain crudely deficient. Research and development programs under the Solid Waste Disposal Act of 1965 have added significantly to our knowledge of more efficient techniques. The Act expires this year. I recommend its extension, and I have already moved to broaden its programs.

I have ordered a re-direction of research under the Solid Waste Disposal Act to place greater emphasis on techniques for re-cycling materials, and on development and use of packaging and other materials which will degrade after use—that is, which will become temporary rather than permanent wastes.

Few of America's eyesores are so unsightly as its millions of junk automobiles.

Ordinarily, when a car is retired from use it goes first to a wrecker, who strips it of its valuable parts, and then to a scrap processor, who reduces the remainder to scrap for sale to steel mills. The prices paid by wreckers for junk cars often are less than the cost of transporting them to the wrecking yard. In the case of a severely damaged or "cannibalized" car, instead of paying for it the wrecker may even charge towing costs. Thus the final owner's economic incentive to deliver his car for processing is slight, non-existent or even negative.

The rate of abandonment is increasing. In New York City, 2,500 cars were towed away as abandoned on the streets in 1960. In 1964, 25,000 were towed away as abandoned; in 1969, more than 50,000.

The way to provide the needed incentive is to apply to the automobile the principle that its price should include not only the cost of producing it, but also the cost of disposing of it.

I have asked the Council on Environmental Quality to take the lead in producing a recommendation for a bounty payment or other system to promote the prompt scrapping of all junk automobiles.

The particular disposal problems presented by the automobile are unique. However, wherever appropriate we should also seek to establish incentives and regulations to encourage the re-use, re-cycling or easier disposal of other commonly used goods.

I have asked the Chairman of the Council on Environmental Quality to work with the Cabinet Committee on the Environment, and with appropriate industry and consumer representatives, toward development of such incentives and regulations for submission to the Congress.

Parks and Public Recreation

Increasing population, increasing mobility, increasing incomes and increasing leisure will all combine in the years ahead to rank recreational facilities among the most vital of our public resources. Yet land suitable for such facilities, especially near heavily populated areas, is being rapidly swallowed up.

Plain common sense argues that we give greater priority to acquiring now the lands that will be so greatly needed in a few years. Good sense also argues that the Federal Government itself, as the nation's largest landholder, should address itself more imaginatively to the question of making optimum use of its own holdings in a recreation-hungry era.

I propose full funding in fiscal 1971 of the $327 million available through the Land and Water Conservation Fund for additional park and recreational facilities, with increased emphasis on locations that can be easily reached by the people in crowded urban areas.

I propose that we adopt a new philosophy for the use of Federally-owned lands, treating them as a precious resource—like money itself—which should be made to serve the highest possible public good.

Acquiring needed recreation areas is a real estate transaction. One third of all the land in the United States—more than 750,000,000 acres—is owned by the Federal Government. Thousands of acres in the heart of metropolitan areas are reserved for only minimal use by Federal installations. To supplement the regularly-appropriated funds available, nothing could be more appropriate than to meet new real estate needs through use of presently-owned real estate, whether by transfer, sale or conversion to a better use.

Until now, the uses to which Federally-owned properties were put has largely been determined by who got them first. As a result, countless properties with enormous potential as recreational areas linger on in the hands of agencies that could just as well—or better—locate elsewhere. Bureaucratic inertia is compounded by a quirk of present accounting procedures, which has the effect of imposing a budgetary penalty on an agency that gives up one piece of property and moves to another, even if the vacated property is sold for 10 times the cost of the new.

The time has come to make more rational use of our enormous wealth of real property, giving a new priority to our newly urgent concern with public recreation—and to make more imaginative use of properties now surplus to finance acquisition of properties now needed.

By Executive Order, I am directing the heads of all Federal agencies and the Administrator of General Services to institute a review of all Federally-owned real properties that should be considered for other uses. The test will be whether a particular property's continued present use or another would better serve the public interest, considering both the agency's needs and the property's location. Special emphasis will be placed on identifying properties that could appropriately be converted to parks and recreation areas, or sold, so that proceeds can be made available to provide additional park and recreation lands.

I am establishing a Property Review Board to review the GSA reports and recommend to me what properties should be converted or sold. This Board will consist of the Director of the Bureau of the Budget, the Chairman of the Council of Economic Advisers, the Chairman of the Council on Environmental Quality and the Administrator of General Services, plus others that I may designate.

I propose legislation to establish, for the first time, a program for relocating Federal installations that occupy locations that could better be used for other purposes.

This would allow a part of the proceeds from the sales of surplus properties to be used for relocating such installations, thus making more land available.

I also propose accompanying legislation to protect the Land and Water Conservation Fund, ensuring that its sources of income would be maintained and possibly increased for purchasing additional parkland.

The net effect would be to increase our capacity to add new park and recreational facilities, by enabling us for the first time to use surplus property sales in a coordinated three-way program: a) by direct conversion from other uses; b) through sale of presently-owned properties and purchase of others with the proceeds; and c) by sale of one Federal property, and use of the proceeds to finance the relocation and conversion costs of making another property available for recreational use.

I propose that the Department of the Interior be given authority to convey surplus real property to State and local governments for pack and recreation purposes at a public benefit discount ranging up to 100 percent.

I propose that Federal procedures be revised to encourage Federal agencies to make efficient use of real property. This revision should remove the budgetary penalty now imposed on agencies relinquishing one site and moving to another.

As one example of what such a property review can make possible, a sizable stretch of one of California's finest beaches has long been closed to the public because it was part of Camp Pendleton. Last month the Defense Department arranged to make more than a mile of that beach available to the State of California for use as a State park. The remaining beach is sufficient for Camp Pendleton's needs; thus the released stretch represents a shift from low-priority to high-priority use. By carefully weighing alternative uses, a priceless recreational resource was returned to the people for recreational purposes.

Another vast source of potential parklands also lies untapped. We have come to realize that we have too much land available for growing crops and not enough land for parks, open space and recreation.

I propose that instead of simply paying each year to keep this land idle, we help local governments buy selected parcels of it to provide recreational facilities for use by the people of towns in rural areas. This program has been tried, but allowed to lapse; I propose that we revive and expand it.

I propose that we also adopt a program of long-term contracts with private owners of idled farmland, providing for its reforestation and public use for such pursuits as hunting, fishing, hiking, and picnicking.

Organizing for Action

The environmental problems we face are deep-rooted and widespread. They can be solved only by a full national effort embracing not only sound, coordinated planning, but also an effective follow-through that reaches into every community in the land. Improving our surroundings is necessarily the business of us all.

At the Federal level, we have begun the process of organizing for this effort.

The Council on Environmental Quality has been established. This Council will be the keeper of our environmental conscience, and a goad to our ingenuity; beyond this, it will have responsibility for ensuring that all our programs and actions are undertaken with a careful respect for the needs of environmental quality. I have already assigned it major responsibilities for new program development, and I shall look to it increasingly for new initiatives.

The Cabinet Committee on the Environment, which I created last year, acts as a coordinating agency for various departmental activities affecting the environment.

To meet future needs, many organizational changes will still be needed. Federal institutions for dealing with the environment and natural resources have developed piecemeal over the years in response to specific needs, not all of which were originally perceived in the light of the concerns we recognize today. Many of their missions appear to overlap, and even to conflict. Last year I asked the President's Advisory Council on Executive Organization, headed by Mr. Roy Ash, to make an especially thorough study of the organization of Federal environmental natural resource and oceanographic programs, and to report its recommendations to me by April 15. After receiving their report, I shall recommend needed reforms, which will involve major reassignments of responsibilities among Departments.

For many of the same reasons, overlaps in environmental programs extend to the Legislative as well as the Executive branch, so that close consultation will be necessary before major steps are taken.

No matter how well organized government itself might be, however, in the final analysis the key to success lies with the people of America.

Private industry has an especially crucial role. Its resources, its technology, its demonstrated ingenuity in solving problems others only talk about—all these are needed, not only in helping curb the pollution industry itself creates but also in helping devise new and better ways of enhancing all aspects of our environment.

I have ordered that the United States Patent Office give special priority to the processing of applications for patents which could aid in curbing environmental abuses.

Industry already has begun moving swiftly toward a fuller recognition of its own environmental responsibilities, and has made substantial progress in many areas. However, more must be done.

Mobilizing industry's resources requires organization. With a remarkable degree of unanimity, its leaders have indicated their readiness to help.

I will shortly ask a group of the nation's principal industrial leaders to join me in establishing a National Industrial Pollution Control Council.

The Council will work closely with the Council on Environmental Quality, the Citizens' Advisory Committee on Environmental Quality, the Secretary of Commerce and others as appropriate in the development of effective policies for the curbing of air, water, noise and waste pollution from industrial sources. It will work to enlist increased support from business and industry in the drive to reduce pollution, in all its forms, to the minimum level possible. It will provide a mechanism through which, in many cases, government can work with key leaders in various industries to establish voluntary programs for accomplishing desired pollution-control goals.

Patterns of organization often turn out to be only as good as the example set by the organizer. For years, many Federal facilities have themselves been among the worst polluters. The Executive Order I issued last week not only accepts responsibility for putting a swift end to Federal pollution, but puts teeth into the commitment.

I hope this will be an example for others.

At the turn of the century, our chief environmental concern was to conserve what we had—and out of this concern grew the often embattled but always determined "conservation" movement. Today, "conservation" is as important as ever—but no longer is it enough to conserve what we have; we must also restore what we have lost. We have to go beyond conservation to embrace restoration.

The task of cleaning up our environment calls for a total mobilization by all of us. It involves governments at every level; it requires the help of every citizen. It cannot be a matter of simply sitting back and blaming someone else. Neither is it one to be left to a few hundred leaders. Rather, it presents us with one of those rare situations in which each individual everywhere has an opportunity to make a special contribution to his country as well as his community.

Through the Council on Environmental Quality, through the Citizens' Advisory Committee on Environmental Quality, and working with Governors and Mayors and county officials and with concerned private groups, we shall be reaching out in an effort to enlist millions of helping hands, millions of willing spirits—millions of volunteer citizens who will put to themselves the simple question: "What can *I* do?"

It is in this way—with vigorous Federal leadership, with active enlistment of governments at every level, with the aid of industry and private groups, and above all with the determined participation by individual citizens in every state and every community, that we at last will succeed in restoring the kind of environment we want for ourselves, and the kind of generations that come after deserve to inherit.

This task is ours together. It summons our energy, our ingenuity and our conscience in a cause as fundamental as life itself.

RICHARD NIXON.

The White House.

APPENDIX E:

State of the Union Address, Extract on Environment, January 22, 1970

I am confident that the Congress will act now to adopt the legislation I placed before you last year. We in the Executive have done everything we can under existing law, but new and stronger weapons are needed in that fight.

While it is true that state and local law enforcement agencies are the cutting edge in the effort to eliminate street crime, burglaries, and murder, my proposals to you have embodied my belief that the Federal government should play a greater role in working in partnership with these agencies.

That is why 1971 Federal spending for aiding local law enforcement will double that budgeted for 1970.

The primary responsibility for crimes that affect individuals is with local and state rather than with Federal government. But in the field of organized crime, narcotics and pornography, the Federal government has a special responsibility it should fulfill. And we should make Washington, D. C., where we have the primary responsibility, an example to the nation and the world of respect for law rather than lawlessness.

I now turn to a subject which, next to our desire for peace, may well become the major concern of the American people in the decade of the seventies.

In the next ten years we shall increase our wealth by fifty percent. The profound question is—does this mean we will be fifty percent richer in a real sense, fifty percent better off, fifty percent happier?

Or, does it mean that in the year 1980 the President standing in this place will look back on a decade in which seventy percent of our people lived in metropolitan areas choked by traffic, suffocated by smog, poisoned by water, deafened by noise and terrorized by crime?

These are not the great questions that concern world leaders at summit conferences. But people do not live at the summit. They live in the foothills of everyday experience. It is time for us all to concern ourselves with the way real people live in real life.

The great question of the seventies is, shall we surrender to our surroundings, or shall we make our peace with nature and begin to make reparations for the damage we have done to our air, to our land and to our water?

Restoring nature to its natural state is a cause beyond party and beyond factions. It has become a common cause of all the people of this country. It is a cause of particular concern to young Americans—because they more than we will reap the grim consequences of our failure to act on programs which are needed now if we are to prevent disaster later.

Clean air, clean water, open spaces—these should once again be the birthright of every American. If we act now—they can be.

We still think of air as free. But clean air is not free, and neither is clean water. The price tag on pollution control is high. Through our years of past carelessness we incurred a debt to nature, and now that debt is being called.

The program I shall propose to Congress will be the most comprehensive and costly program in this field in America's history.

It is not a program for just a year. A year's plan in this field is no plan at all. This is a time to look ahead not a year, but five or ten years—whatever time is required to do the job.

I shall propose to this Congress a ten billion dollar nation-wide clean waters program to put modern municipal waste treatment plants in every place in America where they are needed to make our waters clean again, and to do it now.

We have the industrial capacity, if we begin now, to build them all within five years. This program will get them built within five years.

As our cities and suburbs relentlessly expand, those priceless open spaces needed for recreation areas accessible to their people are swallowed up—often forever. Unless we preserve these spaces while they are still available, we will have none to preserve. Therefore, I shall propose new financing methods for purchasing open space and park lands, now, before they are lost to us.

The automobile is our worst polluter of the air. Adequate control requires further advances in engine design and fuel composition. We shall intensify our research, set increasingly strict standards and strengthen enforcement procedures—and we shall do it now.

We no longer can afford to consider air and water common property, free to be abused by anyone without regard to the consequences. Instead, we should begin now to treat them as scarce resources, which we are no more free to contaminate than we are free to throw garbage in our neighbor's yard.

This requires comprehensive new regulations. It also requires that, to the extent possible, the price of goods should be made to include the costs of producing and disposing of them without damage to the environment.

Now I realize that the argument is often made that there is a fundamental contradiction between economic growth and the quality of life, so that to have one we must forsake the other.

The answer is not to abandon growth, but to redirect it. For example, we should turn toward ending congestion and eliminating smog the same reservoir of inventive genius that created them in the first place.

Continued vigorous economic growth provides us with the means to enrich life itself and to enhance our planet as a place hospitable to man.

Each individual must enlist in this fight if it is to be won.

It has been said that no matter how many national parks and historical monuments we buy and develop, the truly significant environment for each of us is that in which we spend eighty percent of our time—in our homes, in our places of work and the streets over which we pass.

Street litter, rundown parking strips and yards, dilapidated fences, broken windows, smoking automobiles, dingy working places, all should be the object of our fresh view.

We have been too tolerant of our surroundings and too willing to leave it to others to clean up our environment. It is time for those who make massive demands on society to make some minimal demands on themselves. Each of us must resolve that each day he will leave his home, his property, the public places of his city or town a little cleaner, a little better, a little more pleasant for himself and those around him.

With the help of people we can do anything. Without their help we can do nothing. In this spirit, together, we can reclaim our land for ours and generations to come.

Between now and the year 2000, over one-hundred-million children will be born in the United States. Where they group up—and how— will, more than any one thing, measure the quality of American life in these years ahead.

This should be a warning to us.

For the past thirty years our population has also been growing and shifting. The result is exemplified in the vast areas of rural America emptying out of people and of promise—a third of our counties lost population in the 1960's.

The violent and decayed central cities of our great metropolitan complexes are the most conspicuous area of failure in American life today.

I propose that before these problems become insoluble, the nation develop a national growth policy.

In the future, decisions as to where to build highways, locate airports, acquire land or sell land should be made with a clear objective of aiding a balanced growth.

In particular, the Federal Government must be in a position to assist in the building of new cities and the rebuilding of old ones.

At the same time, we will carry our concern with the quality of life in America to the farm as well as the suburb, to the village as well as the city. What rural America needs most is a new kind of assistance. It needs to be dealt with, not as a separate nation, but as part of an overall growth policy for America. We must create a new rural environment that will not only stem the migration to urban centers, but reverse it. If we seize our growth as a challenge, we can make the 1970s an historic period when by conscious choice we transformed our land into what we want it to become.

America, which has pioneered in the new abundance, and in the new technology, is called upon today to pioneer in meeting the concerns which have followed in their wake—in turning the wonders of science to the service of man.

In the majesty of this great chamber we hear the echoes of America's history, of debates that rocked the Union and those that repaired it, of the summons to war and the search for peace, of the uniting of the people and the building of a nation.

Those echoes of history remind us of our roots and our strengths.

They remind us also of that special genius of American democracy, which at one critical turning point after another has led us to spot the new road to the future and given us the wisdom and courage to take it.

As I look down that new road which I have tried to map out today, I see a new America as we celebrate our two hundredth birthday six years from now.

I see an America in which we have abolished hunger, provided the means for every family in the nation to obtain a minimum income, made enormous progress in providing better housing, faster transportation, improved health and superior education.

I see an America in which we have checked inflation, and waged a winning war against crime.

I see an America in which we have made great strides in stopping the pollution of our air, cleaning up our water, opening up new parks, and continuing to explore in space.

Most important, I see an America at peace with all the nations of the world.

This is not an impossible dream. These goals are all within our reach.

In times past, our forefathers had the vision but not the means to achieve such goals.

APPENDIX F:

The President's Message to the Congress Transmitting the Report of the Council on Environmental Quality, Ocean Dumping: A National Policy, October 7, 1970

To the Congress of the United States:

The oceans, covering nearly three-quarters of the world's surface, are critical to maintaining our environment, for they contribute to the basic oxygen-carbon dioxide balance upon which human and animal life depends. Yet man does not treat the oceans well. He has assumed that their capacity to absorb wastes is infinite, and evidence is now accumulating on the damage that he has caused. Pollution is now visible even on the high seas—long believed beyond the reach of man's harmful influence. In recent months, worldwide concern has been expressed about the dangers of dumping toxic wastes in the oceans.

In view of the serious threat of ocean pollution, I am today transmitting to the Congress a study I requested from the Council on Environmental Quality. This study concludes that:

– the current level of ocean dumping is creating serious environmental damage in some areas.
– the volume of wastes dumped in the ocean is increasing rapidly.
– a vast new influx of wastes is likely to occur as municipalities and industries turn to the oceans as a convenient sink for their wastes.
– trends indicate that ocean disposal could become a major, nationwide environmental problem.
– unless we begin now to develop alternative methods of disposing of these wastes, institutional and economic obstacles will make it extremely difficult to control ocean dumping in the future.
– the nation must act now to prevent the problem from reaching unmanageable proportions.

The study recommends legislation to ban the unregulated dumping of all materials in the oceans and to prevent or rigorously limit the dumping of harmful materials. The recommended legislation would call for permits by the Administrator of the Environmental Protection Agency for the transportation and dumping of all materials in the oceans and in the Great Lakes.

I endorse the Council's recommendations and will submit specific legislative proposals to implement them to the next Congress. These recommendations will supplement legislation my Administration submitted to the Congress in November, 1969 to provide comprehensive management by the States of the land and waters of the coastal zone and in April, 1970 to control dumping of dredge spoil in the Great Lakes.

The program proposed by the Council is based on the premise that we should take action before the problem of ocean dumping becomes acute. To date, most of our energies have been spent cleaning up mistakes of the past. We have failed to recognize problems and to take corrective action before they became serious. The resulting signs of environmental decay are all around us, and remedial actions heavily tax our resources and energies.

The legislation recommended would be one of the first new authorities for the Environmental Protection Agency. I believe it is fitting that in this recommended legislation, we will be acting—rather than reacting—to prevent pollution before it begins to destroy the waters that are so critical to all living things.

Richard Nixon

The White House
October 7, 1970

NOTE: The report is entitled "Ocean Dumping: A National Policy" (Government Printing Office, 45 pp.).

APPENDIX G:

Excerpt from Report of the Council on Environmental Quality, "Ocean Dumping: A National Policy"

Findings and Recommendations

The Council on Environmental Quality concludes that there is a critical need for a national policy on ocean dumping. It is not a serious, nation-wide problem now, but the decisions made by municipalities and industries in the next few years could lead to dramatic increases in the level of dumping. Once these decisions are made and ocean dumping proceeds, it will be costly and difficult to shift to land-based disposal at some future date.

Ocean-dumped wastes are heavily concentrated and contain materials that have a number of adverse effects. Many are toxic to human and marine life, deplete oxygen necessary to maintain the marine eco-system, reduce populations of fish and other economic resources, and damage esthetic values. In some areas, the environmental conditions created by ocean disposal of wastes are serious.

The Council study indicates that the volume of waste materials dumped in the ocean is growing rapidly. Because the capacity of land-based waste disposal sites is becoming exhausted in some coastal cities, communities are looking to the ocean as a dumping ground for their wastes. Faced with higher water quality standards, industries may also look to the ocean for disposal. The result could be a massive increase in the already growing level of ocean dumping. If this occurs, environmental deterioration will become widespread.

In most cases, feasible and economic land-based disposal methods are available for wastes currently being dumped in the ocean. In many cases, alternatives to ocean dumping can be applied positively for purposes such as land reclamation and recycling to recover valuable waste components.

Current regulatory activities and authorities are not adequate to handle the problem of ocean dumping. States do not exercise control over ocean dumping, and generally their authority extends only within the 3-mile territorial sea. The Army Corps of Engineers authority to regulate ocean dumping is also largely confined to the territorial sea. The Corps has responsibility to facilitate navigation, chiefly by dredging navigation channels. As such, it is in the position of regulating activities over which it also has operational responsibility. The Coast Guard enforces several Federal laws regarding pollution but has no direct authority to regulate ocean dumping. The authority of the Federal Water Quality Administration does not provide for issuance of permits to control ocean dumping. And the Atomic Energy Commission has authority only for disposal of radioactive materials. The Council believes that new legislative authority is necessary.

Finally, this report recognizes the international character of ocean dumping. Unilateral action by the United States can deal with only a part—although an important part—of the problem. Effective international action will be necessary if damage to the marine environment from ocean dumping is to be averted.

POLICY AND REGULATORY RECOMMENDATIONS

The Council on Environmental Quality recommends a comprehensive national policy on ocean dumping of wastes to ban unregulated ocean dumping of all materials and strictly limit ocean disposal of any materials harmful to the marine environment. In order to implement the policy, new regulatory authority is necessary. The Council on Environmental Quality recommends legislation that would:

Require a permit from the Administrator of the Environmental Protection Agency for the transportation or dumping of all materials in the oceans, estuaries, and the Great Lakes.

Authorize the Administrator to ban ocean dumping of specific materials and to designate safe sites.

Establish penalties for violation of regulations.

Provide for enforcement by the Coast Guard.

The Administrator of the Environmental Protection Agency would be guided by the following principles in exerting his authority:

Ocean dumping of materials clearly identified as harmful to the marine environment or man should be stopped.

When existing information on the effects of ocean dumping are inconclusive, yet the best indicators are that the materials could create adverse conditions if dumped, such dumping should be phased out.

When further information conclusively proves that such dumping does not damage the environment, including cumulative and long-term damage, ocean dumping could be conducted under regulation. The criteria for setting standards for disposing of materials in the ocean and for determining the urgency of terminating disposal operations should include:

1. Present and future impact on the marine environment, human health, welfare, and amenities.
2. Irreversibility of the impact of dumping.
3. Volume and concentration of materials involved.
4. Location of disposal, i.e., depth and potential impact of one location relative to others.

High priority should be given to protecting those portions of the marine environment which are biologically most active, namely the estuaries and the shallow, nearshore areas in which many marine organisms breed or spawn. These biologically critical areas should be delimited and protected.

The Council on Environmental Quality recommends the following policies relating to specific types of wastes currently being dumped in the ocean, in estuaries, and in the Great Lakes:

Ocean dumping of digested or other stabilized sludge should be phased out and no new sources allowed. In cases in which substantial facilities and/or significant commitments exist, continued ocean dumping may be necessary until alternatives can be developed and implemented. But continued dumping should be considered an interim measure.

Ocean dumping of existing sources of solid waste should be stopped as soon as possible. No new sources should be allowed, i.e., no dumping by any municipality that currently does not do so, nor any increase in the volume by existing municipalities.

Ocean dumping of polluted dredge spoils should be phased out as soon as alternatives can be employed. In the interim, dumping should minimize ecological damage. The current policy of the Corps of Engineers on dredging highly polluted areas only when absolutely necessary should be continued, and even then, navigational benefits should be weighed carefully against damages.

The current policy of prohibiting ocean dumping of high-level radioactive wastes should be continued. Low-level liquid discharges to the ocean from vessels and land-based nuclear facilities are, and should continue to be, controlled by Federal regulations and international standards. The adequacy of such standards should be continually reviewed. Ocean dumping of other radioactive wastes should be prohibited. In a very few cases, there may be no alternative offering less harm to man or the environment. In these cases ocean disposal should be allowed only when the lack of alternatives has been demonstrated. Planning of activities which will result in production of radioactive wastes should include provisions to avoid ocean disposal. No ocean dumping of chemical warfare materials should be permitted. Biological warfare materials have not been disposed of at sea and should not be in the future. Ocean disposal of explosive munitions should be terminated as soon as possible.

Ocean dumping of industrial wastes should be stopped as soon as possible. Ocean dumping of toxic industrial wastes should be terminated immediately, except in those cases in which no alternative offers less harm to man or the environment.

Ocean dumping of unpolluted dredge spoils, construction and demolition debris, and similar wastes which are inert and nontoxic should be regulated to prevent damage to estuarine and coastal areas.

Use of waste materials to rehabilitate or enhance the marine environment, as opposed to activities primarily aimed at waste disposal, should be conducted under controlled conditions. Such operations should be regulated, requiring proof by the applicant of no adverse effects on the marine environment, human health, safety, welfare, and amenities.

RESEARCH NEEDS

In the long term, additional information is required in the implementation of this policy. Serious information deficiencies exist, and research is required in the following major areas:

Broad-based ecological research is needed to understand the pathways of waste materials in marine ecosystems. Such studies should be directed to a better understanding of the food chain from microscopic plants and animals to high predators; how pollutants concentrate in the food chain; the origin and ultimate fate of pollutants in the oceans; and the effects of concentration on the marine environment and eventually man.

Marine research preserves should be established to protect representative marine ecosystems for research and to serve as ecological reference points—baselines by which man-induced changes may be evaluated.

Oceanographic studies of basic physical and chemical processes should be directed toward gaining a thorough understanding of the marine environment, with special emphasis on estuaries and coastal areas.

Toxic materials should be identified and their lethal, sublethal and chronic long-term effects on marine life investigated. Information is needed on the persistence of toxic substances; how pollutants are degraded chemically and biologically; the effects of radioactivity on the marine environment and man; and the capacity of waters to assimilate waste materials.

More information is needed about public health risks from ocean pollution. Studies should determine what pathogens are transported in marine ecosystems and how. Better methods of measuring public health dangers are also needed.

Research is needed on the recycling of wastes and the development of alternatives to ocean dumping. Technical problems must be solved, but there is also a great need to study the social, institutional, and economic aspects of waste management.

Effective national and international monitoring systems need to be developed. Research is necessary to develop improved methods and technology so that alterations in the marine environment may be detected. But there is also a need for data coordination so that data gathering and analysis efforts are not duplicated.

SUMMARY

The Nation has an opportunity unique in history—the opportunity to act to prevent an environmental problem which otherwise will grow to a great magnitude. In the past, we have failed to recognize problems and to take corrective action before they became serious. The resulting signs of environmental degradation are all around us, and remedial actions heavily tax our resources. This is clearly the time for a conscious national decision to control ocean dumping.

Russell E. Train, *Chairman*
Robert Cahn
Gordon J. MacDonald

APPENDIX H:

Executive Order 11507

Prevention, Control, and Abatement of Air and Water Pollution at Federal Facilities, February 4, 1970

By virtue of the authority vested in me as President of the United States and in furtherance of the purpose and policy of the Clean Air Act, as amended (42 U.S.C. 1857), the Federal Water Pollution Control Act, as amended (33 U.S.C. 466), and the National Environmental Policy Act of 1969 (Public Law No. 91–190, approved January 1, 1970), it is ordered as follows:

Section 1. *Policy.* It is the intent of this order that the Federal Government in the design, operation, and maintenance of its facilities shall provide leadership in the nationwide effort to protect and enhance the quality of our air and water resources.

Sec. 2. *Definitions.* As used in this order:

a. The term "respective Secretary" shall mean the Secretary of Health, Education, and Welfare in matters pertaining to air pollution control and the Secretary of the Interior in matters pertaining to water pollution control.

b. The term "agencies" shall mean the departments, agencies, and establishments of the executive branch.

c. The term "facilities" shall mean the buildings, installations, structures, public works, equipment, aircraft, vessels, and other vehicles and property, owned by or constructed or manufactured for the purpose of leasing to the Federal Government.

d. The term "air and water quality standards" shall mean respectively the quality standards and related plans of implementation, including emission standards, adopted pursuant to the Clean Air Act, as amended, and the Federal Water Pollution Control Act, as amended, or as prescribed pursuant to section 4 (b) of this order.

e. The term "performance specifications' shall mean permissible limits of emissions, discharges, or other values applicable to a particular Federal facility that would, as a minimum, provide for conformance with air and water quality standards as defined herein.

f. The term "United States" shall mean the fifty States, the District of Columbia, the Commonwealth of Puerto Rico, the Virgin Islands, and Guam.

Sec. 3. *Responsibilities.* a. Heads of agencies shall, with regard to all facilities under their jurisdiction:

1. Maintain review and surveillance to ensure that the standards set forth in section 4 of this order are met on a continuing basis.
2. Direct particular attention to identifying potential air and water quality problems associated with the use and production of new materials and make provisions for their prevention and control.
3. Consult with the respective Secretary concerning the best techniques and methods available for the protection and enhancement of air and water quality.
4. Develop and publish procedures, within six months of the date of this order, to ensure that the facilities under their jurisdiction are in conformity with this order. In the preparation of such procedures there shall be timely and appropriate consultation with the respective Secretary.

b. The respective Secretary shall provide leadership in implementing this order, including the provision of technical advice and assistance to the heads of agencies in connection with their duties and responsibilities under this order.

c. The Council on Environmental Quality shall maintain continuing review of the implementation of this order and shall, from time to time, report to the President thereon.

Sec. 4. *Standards.* a. Heads of agencies shall ensure that all facilities under their jurisdiction are designed, operated, and maintained so as to meet the following requirements:

1. Facilities shall conform to air and water quality standards as defined in section 2(d) of this order. In those cases where no such air or water quality standards are in force for a particular geographical area, Federal facilities in that area shall conform to the standards established pursuant to subsection (b) of this section. Federal facilities shall also conform to the performance specifications provided for in this order.
2. Actions shall be taken to avoid or minimize wastes created through the complete cycle of operations of each facility.
3. The use of municipal or regional waste collection or disposal systems shall be the preferred method of disposal of wastes from Federal facilities. Whenever use of such a system is not feasible or appropriate, the heads of agencies concerned shall take necessary measures for the satisfactory disposal of such wastes, including:
   A. When appropriate, the installation and operation of their own

waste treatment and disposal facilities in a manner consistent with this section.

B. The provision of trained manpower, laboratory and other supporting facilities as appropriate to meet the requirements of this section.

C. The establishment of requirements that operators of Federal pollution control facilities meet levels of proficiency consistent with the operator certification requirements of the State in which the facility is located. In the absence of such State requirements the respective Secretary may issue guidelines, pertaining to operator qualifications and performance, for the use of heads of agencies.

4. The use, storage, and handling of all materials, including but not limited to, solid fuels, ashes, petroleum products, and other chemical and biological agents, shall be carried out so as to avoid or minimize the possibilities for water and air pollution. When appropriate, preventive measures shall be taken to entrap spillage or discharge or otherwise to prevent accidental pollution. Each agency, in consultation with the respective Secretary, shall establish appropriate emergency plans and procedures for dealing with accidental pollution.

5. No waste shall be disposed of or discharged in such a manner as could result in the pollution of ground water which would endanger the health or welfare of the public.

6. Discharges of radioactivity shall be in accordance with the applicable rules, regulations, or requirements of the Atomic Energy Commission and with the policies and guidance of the Federal Radiation Council as published in the Federal Register.

b. In those cases where there are no air or water quality standards as defined in section 2(d) of this order in force for a particular geographic area or in those cases where more stringent requirements are deemed advisable for Federal facilities, the respective Secretary, in consultation with appropriate Federal, State, interstate, and local agencies, may issue regulations establishing air or water quality standards for the purpose of this order, including related schedules for implementation.

c. The heads of agencies, in consultation with the respective Secretary, may from time to time identify facilities or uses thereof which are to be exempted, including temporary relief, from provisions of this order in the interest of national security or in extraordinary cases where it is in the national interest. Such exemptions shall be reviewed periodically by the respective Secretary and the heads of the agencies concerned. A report on exemptions granted shall be submitted to the Council on Environmental Quality periodically.

Sec. 5. *Procedures for abatement of air and water pollution at existing Federal facilities.* a. Actions necessary to meet the requirements of subsections (a) (1) and (b) of section 4 of this order pertaining to air and water pollution at existing facilities are to be completed or under way no later than December 31, 1972. In cases where an enforcement conference called pursuant to law or air and water quality standards require earlier actions, the earlier date shall be applicable.

b. In order to ensure full compliance with the requirements of section 5(a) and to facilitate budgeting for necessary corrective and preventive measures, heads of agencies shall present to the Director of the Bureau of the Budget by June 30, 1970, a plan to provide for such improvements as may be necessary to meet the required date. Subsequent revisions needed to keep any such plan up-to-date shall be promptly submitted to the Director of the Bureau of the Budget.

c. Heads of agencies shall notify the respective Secretary as to the performance specifications proposed for each facility to meet the requirements of subsections (a) (1) and (b) of section 4 of this order. Where the respective Secretary finds that such performance specifications are not adequate to meet such requirements, he shall consult with the agency head and the latter shall thereupon develop adequate performance specifications.

d. As may be found necessary, heads of agencies may submit requests to the Director of the Bureau of the Budget for extensions of time for a project beyond the time specified in section 5(a). The Director, in consultation with the respective Secretary, may approve such request if the Director deems that such project is not technically feasible or immediately necessary to meet the requirements of subsections 4 (a) and (b). Full justification as to the extraordinary circumstances necessitating any such extension shall be required.

e. Heads of agencies shall not use for any other purpose any of the amounts appropriated and apportioned for corrective and preventive measures necessary to meet the requirements of subsection (a) for the fiscal year ending June 30, 1971, and for any subsequent fiscal year.

Sec. 6. *Procedures for new Federal facilities.* a. Heads of agencies shall ensure that the requirements of section 4 of this order are considered at the earliest possible stage of planning for new facilities.

b. A request for funds to defray the cost of designing and constructing new facilities in the United States shall be included in the annual budget estimates of an agency only if such request includes funds to defray the costs of such measures as may be necessary to assure that the new facility will meet the requirements of section 4 of this order.

c. Heads of agencies shall notify the respective Secretary as to the performance specifications proposed for each facility when action is necessary to meet the requirements of subsections (a) (1) and (b) of section 4 of this order. Where the respective Secretary finds that such performance specifications are not adequate to meet such requirements he shall consult with the agency head and the latter shall thereupon develop adequate performance specifications.

d. Heads of agencies shall give due consideration to the quality of air and water resources when facilities are constructed or operated outside the United States.

Sec. 7. *Procedures for Federal water resources projects.* a. All water resources projects of the Departments of Agriculture, the Interior, and the Army, the Tennessee Valley Authority, and the United States Section of the International Boundary and Water Commission shall be consistent with the requirements of section 4 of this order. In addition, all such projects shall be presented for the consideration of the Secretary of the Interior at the earliest feasible stage if they involve proposals or recommendations with respect to the authorization or construction of any Federal water resources project in the United States. The Secretary of the Interior shall review plans and supporting data for all such projects relating to water quality, and shall prepare a report to the head of the responsible agency describing the potential impact of the project on water quality, including recommendations concerning any changes or other measures with respect thereto which he considers to be necessary in connection with the design, construction, and operation of the project.

b. The report of the Secretary of the Interior shall accompany at the earliest practicable stage any report proposing authorization or construction, or a request for funding, of such a water resource project. In any case in which the Secretary of the Interior fails to submit a report within 90 days after receipt of project plans, the head of the agency concerned may propose authorization, construction, or funding of the project without such an accompanying report. In such a case, the head of the agency concerned shall explicitly state in his request or report concerning the project that the Secretary of the Interior has not reported on the potential impact of the project on water quality.

Sec. 8. *Saving provisions.* Except to the extent that they are inconsistent with this order, all outstanding rules, regulations, orders, delegations, or other forms of administrative action issued, made, or otherwise taken under the orders superseded by section 9 hereof or relating to the subject of this order shall remain in full force and effect until amended, modified, or terminated by proper authority.

Sec. 9. *Orders superseded.* Esecutive Order No. 11282 of May 26, 1966, and Executive Order No. 11288 of July 2, 1966, are hereby superseded.

Richard Nixon

The White House

APPENDIX I:

Executive Order 11514

Protection and Enhancement of Environmental Quality, March 5, 1970

By virtue of the authority vested in me as President of the United States and in furtherance of the purpose and policy of the National Environmental Policy Act of 1969 (Public Law No. 91–190, approved Jannuary 1, 1970), it is ordered as follows:

Section 1. *Policy.* The Federal Government shall provide leadership in protecting and enhancing the quality of the Nation's environment to sustain and enrich human life. Federal agencies shall initiate measures needed to direct their policies, plans and programs so as to meet national environmental goals. The Council on Environmental Quality, through the Chairman, shall advise and assist the President in leading this national effort.

Sec. 2. *Responsibilities of Federal agencies.* Consonant with Title I of the National Environmental Policy Act of 1969, hereafter referred to as the "Act", the heads of Federal agencies shall:

a. Monitor, evaluate, and control on a continuing basis their agencies' activities so as to protect and enhance the quality of the environment. Such activities shall include those directed to controlling pollution and enhancing the environment and those designed to accomplish other program objectives which may affect the quality of the environment. Agencies shall develop programs and measures to protect and enhance environmental quality and shall assess progress in meeting the specific objectives of such activities. Heads of agencies shall consult with appropriate Federal, State and local agencies in carrying out their activities as they affect the quality of the environment.

b. Develop procedures to ensure the fullest practicable provision of timely public information and understanding of Federal plans and programs with environmental impact in order to obtain the views of interested parties. These procedures shall include, whenever appropriate, provision for public hearings, and shall provide the public with relevant information, including information on alternative courses of action. Federal agencies shall also encourage State and local agencies to adopt similar procedures for informing the public concerning their activities affecting the quality of the environment.

c. Insure that information regarding existing or potential environmental problems and control methods developed as part of research, development, demonstration, test, or evaluation activities is made available to Federal agencies, States, counties, municipalities, institutions, and other entities, as appropriate.

d. Review their agencies' statutory authority, administrative regulations, policies, and procedures, including those relating to loans, grants, contracts, leases, licenses, or permits, in order to identify any deficiencies or inconsistencies therein which prohibit or limit full compliance with the purposes and provisions of the Act. A report on this review and the corrective actions taken or planned, including such measures to be proposed to the President as may be necessary to bring their authority and policies into conformance with the intent, purposes, and procedures of the Act, shall be provided to the Council on Environmental Quality not later than September 1, 1970.

e. Engage in exchange of data and research results, and cooperate with agencies of other governments to foster the purposes of the Act.

f. Proceed, in coordination with other agencies, with actions required by section 102 of the Act.

Sec. 3. *Responsibilities of Council on Environmental Quality.* The Council on Environmental Quality shall:

a. Evaluate existing and proposed policies and activities of the Federal Government directed to the control of pollution and the enhancement of the environment and to the accomplishment of other objectives which affect the quality of the environment. This shall include continuing review of procedures employed in the development and enforcement of Federal Standards affecting environmental quality. Based upon such evaluations the Council shall, when appropriate, recommend to the President policies and programs to achieve more effective protection and enhancement of environmental quality and shall, where appropriate, seek resolution of significant environmental issues.

b. Recommend to the President and to the agencies priorities among programs designed for the control of pollution and for enhancement of the environment.

c. Determine the need for new policies and programs for dealing with environmental problems not being adequately addressed.

d. Conduct, as it determines to be appropriate, public hearings or conferences on issues of environmental significance.

e. Promote the development and use of indices and monitoring systems (1) to assess environmental conditions and trends, (2) to predict the environmental impact of proposed public and private action, and (3) to determine the effectiveness of programs for protecting and enhancing environmental quality.

    f. Coordinate Federal programs related to environmental quality.

    g. Advise and assist the President and the agencies in achieving international cooperation for dealing with environmental problems, under the foreign policy guidance of the Secretary of State.

    h. Issue guidelines to Federal agencies for the preparation of detailed statements on proposals for legislation and other Federal actions affecting the environment, as required by section 102(2) (C) of the Act.

    i. Issue such other instructions to agencies, and request such reports and other information from them, as may be required to carry out the Council's responsibilities under the Act.

    j. Assist the President in preparing the annual Environmental Quality Report provided for in section 201 of the Act.

    k. Foster investigations, studies, surveys, research, and analyses relating to (i) ecological systems and environmental quality, (ii) the impact of new and changing technologies thereon, and (iii) means of preventing or reducing adverse effects from such technologies.

    Sec. 4. *Amendments of E.O. 11472.* Executive Order No. 11472 of May 29, 1969, including the heading thereof, is hereby amended:

    1. By substituting for the term "the Environmental Quality Council", wherever it occurs, the following: "the Cabinet Committee on the Environment".

    2. By Substituting for the term "the Council", wherever it occurs, the following: "the Cabinet Committee".

    3. By inserting in subsection (f) of section 101, after "Budget,", the following: "the Director of the Office of Science and Technology,".

    4. By substituting for subsection (g) of section 101 the following:

    "(g) The Chairman of the Council on Environmental Quality (established by Public Law 91–190) shall assist the President in directing the affairs of the Cabinet Committee."

    5. By deleting subsection (c) of section 102.

    6. By substituting for "the Office of Science and Technology", in section 104, the following: "the Council on Environmental Quality (established by Public Law 91–190)".

    7. By substituting for "(hereinafter referred to as the 'Committee')", in section 201, the following: "(hereinafter referred to as the 'Citizens' Committee')".

    8. By substituting for the term "the Committee", wherever it occurs, the following: "the Citizens' Committee".

Richard Nixon   The White House, *March 5, 1970*

APPENDIX J:

Reorganization Plan No. 3 of 1970

Prepared by the President and transmitted to the Senate and the House of Representatives in Congress assembled, July 9, 1970, pursuant to the provisions of chapter 9 of title 5 of the United States Code

Environmental Protection Agency

Section 1. *Establishment of Agency.* a. There is hereby established the Environmental Protection Agency, hereinafter referred to as the "Agency."

b. There shall be at the head of the Agency the Administrator of the Environmental Protection Agency, hereinafter referred to as the "Administrator." The Administrator shall be appointed by the President, by and with the advice and consent of the Senate, and shall be compensated at the rate now or hereafter provided for Level II of the Executive Schedule Pay Rates (5 U.S.C. 5313).

c. There shall be in the Agency a Deputy Administrator of the Environmental Protection Agency who shall be appointed by the President, by and with the advice and consent of the Senate, and shall be compensated at the rate now or hereafter provided for Level III of the Executive Schedule Pay Rates (5 U.S.C. 5314). The Deputy Administrator shall perform such functions as the Administrator shall from time to time assign or delegate, and shall act as Administrator during the absence or disability of the Administrator or in the event of a vacancy in the office of Administrator.

d. There shall be in the Agency not to exceed five Assistant Administrators of the Environmental Protection Agency who shall be appointed by the President, by and with the advise and consent of the Senate, and shall be compensated at the rate now or hereafter provided for Level IV of the Executive Schedule Pay Rates (5 U.S.C. 5315). Each Assistant Administrator shall perform such functions as the Administrator shall from time to time assign or delegate.

Sec. 2. *Transfers to Environmental Protection Agency.* a. There are hereby transferred to the Administrator:

1. All functions vested by law in the Secretary of the Interior and the Department of the Interior which are administered through the Federal Water Quality Administration, all functions which were

transferred to the Secretary of the Interior by Reorganization Plan No. 2 of 1966 (80 Stat. 1608), and all functions vested in the Secretary of the Interior or the Department of the Interior by the Federal Water Pollution Control Act or by provisions of law amendatory or supplementary thereof.

2. (i) The functions vested in the Secretary of the Interior by the Act of August 1, 1958, 72 Stat. 479, 16 U.S.C. 742d–1 (being an Act relating to studies on the effects of insecticides, herbicides, fungicides, and pesticides upon the fish and wildlife resources of the United States), and (ii) the functions vested by law in the Secretary of the Interior and the Department of the Interior which are administered by the Gulf Breeze Biological Laboratory of the Bureau of Commercial Fisheries at Gulf Breeze, Florida.

3. The functions vested by law in the Secretary of Health, Education, and Welfare or in the Department of Health, Education, and Welfare which are administered through the Environmental Health Service, including the functions exercised by the following components thereof:

 (i) The National Air Pollution Control Administration,

 (ii) The Environmental Control Administration:

  (A) Bureau of Solid Waste Management,

  (B) Bureau of Water Hygiene,

  (C) Bureau of Radiological Health,

except that functions carried out by the following components of the Environmental Control Administration of the Environmental Health Service are not transferred: (i) Bureau of Community Environmental Management, (ii) Bureau of Occupational Safety and Health, and (iii) Bureau of Radiological Health, insofar as the functions carried out by the latter Bureau pertain to (A) regulation of radiation from consumer products, including electronic product radiation, (B) radiation as used in the healing arts, (C) occupational exposures to radiation, and (D) research, technical assistance, and training related to clauses (A), (B), and (C).

4. The functions vested in the Secretary of Health, Education, and Welfare of establishing tolerances for pesticide chemicals under the Federal Food, Drug, and Cosmetic Act, as amended, 21 U.S.C. 346, 346a, and 348, together with authority, in connection with the functions transferred, (i) to monitor compliance with the tolerances and the effectiveness of surveillance and enforcement, and (ii) to provide technical assistance to the States and conduct

research under the Federal Food, Drug, and Cosmetic Act, as amended, and the Public Health Service Act, as amended.

5. So much of the functions of the Council on Environmental Quality under section 204(5) of the National Environmental Policy Act of 1969 (Public Law 91−190, approved January 1, 1970, 83 Stat. 855), as pertains to ecological systems.

6. The functions of the Atomic Energy Commission under the Atomic Energy Act of 1954, as amended, administered through its Division of Radiation Protection Standards, to the extent that such functions of the Commission consist of establishing generally applicable environmental standards for the protection of the general environment from radioactive material. As used herein, standards mean limits on radiation exposures or levels, or concentrations or quantities of radioactive material, in the general environment outside the boundaries of locations under the control of persons possessing or using radioactive material.

7. All functions of the Federal Radiation Council (42 U.S.C. 2021(h)).

8. (i) The functions of the Secretary of Agriculture and the Department of Agriculture under the Federal Insecticide, Fungicide, and Rodenticide Act, as amended (7 U.S.C. 135−135k), (ii) the functions of the Secretary of Agriculture and the Department of Agriculture under section 408(*l*) of the Federal Food, Drug, and Cosmetic Act, as amended (21 U.S.C. 346a(*l*)), and (iii) the functions vested by law in the Secretary of Agriculture and the Department of Agriculture which are administered through the Environmental Quality Branch of the Plant Protection Division of the Agricultural Research Service.

9. So much of the functions of the transferor officers and agencies referred to in or affected by the foregoing provisions of this section as is incidental to or necessary for the performance by or under the Administrator of the functions transferred by those provisions or relates primarily to those functions. The transfers to the Administrator made by this section shall be deemed to include the transfer of (1) authority, provided by law, to prescribe regulations relating primarily to the transferred functions, and (2) the functions vested in the Secretary of the Interior and the Secretary of Health, Education, and Welfare by section 169(d) (1) (1) (B) and (3) of the Internal Revenue Code of 1954 (as enacted by section 704 of the Tax Reform Act of 1969, 83 Stat. 668); but

shall be deemed to exclude the transfer of the functions of the Bureau of Reclamation under section 3(b) (1) of the Water Pollution Control Act (33 U.S.C. 466a(b) (1)).

b. There are hereby transferred to the Agency:

1. From the Department of the Interior, (i) the Water Pollution Control Advisory Board (33 U.S.C. 466f), together with its functions, and (ii) the hearing boards provided for in sections 10(c) (4) and 10(f) of the Federal Water Pollution Control Act, as amended (33 U.S.C. 466g(c) (4); 466g(f). The functions of the Secretary of the Interior with respect to being or designating the Chairman of the Water Pollution Control Advisory Board are hereby transferred to the Administrator.

2. From the Department of Health, Education, and Welfare, the Air Quality Advisory Board (42 U.S.C. 1857e), together with its functions. The functions of the Secretary of Health, Education, and Welfare with respect to being a member and the Chairman of that Board are hereby transferred to the Administrator.

Sec. 3. *Performance of transferred functions.* The Administrator may from time to time make such provisions as he shall deem appropriate authorizing the performance of any of the functions transferred to him by the provisions of this reorganization plan by any other officer, or by any organizational entity or employee, of the Agency.

Sec. 4. *Incidental transfers.* a. So much of the personnel, property, records, and unexpended balances of appropriations, allocations, and other funds employed, used, held available, or to be made available in connection with the functions transferred to the Administrator or the Agency by this reorganization plan as the Director of the Office of Management and Budget shall determine shall be transferred to the Agency at such time or times as the Director shall direct.

b. Such further measures and dispositions as the Director of Office of Management and Budget shall deem to be necessary in order to effectuate the transfers referred to in subsection (a) of this section shall be carried out in such manner as he shall direct and by such agencies as he shall designate.

Sec.5. *Interim officers.* a. The President may authorize any person who immediately prior to the effective date of this reorganization plan held a position in the executive branch of the Government to act as Administrator until the office of Administrator is for the first time filled pursuant to the provisions of this reorganization plan or by recess appointment, as the case may be.

b. The President may similarly authorize any such person to act as Deputy Administrator, authorize any such person to act as Assistant Administrator, and authorize any such person to act as the head of any principal constituent organizational entity of the Administration.

c. The President may authorize any person who serves in an acting capacity under the foregoing provisions of this section to receive the compensation attached to the office in respect of which he so serves. Such compensation, if authorized, shall be in lieu of, but not in addition to, other compensation from the United States to which such person may be entitled.

Sec. 6. *Abolitions.* a. Subject to the provisions of this reorganization plan, the following, exclusive of any functions, are hereby abolished:

1. The Federal Water Quality Administration in the Department of the Interior (33 U.S.C. 466–1).

2. The Federal Radiation Council (73 Stat. 690; 42 U.S.C. 2021(h)).

b. Such provisions as may be necessary with respect to terminating any outstanding affairs shall be made by the Secretary of the Interior in the case of the Federal Water Quality Administration and by the Administrator of General Services in the case of the Federal Radiation Council.

Sec. 7. *Effective date.* The provisions of this reorganization plan shall take effect sixty days after the date they would take effect under 5 U.S.C. 906(a) in the absence of this section.

191

APPENDIX K:

White House Press Release on Designation of Administrator, Environmental Protection Agency

Office of the White House Press Secretary

THE WHITE HOUSE

The President today announced his intention to nominate William D. Ruckelshaus as Administrator of the Environmental Protection Agency. Mr. Ruckelshaus is now Assistant Attorney General, Civil Division, Department of Justice.

The Environmental Protection Agency brings together, in a single organization, the major Federal pollution control programs now existing in four separate agencies and one inter-agency council. The Environmental Protection Agency will begin operations on December 2, 1970. It was proposed by President Nixon in a reorganization plan which was transmitted to the Congress on July 9, 1970. The Plan won Congressional concurrence on October 2, 1970, and provides a 60-day planning period before the new agency begins formal operations.

Mr. Ruckelshaus was formerly Assistant Attorney General, State of Indiana, assigned to the State Health Department where he prosecuted water polluters and other violators of State health and environmental control laws and regulations. He wrote the State Air Pollution Control law in 1963. In his capacity as Assistant Attorney General, Mr. Ruckelshaus became intimately involved with the administrative and legislative process of environmental health planning, budgeting, appropriations and operations.

He served from 1966-1969 as Majority Leader in the Indiana Legislature before becoming Assistant Attorney General, Civil Division, Department of Justice. Mr. Ruckelshaus is 38 years old, holds an A.B. Cum Laude from Princeton and a L.L.B. from Harvard University. He is married to the former Jill Elizabeth Strickland. They have five children: Catherine 9, Mary 9, Jennifer 7, William 6, and Robin 2, and they reside in Rockville, Maryland.

APPENDIX L:

Reorganization Plan No. 4 of 1970

Prepared by the President and transmitted to the Senate and the House of Representatives in Congress assembled, July 9, 1970, pursuant to the provisions of chapter 9 of title 5 of the United States Code

National Oceanic and Atmospheric Administration

Section 1. *Transfers to Secretary of Commerce.* The following are hereby transferred to the Secretary of Commerce:

a. All functions vested by law in the Bureau of Commercial Fisheries of the Department of the Interior or in its head, together with all functions vested by law in the Secretary of the Interior or the Department of the Interior which are administered through that Bureau or are primarily related to the Bureau, exclusive of functions with respect to (1) Great Lakes fishery research and activities related to the Great Lakes Fisheries Commission, (2) Missouri River Reservoir research, (3) the Gulf Breeze Biological Laboratory of the said Bureau at Gulf Breeze, Florida, and (4) Trans-Alaska pipeline investigations.

b. The functions vested in the Secretary of the Interior by the Act of September 22, 1959 (Public Law 86–359, 73 Stat, 642, 16 U.S.C. 760e–760g; relating to migratory marine species of game fish).

c. The functions vested by law in the Secretary of the Interior, or in the Department of the Interior or in any officer or instrumentality of that Department, which are administered through the Marine Minerals Technology Center of the Bureau of Mines.

d. All functions vested in the National Science Foundation by the National Sea Grant College and Program Act of 1966 (80 Stat. 998), as amended (33 U.S.C. 1121 et seq.).

e. Those functions vested in the Secretary of Defense or in any officer, employee, or organizational entity of the Department of Defense by the provision of Public Law 91–144, 83 Stat. 326, under the heading "Operation and maintenance, general" with respect to "surveys and charting of northern and northwestern lakes and connecting waters," or by other law, which come under the mission assigned as of July 1, 1969, to the United States Army Engineer District, Lake Survey, Corps of Engineers, Department of the Army and relate to (1) the conduct of hydrographic surveys of the Great Lakes and their outflow rivers, Lake Champlain, New York State Barge Canals, and the Minnesota-Ontario border lakes, and the compilation and publication of navigation charts, including recreational aspects, and the Great Lakes Pilot for the benefit and use of the public, (2) the conception, planning, and conduct of basic research and development in the fields of water motion, water characteristics, water quantity, and ice and snow, and (3) the publication of data and the results of research projects in forms useful to the Corps of Engineers and the public, and the operation of a Regional Data Center for the collection, coordination, analysis, and the furnishing to interested agencies of data relating to water resources of the Great Lakes.

f. So much of the functions of the transferor officers and agencies referred to in or affected by the foregoing provisions of this section as is incidental to or necessary for the performance by or under the Secretary of Commerce of the functions transferred by those provisions or relates primarily to those functions. The transfers to the Secretary of Commerce made by this section shall be deemed to include the transfer of authority, provided by law, to prescribe regulations relating primarily to the transferred functions.

Sec. 2. *Establishment of Administration.* a. There is hereby established in the Department of Commerce an agency which shall be known as the National Oceanic and Atmospheric Administration, hereinafter referred to as the "Administration."

b. There shall be at the head of the Administration the Administrator of the National Oceanic and Atmospheric Administration, hereinafter referred to as the "Administrator." The Administrator shall be appointed by the President, by and with the advice and consent of the Senate, and shall be compensated at the rate now or hereafter provided for Level III of the Executive Schedule Pay Rates (5 U.S.C. 5314).

c. There shall be in the Administration a Deputy Administrator of the National Oceanic and Atmospheric Administration who shall be appointed by the President, by and with the advice and consent of the Senate, and shall be compensated at the rate now or hereafter provided for Level IV of the Executive Schedule Pay Rates (5 U.S.C. 5315). The Deputy Administrator shall perform such functions as the Administrator shall from time to time assign or delegate, and shall act as Administrator during the absence or disability of the Administrator or in the event of a vacancy in the office of Administrator.

d. There shall be in the Administration an Associate Administrator of the National Oceanic and Atmospheric Administration who shall be appointed by the President, by and with the advice and consent of the Senate, and shall be compensated at the rate now or hereafter provided for Level V of the Executive Schedule Pay Rates (5 U.S.C. 5316). The Associate Administrator shall perform such functions as the Administrator shall from time to time assign or delegate, and shall act as Administrator during the absence or disability of the Administrator and Deputy Administrator. The office of Associate Administrator may be filled at the discretion of the President by appointment (by and with the advice and consent of the Senate) from the active list of commissioned officers of the Administration in which case the appointment shall create a vacancy on the active list and while holding the office of Associate Administrator the officer shall have rank, pay, and allowances not exceeding those of a vice admiral.

e. There shall be in the Administration three additional officers who shall perform such functions as the Administrator shall from time to time assign or delegate. Each such officer shall be appointed by the Secretary, subject to the approval of the President, under the classified civil service, shall have such title as the Secretary shall from time to time determine, and shall receive compensation at the rate now or hereafter provided for Level V of the Executive Schedule Pay Rates (5 U.S.C. 5316).

f. The President may appoint in the Administration, by and with the advice and consent of the Senate, two commissioned officers to serve at any one time as the designated heads of two principal constituent organizational entities of the Administration, or the President may designate one such officer as the head of such an organizational entity and the other as the head of the commissioned corps of the Administration. Any such designation shall create a vacancy in the active list and the officer while serving under this subsection shall have the rank, pay, and allowances of a rear admiral (upper half).

g. Any commissioned officer of the Administration who has served under (d) or (f) and is retired while so serving or is retired after the completion of such service while serving in a lower rank or grade, shall be retired with the rank, pay, and allowances authorized by law for the highest grade and rank held by him; but any such officer, upon termination of his appointment in a rank above that of captain, shall, unless appointed or assigned to some other position for which a higher rank or grade is provided, revert to the grade and number he would have occupied had he not served in a rank above that of captain and such officer shall be an extra number in that grade.

Sec. 3. *Performance of transferred functions.* The provisions of sections 2 and 4 of Reorganization Plan No. 5 of 1950 of 1950 (64 Stat. 1263) shall be applicable to the functions transferred hereunder to the Secretary of Commerce.

Sec. 4. *Incidental transfers.* a. So much of the personnel, property, records, and unexpended balances of appropriations, allocations, and other funds employed, used, held, available, or to be made available in connection with the functions transferred to the Secretary of Commerce by this reorganization plan as the Director of the Office of Management and Budget,shall determine shall be transferred to the Department of Commerce at such time or times as the Director shall direct.

b. Such further measures and dispositions as the Director of the Office of Management and Budget shall deem to be necessary in order to effectuate the transfers referred to in subsection (a) of this section shall be carried out in such manner as he shall direct and by such agencies as he shall designate.

c. The personnel, property, records, and unexpended balances of appropriations, allocations, and other funds of the Environmental Science Services Administration shall become personnel, property, records, and unexpended balances of the National Oceanic and Atmospheric Administration or of such other organizational entity or entities of the Department of Commerce as the Secretary of Commerce shall determine.

d. The Commissioned Officer Corps of the Environmental Science Services Administration shall become the Commissioned Officer Corps of the National Oceanic and Atmospheric Administration. Members of the Corps, including these appointed hereafter, shall be entitled to all rights, privileges, and benefits heretofore available under any law to commissioned officers of the Environmental Science Services Administration, including those rights, privileges, any benefits heretofore accorded by law to commissioned officers of the former Coast and Geodetic Survey.

e. Any personnel, property, records, and unexpended balances of appropriations, allocations, and other funds of the Bureau of Commercial Fisheries not otherwise transferred shall become personnel, property, records, and unexpended balances of such organizational entity or entities of the Department of the Interior as the Secretary of the Interior shall determine.

Sec. 5. *Interim officers.* a. The President may authorize any person who immediately prior to the effective date of this reorganization plan held a position in the executive branch of the Government to act as Administrator until the office of Administrator is for the first time filled pursuant to provisions of this reorganization plan or by recess appointment, as the case may be.

b. The President may similarly authorize any such person to act as Deputy Administrator and authorize any such person to act as Associate Administrator.

c. The President may similarly authorize a member of the former Commissioned Officer Corps of the Environmental Science Services Administration to act as the head of one principal constituent organizational entity of the Administration.

d. The President may authorize any person who serves in an acting capacity under the foregoing provisions of this section to receive the compensation attached to the office in respect of which he so serves. Such compensation, if authorized, shall be in lieu of, but not in addition to, other compensation from the United States to which such person may be entitled.

Sec. 6. *Abolitions.* a. Subject to the provisions of this reorganization plan, the following, exclusive of any functions, are hereby abolished:

1. The Environmental Science Services Administration in the Department of Commerce (established by Reorganization Plan No. 2 of 1965, 79 Stat. 1318), including the offices of Administrator of the Environmental Science Services Administration and Deputy Administrator of the Environmental Science Services Administration.

2. The Bureau of Commercial Fisheries in the Department of the Interior (16 U.S.C. 742b), including the office of Director of the Bureau of Commercial Fisheries.

b. Such provisions as may be necessary with respect to terminating any outstanding affairs shall be made by the Secretary of Commerce in the case of the Environmental Science Services Administration and by the Secretary of the Interior in the case of the Bureau of Commercial Fisheries.

APPENDIX M:

U.S. Department of Commerce

Interim Organization of The National Oceanic and Atmospheric Administration, October 1970

NOAA, the National Oceanic and Atmospheric Administration, was created within the U.S. Department of Commerce on October 3, 1970, by Presidential Reorganization Plan Number 4 of 1970.

Its formation brought together the functions of the Commerce Department's Environmental Science Services Administration (including its major elements: the Weather Bureau, Coast and Geodetic Survey, Environmental Data Service, National Environmental Satellite Center, and Research Laboratories); the Interior Department's Bureau of Commercial Fisheries, Marine Game Fish Research Program, and Marine Minerals Technology Center; the Navy-administered National Oceanographic Data Center and National Oceanographic Instrumentation Center; the Coast Guard's National Data Buoy Development Project; the National Science Foundation's National Sea Grant Program; and elements of the Army Corps of Engineers' U.S. Lake Survey.

The President's reorganization plan, dated July 9, 1970, was sent to the Congress with this description of the new agency:

"[NOAA] would make possible a balanced Federal program to improve our understanding of the resources of the sea, and permit their development and use while guarding against the sort of thoughtless exploitation that in the past laid waste to so many of our precious natural assets. It would make possible a consolidated program for achieving a more comprehensive understanding of oceanic and atmospheric phenomena, which so greatly affect our lives and activities. It would facilitate the cooperation between public and private interests that can best serve the interests of all.

"I expect that NOAA would exercise leadership in developing a national oceanic and atmospheric program of research and development. It would coordinate its own scientific and technical resources with the technical and operational capabilities of other government agencies and private institutions. As important, NOAA would continue to provide those services to other agencies of government, industry, and to private individuals which have become essential to the efficient operation of our transportation systems, our agriculture, and our national security."

Interim Organization

Functions combined in the new agency are being reshaped to meet the broad NOAA mission. NOAA's interim organization includes: the National Ocean Survey, combining the activities of the ESSA Coast and Geodetic Survey and the U.S. Lake Survey; the National Weather Service, formerly the ESSA Weather Bureau; the National Marine Fisheries Service, composed of the Bureau of Commercial Fisheries and Marine Game Fish Research Program; the National Environmental Satellite Service, formerly ESSA's National Environmental Satellite Center; the Environmental Research Laboratories, formerly ESSA's Research Laboratories; and the Environmental Data Service, combining the ESSA Environmental Data Service and the National Oceanographic Data Center.

The interim organization establishes staff locations for other new functions. The Office of Sea Grant administers and directs the National Sea Grant Program, and the National Oceanographic Instrumentation Center, Marine Minerals Technology Center, and Data Buoy Project Office are attached to the office of the Assistant Administrator for Environmental Systems.

The functions of each element and new staff activity of NOAA are described below.

Other staff offices are those of the Assistant Administrator for Plans and Programs, the Assistant Administrator for Administration and Technical Services, and the Director of the NOAA Commissioned Corps. (The smallest of the Nation's seven uniformed services, the NOAA Commissioned Corps began in 1917 as the Coast and Geodetic Survey Commissioned Corps, and was transferred to ESSA when that agency was formed in 1965.)

National Ocean Survey

The National Ocean Survey prepares and distributes nautical and aeronautical charts, conducts precise geodetic, oceanographic, and marine geophysical surveys, monitors the earth's geophysical fields and seismic activity, predicts tides and currents, and issues tsunami warnings to the Pacific Ocean area. It maps and charts American coastal waters, the Great Lakes, and navigable waters of the New York State Barge Canal System, Lake Champlain, and the Minnesota-Ontario Border Lakes. The National Ocean Survey fleet conducts mapping and charting operations and provides ship support to NOAA's Environmental Research Laboratories.

The Survey employs approximately 2,500 persons. Its major facilities include the Atlantic and Pacific Marine Centers, at Norfolk, Va., and Seattle, Wash.; the Albuquerque Seismological Center in New Mexico; the National Tsunami Warning Center in Hawaii; the Great Lakes Research Center in Detroit; and a network of geophysical observatories.

National Weather Service

The National Weather Service reports the weather of the United States and its possessions, provides weather forecasts to the general public, issues warnings against tornadoes, hurricanes, floods, and other weather hazards, and records the climate of the United States. The Weather Service also develops and furnishes specialized weather services which support the needs of agriculture, aviation, maritime, space, and military operations. These services are supported by a national network of observing and forecasting stations, communications links, aircraft, satellite systems, and computers.

The Weather Service's 5,000 employees are located at approximately 400 facilities within the 50 states, at 14 overseas stations, and on 20 ships at sea. Special facilities include the National Meteorological Center in Suitland, Md.; the National Hurricane Center in Miami, Fla.; and the National Severe Storms Forecast Center in Kansas City, Mo.

National Marine Fisheries Service

The National Marine Fisheries Service seeks to discover, describe, develop, and conserve the living resources of the global sea, especially as these affect the American economy and diet.

The Fisheries Service conducts biological research on economically important species, analyzes economic aspects of fisheries operations and rates, develops methods for improving catches, and, in cooperation with the U.S. Department of State, is active in international fisheries affairs. With the U.S. Coast Guard, the National Marine Fisheries Service conducts enforcement and surveillance operations on the high seas and in territorial waters. It also studies game fish behavior and resources, seeks to describe the ecological relationships between game fish and other marine and estuarine organisms, and investigates the effects on game fish of thermal and chemical pollution.

The National Marine Fisheries Service conducts a voluntary grading and inspection program under which fishery products that meet established quality standards and product specifications can bear a special shield that is the shopper's guarantee that the product was of high quality when it left the processor. A staff of marketing specialists and home economists provide services to Federal and state governments, industry, and consumer organizations in the use of fish and fishery products. The Service also maintains a national programs of fishery statistics and market news.

The Service maintains nearly 30 major laboratories and centers and more than 50 lesser installations such as statistics and market news offices, across the nation. It has a fleet of 29 research vessels equipped for various kinds of oceanographic research and fishery exploration.

National Environmental Satellite Service

The National Environmental Satellite Service plans and operates environmental satellite systems, gathers and analyzes satellite data, and develops new methods of using satellites to obtain environmental data. As environmental satellite technology matures, sensors will be added to measure additional atmospheric characteristics, and to provide data on solar, ionospheric, oceanographic, and other geophysical phenomena.

Environmental Research Laboratories

The Environmental Research Laboratories, headquartered in Boulder, Colo., conduct the fundamental investigations needed to improve man's understanding of the physical environment.

The Atmospheric Physics and Chemistry Laboratory (Boulder, Colo.) is NOAA's major focus for developing methods of practical, beneficial weather modification.

The Air Resources Laboratories (Washington, D.C.) house NOAA's principal efforts to identify, detect, predict, and control atmospheric pollution.

The Geophysical Fluid Dynamics Laboratory (Princeton, N.J.) studies the dynamics and physics of geophysical fluid systems to develop predictive mathematical models of ocean and atmosphere.

The National Severe Storms Laboratory (Norman, Okla.) studies tornadoes, squall lines, and other severe local storms with an eye to improved detection and prediction methods.

The Atlantic Oceanographic and Meteorological Laboratories (Miami, Fla.) conduct research toward a fuller understanding of the global ocean and its interactions, study hurricanes and other tropical weather phenomena, and conduct experiments in hurricane modification.

The Pacific Oceanographic Laboratories (Seattle, Wash.) conduct research toward a more complete description of the global ocean and its interactions, including seismic sea waves.

The Earth Science Laboratories (Boulder, Colo.) conduct research in geomagnetism, seismology, geodesy, and related technologies.

The Aeronomy Laboratory (Boulder, Colo.) studies the physical and chemical processes of the ionosphere and exosphere of the earth and other planets.

The Space Disturbances Laboratory (Boulder, Colo.) monitors characteristics of the space environment related to early detection and reporting of important disturbances, and conducts related basic research.

The Research Flight Facility (Miami, Fla.) meets NOAA's requirements for environmental measurements from specially instrumented aircraft. The Facility currently maintains a fleet of four aircraft.

Environmental Data Service

The Environmental Data Service collects, processes, archives, publishes, and issues environmental data gathered on a global scale. The Service maintains data centers for geodetic, geomagnetic, seismological, meteorological, aeronomic, and oceanographic information, providing a single source of readily available environmental data to specialized and general user groups. It also provides administrative support for the corresponding World Data Centers A, which receive data from cooperative investigations and other international sources.

The Environmental Data Service's major facilities include the National Oceanographic Data Center, Washington, D.C.; the National Climatic Center, the Seismological Data Center, and the Geodetic Data Center, Asheville, N.C.; the Geomagnetic Data Center, Rockville, Md.; and the Aeronomy and Space Data Center, Boulder, Colo.

Office of Sea Grant

The Office of Sea Grant administers and directs the National Sea Grant Program. This program provides support for institutions engaged in comprehensive marine research, education, and advisory service programs, supports individual projects in marine research and development, and sponsors education of ocean scientists and engineers, marine technicians, and other specialists at selected colleges and universities.

Data Buoy Project Office

The Data Buoy Project Office manages the National Data Buoy Development Project. It is developing a national system of automatic ocean buoys for obtaining essentially continuous marine environmental data. This work is closely associated with satellite and sensor developments elsewhere in NOAA.

Marine Minerals Technology Center

The Marine Minerals Technology Center at Tiburon, Calif., is concerned with the development of marine mining and related technology, with emphasis on the assessment of environmental impact of mining systems. A related activity is to develop the necessary tools and techniques for accurate delineation and economic evaluation of marine minerals deposits.

National Oceanographic Instrumentation Center

The National Oceanographic Instrumentation Center provides the Nation with a focal point for knowledge of technology related to instrument measurement, evaluation, and the reliability of sensing systems for ocean use. The Center performs laboratory and field testing and calibration, sponsors standards development, and enhances the quality of ocean systems by the dissemination of operational results and technical information.

A Statement of Mission

NOAA will explore, map, and chart the global oceans, their geological cradles, their geophysical forces and fields, and their mineral and living resources. New physical and biological knowledge will be translated into systems capable of assessing the sea's potential yield, and into techniques which the Nation and its industries can employ to manage, use, and conserve these animal and mineral resources.

NOAA will monitor and predict the characteristics of the physical environment — the protean changes of atmosphere and ocean, sun and solid earth, gravity, and geomagnetism — in real time, given sufficiently advanced knowledge and technology. It will warn against impending environmental hazards, and ease the human burden of hurricane, tornado, flood, tsunami, and other destructive natural events.

NOAA will monitor and predict such gradual and inexorable changes as those of climate, seismicity, marine-life distributions, earth tides, continental position, the planet's internal circulations, and the effects of human civilization and industry on the environment and oceanic life.

To accomplish these objectives, NOAA will draw upon the talent and experience of its personnel, the wide range of its facilities, and mutually important links between government, universities, and industry. NOAA and its institutional partners will develop the technology and the systems with which to comprehend this broad province of service and investigation — systems leading to effective resource assessment, utilization of environmental data, environmental monitoring and prediction, and, possibly, environmental modification and control. Here, the growing family of satellites, sensors, ships, data buoys, computers, and simulators, which have enriched scientific understanding and provided the base for essential environmental services in recent decades, will find their best achievement.

In these ways, NOAA will improve the safety and quality of life, the efficiency and timing of oceanic hunts and harvests, and man's comprehension, use, and preservation of his planetary home.

APPENDIX N:

Council on Environmental Quality

Statements on Proposed Federal Actions Affecting the Environment; Interim Guidelines, April 30, 1970

1. *Purpose.* This memorandum provides interim guidelines to Federal departments, agencies and establishments for preparing detailed environmental statements on proposals for legislation and other major Federal actions significantly affecting the quality of the human environment, as required by section 102(2) (C) of the National Environmental Policy Act (Public Law 91–190) (hereafter "the Act"). Underlying the preparation of such environmental statements is the mandate of both the Act and Executive Order 11514 (35 F.R. 4247) of March 5, 1970, that all Federal agencies, to the fullest extent possible, direct their policies, plans and programs so as to meet national environmental goals.

2. *Policy.* Before undertaking major action or recommending or making a favorable report on legislation that significantly affects the environment, Federal agencies will, in consultation with other appropriate Federal, State, and local agencies, assess in detail the potential environmental impact in order that adverse affects are avoided, and environmental quality is restored or enhanced, to the fullest extent practicable. In particular, alternative actions that will minimize adverse impact should be explored and both the long- and short-range implications to man, his physical and social surroundings, and to nature, should be evaluated in order to avoid to the fullest extent practicable undesirable consequences for the environment.

3. *Agency and BOB procedures.* a. Pursuant to section 2(f) of Executive Order 11514, the heads of Federal agencies have been directed to proceed with measures required by section 102(2) (C) of the Act. Consequently, each agency will establish no later than June 1, 1970, its own formal procedures for (1) identifying those agency actions requiring environmental statements, (2) obtaining information required in their preparation, (3) designating the officials who are to be responsible for the statements, (4) consulting with and taking account of the comments of appropriate Federal, State and local agencies, and (5) meeting the requirements of section 2(b) of Executive Order 11514 for providing timely public information on Federal plans and programs with environmental impact. These procedures should be consonant with

the guidelines contained herein. Each agency should file seven (7) copies of all such procedures with the Council on Environmental Quality, which will provide advice to agencies in the preparation of their procedures and guidance on the application and interpretation of the Council's guidelines.

b. Each Federal agency should consult, with the assistance of the Council on Environmental Quality if desired, with other appropriate Federal agencies in the development of the above procedures so as to achieve consistency in dealing with similar activities and to assure effective coordination among agencies in their review of proposed activities.

c. It is imperative that existing mechanisms for obtaining the views of Federal, State, and local agencies on proposed Federal actions be utilized to the extent practicable in dealing with environmental matters. The Bureau of the Budget will issue instructions, as necessary, to take full advantage of existing mechanisms (relating to procedures for handling legislation, preparation of budgetary material, new policies and procedures, water resource and other projects, etc.).

4. *Federal agencies included.* Section 102(2)(C) applies to all agencies of the Federal Government with respect to recommendations or reports on proposals for (i) legislation and (ii) other major Federal actions significantly affecting the quality of the human environment. The phrase "to the fullest extent possible" in section 102(2)(C) is meant to make clear that each agency of the Federal Government shall comply with the requirement unless existing law applicable to the agency's operations expressly prohibits or makes compliance impossible. (Section 105 of the Act provides that "The policies and goals set forth in this Act are supplementary to those set forth in existing authorizations of Federal agencies.")

5. *Actions included.* The following criteria will be employed by agencies in deciding whether a proposed action requires the preparation of an environmental statement:

    a. "Actions" include but not limited to:

        i. Recommendations or reports relating to legislation and appropriations;

        ii. Projects and continuing activities;

            Directly undertaken by Federal agencies;

            Supported in whole or in part through Federal contracts, grants, subsidies, loans, or other forms of funding assistance;

            Involving a Federal lease, permit, license, certificate or other entitlement for use;

iii. Policy—and procedure-making.

b. The statutory clause "major Federal actions significantly affecting the quality of the human environment" is to be construed by agencies with a view to the overall, cumulative impact of the action proposed (and of further actions contemplated). Such actions may be localized in their impact, but if there is potential that the environment may be significantly affected, the statement is to be prepared. Proposed actions the environmental impact of which is likely to be highly controversial should be covered in all cases. In considering what constitutes major action significantly affecting the environment, agencies should bear in mind that the effect of many Federal decisions about a project or complex of projects can be individually limited but cumulatively considerable. This can occur when one or more agencies over a period of years puts into a project individually minor but collectively major resources, when one decision involving a limited amount of money is a precedent for action in much larger cases or represents a decision in principle about a future major course of action, or when several Government agencies individually make decisions about partial aspects of a major action. The lead agency should prepare an environmental statement if it is reasonable to anticipate a cumulatively significant impact on the environment from the Federal action.

c. Section 101(b) of the Act indicates the broad range of aspects of the environment to be surveyed in any assessment of significant effect. The Act also indicates that adverse significant effects include those that degrade the quality of the environment, curtail the range of beneficial uses of the environment or serve short-term, to the disadvantage of long-term, environmental goals. Significant effects can also include actions which may have both beneficial and detrimental effects, even if, on balance, the agency believes that the effect will be beneficial. Significant adverse effects on the quality of the human environment include both those that directly affect human beings and those that indirectly affect human beings through adverse effects on the environment.

d. Because of the Act's legislative history, the regulatory activities of Federal environmental protection agencies (e.g., the Federal Water Quality Administration of the Department of the Interior and the National Air Pollution Control Administration of the Department of Health, Education, and Welfare) are not deemed actions which require the preparation of an environmental statement under section 102(2)(C) of the Act.

6. *Recommendations or reports on proposals for legislation.* The requirement for following the section 102(2) (C) procedure as elaborated in these guidelines applies to both (i) agency recommendations on their own proposals for legislation and (ii) agency reports on legislation initiated elsewhere. (In the latter case only the agency which has primary responsibility for the subject matter involved will prepare an environmental statement.) The Bureau of the Budget will supplement these general guidelines with specific instructions relating to the way in which the section 102(2) (C) procedure fits into its legislative clearance process.

7. *Content of environmental statement.* a. The following points are to be covered:

  i. The probable impact of the proposed action on the environment, including impact on ecological systems such as wildlife, fish and marine life. Both primary and secondary significant consequences for the environment should be included in the analysis. For example, the implications, if any, of the action for population distribution or concentration should be estimated and an assessment made of the effect of any possible change in population patterns upon the resource base, including land use, water, and public services, of the area in question.

  ii. Any probable adverse environmental effects which cannot be avoided (such as water or air pollution, damage to life systems, urban congestion, threats to health or other consequences adverse to the environmental goals set out in section 101(b) of Public Law 91–190).

  iii. Alternatives to the proposed action (section 102(2) (D) of the Act requires the responsible agency to "study, develop and describe appropriate alternatives to recommended courses of action in any proposal which involves unresolved conflicts concerning alternative uses of available resources"). A rigorous exploration and objective evaluation of alternative actions that might avoid some or all of the adverse environmental effects is essential. Sufficient analysis of such alternatives and their costs and impact on the environment should accompany the proposed action through the agency review process in order not to foreclose prematurely options which might have less detrimental effects.

  iv. The relationship between local short-term uses of man's environment and the maintenance and enhancement of long-term productivity. This in essence requires the agency to assess the action for cumulative and long-term effects from the perspective that each generation is trustee of the environment for succeeding generations.

v. Any irreversible and irretrievable commitments of resources which would be involved in the proposed action should it be implemented. This requires the agency to identify the extent to which the action curtails the range of beneficial uses of the environment.

vi. Where appropriate, a discussion of problems and objections raised by other Federal agencies and State and local entities in the review process and the disposition of the issues involved. (This section may be added at the end of the review process in the final text of the environmental statement.)

b. With respect to water quality aspects of the proposed action which have been previously certified by the appropriate State or interstate organization as being in substantial compliance with applicable water quality standards, mere reference to the previous certification is sufficient.

c. Each environmental statement should be prepared in accordance with the precept in section 102(2) (A) of the Act that all agencies of the Federal Government "utilize a systematic interdisciplinary approach which will insure the integrated use of the natural and social sciences and the environmental design arts in planning and decision making which may have an impact on man's environment."

8. *Federal agencies to be consulted in connection with preparation of environmental statement.* The Federal agencies to be consulted in connection with preparation of environmental statements are those which have "jurisdiction by law or special expertise with respect to any environmental impact involved" or "which are authorized to develop and enforce environmental standards". These Federal agencies include components of (depending on the aspect or aspects of the environment involved):

Department of Agriculture.
Department of Commerce.
Department of Defense.
Department of Health, Education, and Welfare.
Department of Housing and Urban Development.
Department of the Interior.
Department of Transportation.

Atomic Energy Commission.

For actions specially affecting the environment of their regional jurisdictions, the following Federal agencies are also to be consulted:

Tennessee Valley Authority.

Appalachian Regional Commission.

Agencies obtaining comment should determine which one or more of the above listed agencies are appropriate to consult. It is recommended that the above listed Departments establish contact points for providing comments and that Departments from which comment is solicited coordinate and consolidate the comments of their component entities. The requirement in section 102(2) (C) to obtain comment from Federal agencies having jurisdiction or special expertise is in addition to any specific statutory obligation of any Federal agency to coordinate or consult with any other Federal or State agency. Agencies seeking comment may establish time limits of not less than thirty days for reply, after which it may be presumed the agency consulted has no comment to make.

9. *State and local review.* Where no public hearing has been held on the proposed action at which the appropriate State and local review has been invited, and where review of the proposed action by State and local agencies authorized to develop and enforce environmental standards is relevant, such State and local review shall be provided for as follows:

a. For direct Federal development projects and projects assisted under programs listed in Attachment D of the Bureau of the Budget Circular No. A–95, review by State and local governments will be through procedures set forth under Part 1 of Circular No. A–95.

b. State and local review of agency procedures, regulations, and policies for the administration of Federal programs of assistance to State and local governments will be conducted pursuant to procedures established by Bureau of the Budget Circular No. A–85.

c. Where these procedures are not appropriate and where the proposed action affects matters within their jurisdiction, review of the proposed action by State and local agencies authorized to develop and enforce environmental standards and their comments on the draft environmental statement may be obtained directly or by publication of a summary notice in the Federal Register (with a copy of the environmental statement and comments of Federal agencies thereon to be supplied on request). The notice in the Federal Register may specify that comments of the relevant State and local agencies must be submitted within 60 days of publication of the notice.

10. *Use of statements in agency review processes; distribution to Council on Environmental Quality.* a. Agencies will need to identify at what stage or stages of a series of actions relating to a particular matter the environmental statement procedures of this directive will be applied. It will often be necessary to use the procedures both in the development of a national program and in the review of proposed projects within the national program. However, where a grant-in-aid program does not entail prior approval by Federal agencies of specific projects, the view of Federal, State, and local agencies in the legislative, and possibly appropriation, process may have to suffice. The principle to be applied is to obtain views of other agencies at the earliest feasible time in the development of program and project proposals. Care should be exercised so as not to duplicate the clearance process, but when actions being considered differ significantly from those that have already been reviewed an environmental statement should be provided.

b. Seven (7) copies of draft environmental statements (when prepared), seven (7) copies of all comments received thereon (when received), and seven (7) copies of the final text of environmental statements should be supplied to the Council on Environmental Quality in the Executive Office of the President (this will serve as making environmental statements available to the President). It is important that draft environmental statements be prepared and circulated for comment and furnished to the Council early enough in the agency review process before an action is taken in order to permit meaningful consideration of the environmental issues involved.

11. *Application of section 102(2) (C) procedure to existing projects and programs.* To the fullest extent possible the section 102(2) (C) procedure should be applied to further major Federal actions having a significant effect on the environment even though they arise from projects or programs initiated prior to enactment of Public Law 91–190 on January 1, 1970. Where it is not practicable to reassess the basic course of action, it is still important that further incremental major actions be shaped so as to minimize adverse environmental consequences. It is also important in further action that account be taken of environmental consequences not fully evaluated at the outset of the project or program.

12. *Availability of environmental statements and comments to public.* The agency which prepared the environmental statement is responsible for making such statement and the comments received avail-

able to the public pursuant to the provisions of the Freedom of Information Act (5 U.S.C. sec 552).

13. *Review of existing authority, policies and procedures in light of National Environmental Policy Act.* Pursuant to section 103 of the Act and section 2(d) of Executive Order 11514, all agencies, as soon as possible, shall review their present statutory authority, administrative regulations, and current policies and procedures, including those relating to loans, grants, contracts, leases, licenses, certificates and permits, for the purpose of determining whether there are any deficiencies or inconsistencies therein which prohibit full compliance with the purposes and provisions of the Act. After such review each agency shall report to the Council on Environmental Quality not later than September 1, 1970, the results of such review and their proposals to bring their authority and policies into conformity with the intent, purposes and procedures set forth in the Act.

14. *Supplementary guidelines; evaluation of procedures.* a. The Council on Environmental Quality after examining environmental statements and agency procedures with respect to such statements will issue such supplements to these guidelines as are necessary.

b. Agencies will assess their experience in the implementation of the section 102(2) (C) provisions of the Act and in conforming with these guidelines and report thereon to the Council on Environmental Quality by December 1, 1970. Such reports should include an identification of problem areas and suggestions for revision or clarification of these guidelines to achieve effective coordination of views on environmental aspects (and alternatives, where appropriate) of proposed actions without imposing unproductive administrative procedures.

Russell E. Train,
Chairman.

[F.R. Doc. 70–5769; Filed, May 11, 1970; 8:46 a.m.]

APPENDIX O:

Citizens' Advisory Committee on Environmental Quality, August 1969

Table of Funding of Federal Environmental Control Programs
(by fiscal years, in millions of dollars)

Solid Waste Disposal Act

Dept. of the Interior	1965	1966	1967	1968	1969	1970
Authorization		3.0	6.0	10.8	12.5	12.3
Appropriation		1.4	4.3	3.4	1.9	1.7[1]
Gap		1.6	1.7	7.4	10.6	10.6

Department of Health, Education and Welfare

	1965	1966	1967	1968	1969	1970
Authorization		7.0	14.0	19.2	20.0	19.8
Appropriation		4.3	12.3	15.4	13.3	14.9[1]
Gap		2.7	1.7	3.8	4.7	4.9

Air Pollution Control

	1965	1966	1967	1968	1969	1970
Authorization	25.5	30.5	46.0	109.0	185.0	134.3
Appropriation	21.0	26.6	40.1	64.2	88.7	95.8[1]
Gap	4.5	3.9	5.9	44.8	96.3	38.5

Land and Water Conservation Fund

	1965	1966	1967	1968	1969	1970
Authorization[2]					260.0	200.0
Appropriation		122.1	95.0	113.1	164.5	124.0[3]
Gap					95.5	76.0

Highway Beautification Act

	1965	1966	1967	1968	1969	1970
Authorization		160.0	160.0	[4]	26.1	31.3
Appropriation		70.8	81.5	[4]	0	N.A.
Gap		89.2	78.5		26.1	

Treatment Plant Grants

	1965	1966	1967	1968	1969	1970
Authorization		150	150	450	700	1,000
Appropriation		141	173[5]	203	214	214[1]
Gap		9		247	486	786

Water and Sewer Grants

	1965	1966	1967	1968	1969	1970
Authorization		200	200	200	420	605
Appropriation			100	165	165	135[1]
Gap		200	100	35	255	470

1 Estimated.
2 In fiscal years 1966-1968 program level was determined by actual receipts to the fund plus receipts in excess of appropriations for prior years. Amendments to the Act in fiscal year 1969 guaranteed an annual income to the fund of $200 million for five years.
3 House Committee allowance 7/10/69.
4 Amendments to the 1965 Act changed funding from straight authorization to contract authorization. No new funds appropriated in FY 1968.
5 Appropriation higher than authorization shown because of open-ended authorizing provision then in law.

APPENDIX P:

Budget Analysis

TABLE 1.—*Estimated Federal Funding for Pollution Control and Abatement Programs, Fiscal Years 1969, 1970, 1971 by Type of Activity*

[In millions of dollars]

Type of activity	Budget authority			Obligations			Outlays		
	1969	1970	1971	1969	1970	1971	1969	1970	1971
I. Assistance for State, interstate, and local governments [1]	289	887	4,089	312	626	1,336	217	255	649
a. Funds for capital investments; e.g., treatment facilities	232	825	4,020	256	564	1,265	170	199	580
b. Funds for operations of pollution control agencies	36	39	45	35	39	46	25	35	45
c. Technical assistance	21	23	25	21	23	25	22	21	24
II. Research, development, and demonstration [1]	319	319	346	330	332	361	292	317	339
a. Primarily for pollution control and abatement	249	241	267	253	251	277	220	242	259
b. For some other primary purpose but contributing to pollution control and abatement	70	78	79	77	81	84	72	75	80
III. Monitoring and surveillance [1]	49	46	50	48	46	51	48	46	51
a. Primarily for pollution control and abatement	41	38	40	40	38	41	40	38	41
b. For some other primary purpose but contributing to pollution control and abatement	8	8	10	8	8	10	8	8	10
IV. Standards promulgation and enforcement	23	27	32	22	28	32	22	26	31
V. Manpower development	17	18	19	16	18	19	17	17	18
VI. Remedial actions to control pollution at Federal facilities	50	88	130	77	108	153	63	103	144
VII. Other:									
a. Program administration and education	25	31	30	22	29	30	19	20	33
b. Direct actions by AEC to control pollution from radioactive wastes	22	29	37	22	30	38	19	26	32
c. Financial and technical assistance by Soil Conservation Service to control sediment and agriculturally related pollutants	68	75	79	68	75	79	66	75	83
Total	862	1,520	4,813	916	1,291	2,100	763	885	1,380

[1] Totals of amounts below.

NOTE.—Details in the tables may not add exactly to the totals due to rounding.

Source: Compiled from data supplied by the Office of Management and Budget, July 1970.

TABLE 2.—*Estimated Federal Funding for Pollution Control and Abatement, by Agency and by Polluted Medium and Selected Pollutants (Fiscal Year 1970 Obligations)*

[In millions of dollars]

Agency	Polluted medium			Selected pollutants [1]						
	Air	Water	Land	Pesti-cides	Radia-tion	Solid wastes	Noise	Ther-mal	Other	Total
Interior	4.0	629.9	2.6	5.2	0.2	5.7		2.4		650.0
AEC	4.6	5.8	.2	.1	133.3	2.1		1.8		147.9
HEW	94.2	3.5		11.7	18.6	15.2	0.1		7.9	151.2
DOD-military	19.9	35.5		.7	.8	.2	12.5		.1	69.7
Agriculture	12.0	120.7	7.9	23.2	.7	2.6			.4	167.5
Transportation	5.8	6.0		.2		.4	7.3			19.7
NASA	2.3	.9				.1	14.0			17.3
Appalachian Region-al Commission		4.6	6.5			1.0				12.1
TVA	14.5	10.2	.1		1.4	.1		6.8		33.1
Corps of Engineers	.4	3.0				1.8				5.2
Commerce	1.7	3.4	.2		.1	.2	.2		.4	6.2
Justice	.3					.9				1.2
Other	3.5	5.0	.2	.1	.2	.4			.4	9.8
Total	163.2	828.5	17.7	41.2	155.3	30.0	34.1	11.0	9.2	1,290.9

[1] Excluding funds reported in media columns.

Source: Compiled from data supplied by the Office of Management and Budget, July 1970.

TABLE 3.—Estimated Federal Funding (Fiscal Year 1970 Obligations) for Pollution Control and Abatement, by Agency and by Type of Activity

[In millions of dollars]

Agency	Aid to State, regional, and local governments — Capital funds	Operating funds	Technical assistance	Sub-total	Research, development demonstration — Primarily for pollution control	Contributing to pollution control	Sub-total	Monitoring and surveillance — Primarily for pollution control	Contributing to pollution control	Sub-total	Standards and enforcement	Manpower development	Pollution control: Remedial actions at Federal facilities	Other — Program administration and education	AEC control of radioactive wastes	Financial-technical assistance by SCS	Grand total
Interior	514.8	12.5	11.4	538.7	57.4	16.2	73.6	4.4	5.5	9.9	4.4	6.2	7.6	9.8			650.0
AEC			.1	.1	71.2	17.1	88.3	15.9		15.9	11.7		1.5		30.4		147.9
HEW		26.7	10.6	37.3	62.8	7.0	69.8	10.0	1.0	11.0	7.4	11.1		13.9			150.4
DOD-military					.5	6.5	7.0	4.6	.3	4.9		.4	57.8	.1			70.1
Agriculture	32.3			32.3	32.8	17.7	50.5	.7	1.2	1.9	3.2		3.1	1.2		75.1	167.2
TVA			.3	.3	.8	3.6	4.4	1.5		1.5			26.9				33.1
Transportation					9.4	7.1	16.5				.9		.5	1.8			19.7
NASA					14.1	3.1	17.2						.1				17.3
Appalachian Regional Commission	10.4			10.4										1.8			12.1
Commerce	2.3		.4	2.7	.5	2.7	3.2	.2	.2	.4			.2				6.5
Corps of Engineers								1.0		1.0			4.2				5.2
GSA													2.3				2.3
HUD	2.5			2.5													2.5
VA													1.8				1.8
Post Office	.5			.5									1.4				1.6
Justice	.8			.8							.1		.7				1.2
State					.2		.2		.1	.1							1.0
NSF					.8		.8										.8
Smithsonian					.2		.2										.2
Total	563.5	39.2	22.8	625.5	250.5	81.0	331.5	38.3	8.1	46.4	27.7	17.7	108.1	28.5	30.4	75.1	1,290.9

Source: Compiled from data supplied by the Office of Management and Budget, July 1970.

TABLE 4.—*Estimated Federal Funding (Fiscal Year 1970 Obligations) for Other Environmentally Related Activities, by Agency and by Selected Activities*

[In millions of dollars]

Agency	Preventing side effects[1][2]		Enhancing the environment[1][3]			Weather modification	Understanding, predicting the environment[4]				Population control and distribution	Management of public lands	Environmental health	Environmental education	Pest control	Water, sewer grants, loans	Agriculture conservation program	Major civilian technology and development programs[1]
	A	B	A	B	C		A	B	C	D								
Interior	18.0	8.2	221.5	106.7		4.8	1.4	90.5		4.3		170.3	0.6	1.5	0.5	2.4		11.6
Agriculture	203.1	20.5	90.0	9.8	13.1	.5	1.0	29.6		4.6	0.3	16.7	175.5	23.9	60.5	138.1	233.1	
DOT		227.0	13.0		146.2		19.1				.2							72.5
DOD				1.0	1.8	.2	237.2				64.2	24.1	20.8		2.7			
HEW		82.8							21.7				22.1	11.2	16.1			
Corps of Engineers	.4		65.2		3.6		5.3											
HUD			60.6		15.4						2.5					185.4		
Commerce			12.5	.1		1.4	130.0	10.9	3.4				.4	1.1		63.4		
NSF						2.5	15.6		8.0	65.8	1.0		.5		.1			
OEO							46.7				22.0			2.9				
NASA	3.2	1.3	4.9		55.0			30.4										
Smithsonian			4.4	.3				2.4										
TVA							1.0		1.7	3.5			2.6	7.7				
Appalachian Regional Commission	1.8										.1					1.5		
Labor			.1															
AEC	49.8												3.4					203.4
FPC	.5											.1						
Total	276.8	339.8	472.2	117.9	235.1	9.4	457.3	163.8	34.8	78.2	90.3	211.2	225.9	48.3	79.9	390.8	233.1	287.5

[1] Projects which have an environmental or natural resource conservation impact but are primarily for some other purpose.

[2] Preventing, controlling, or correcting environmental degradation (i.e., side effects caused by: A. Non-Federal natural resource exploitation activities. B. Direct Federal public works activities and public works activities supported by the Federal Government under grants or loans.

[3] Enhancing the environment: A. Recreation resources, B. Fisheries and Wildlife pres-ervation. C. "Natural Beauty"; e.g., highway beautification activities.

[4] Understanding, describing, predicting the environment: A. Environmental observation and measurement for the purpose of describing and predicting weather and ocean activities. B. Locating and describing natural resources. C. Research on the impact of the environment on man. D. Ecology and other basic environmental research.

Source: Compiled from data supplied by the Office of Management and Budget, July 1970.

APPENDIX Q:

Federal Expenditures on Research, Development, and Demonstration Related to Pollution
For Fiscal Years 1969 and 1970: A Report

Prepared by

Research, Development, and Demonstration Subcommittee on Environmental Quality, of the Federal Council on Science and Technology.

FEDERAL COUNCIL FOR SCIENCE AND TECHNOLOGY
EXECUTIVE OFFICE BUILDING
WASHINGTON, D.C. 20506

This preliminary report summarizes the results of a survey of federal research, development, and demonstration activities related to environmental pollution. Each Federal agency and department known to have programs in this area, has completed a comprehensive questionnaire, and these have been compiled.

The results of the survey show the amount of RD&D done directly in the field of environmental pollution mainly by agencies with mission responsibilities. (Tables I, II, and V.) Also shown is the amount of RD&D not directly conducted for pollution-related purposes, but which contributes to understanding or controlling pollution. (Tables II, IV, and VI.) These data do not include federal funds used in monitoring or surveillance or in control of pollution. The funds shown are those appropriated to each agency and are obligations rather than expenditures. Funds received by federal agencies by interagency transfer of funds are not included to prevent any duplication, but these transfer funds have been identified and are on record. In addition, data are on file on internal use of funds (in-house with federal employees), and extra-mural grants and contracts.

Summaries of the results of the survey are shown in accompanying charts. Fig. 1 shows the annual total expenditures in federal RD&D for 1967-1970. Fig. 2 shows the RD&D effort, both direct and indirect (related) for each of the federal agencies. Fig. 3 indicates the RD&D by classification of functional areas of pollution. Fig. 4 shows a breakdown of the amounts expended in each type of pollution activity, eg., air, water, land, etc. These summary figures are based on the more comprehensive data in Tables I–VI.

Different functional areas in the field of pollution, have been classified into six different categories as follows:

1. *Sources of Pollution.* Includes RD&D devoted to detecting and/or measuring the contributions from different sources of the same pollutant. For example, CO_2 may come from many sources such as respiration, volcanos, forest fires, and many different activities of man, such as power generation.

2. *Transport and Fate.* Includes the whole array of physical, chemical, and biological processes which are involved in the initial distribution, redistribution cycling, and ultimate fate, including degradation of pollutions in natural environments.

3. *Measuring and Monitoring.* Includes all RD&D devoted to providing new or improved methods for detecting, identifying or quantifying pollutants and for monitoring the effects of pollutants.

4. *Evaluation of Effects.* Includes research conducted to develop and advance understanding of the effects of pollutants.

5. *Prevention and Control Technology.* Includes RD&D conducted to discover, develop, and test methods to prevent or manage pollution problems, and to restore environments that have been harmed by pollutants.

6. *Standards and Regulations.* Includes RD&D conducted specifically for the purpose of establishing or improving pollution control standards or regulations.

The data in this report are presented to show the amount of RD&D effort by federal government agencies in FY 1969 and FY 1970. The information is being evaluated by the RD&D Subcommittee to determine the scope of effort, to analyse expenditures in relation to suggested goals, to determine the balance and relative efforts, and identification of areas not receiving sufficient support. For example, on the basis of data at hand, it appears that in the important area of thermal pollution, less than one million dollars per year is being spent on RD&D by all federal agencies.

A comprehensive report is now being prepared analysing all of the collected data, which should be of value in considering research needs in future years.

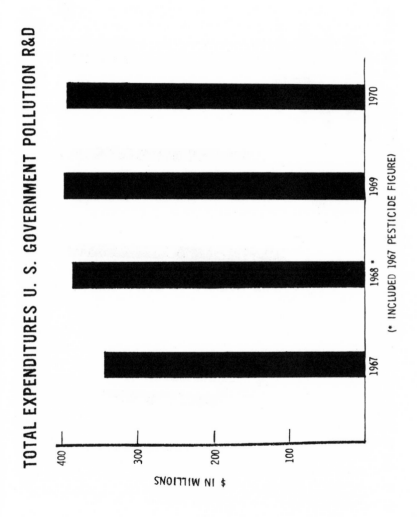

TOTAL EXPENDITURES U. S. GOVERNMENT POLLUTION R&D

$ IN MILLIONS

400

300

200

100

1967

1968 *

1969

1970

(* INCLUDED 1967 PESTICIDE FIGURE)

219

U. S. GOVERNMENT POLLUTION RESEARCH - DEVELOPMENT 1969-1970

TOTAL (MIL)

$ 328.2   '69 DIRECT
$ 318.7   '70 DIRECT
$ 69.3   '69 RELATED
$ 75.9   '70 RELATED

$ IN MILLIONS

FEDERAL AGENCY

USDA   AEC   COMM   DOD   DHEW   HUD   USDI   NSF   NASA   DOT

220

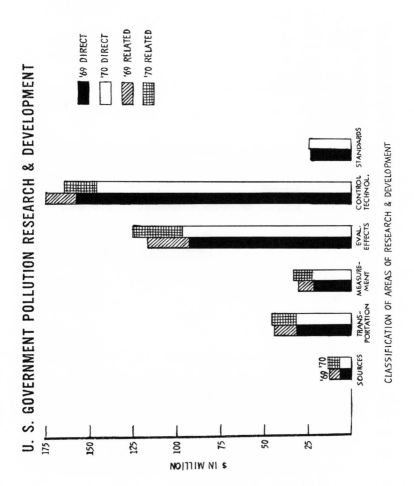

U. S. GOVERNMENT POLLUTION RESEARCH & DEVELOPMENT

'69 DIRECT
'70 DIRECT
'69 RELATED
'70 RELATED

$ IN MILLION

175
150
125
100
75
50
25

'69 '70

SOURCES
TRANS-PORTATION
MEASURE-MENT
EVAL. EFFECTS
CONTROL TECHNOL.
STANDARDS

CLASSIFICATION OF AREAS OF RESEARCH & DEVELOPMENT

221

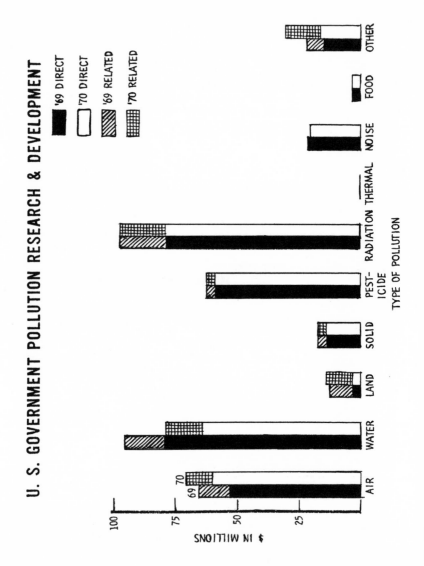

U. S. GOVERNMENT POLLUTION RESEARCH & DEVELOPMENT

'69 DIRECT
'70 DIRECT
'69 RELATED
'70 RELATED

$ IN MILLIONS

TYPE OF POLLUTION

AIR WATER LAND SOLID PEST-ICIDE RADIATION THERMAL NOISE FOOD OTHER

TABLE 1 – POLLUTION RESEARCH, DEVELOPMENT & DEMONSTRATION CONDUCTED OR SUPPORTED BY THE U.S. FEDERAL GOVERNMENT

(costs in thousands of dollars)

	(1) USDA	(2) AEC	(3) COMM	(4) FPC	(5) DOD	(6) DHEW	(7) HUD	(8) USDI	(9) NSF	(10) NASA	(11) State	(12) Trans.	Total
1969													
Sources of Pollution	460	87	15			4,280		673		1,615			7,130
Transportation & Fate	5,365	14,510	69		1,000	6,644		2,238	252	50		50	30,178
Measurement & Monitoring	1,130	9,011	420		93	6,333		2,242	29	970		219	20,447
Evaluation of Effects	9,380	43,050	115		135	26,403	100	11,670	50	773			91,676
Prevention & Control Technology	42,575	5,024	122		622	34,689	320	57,043	15	15,660	38	1,809	157,917
Standards & Regulations	110					16,295	190	1,810				2,413	20,818
Total	29,020	71,682	741		1,850	94,644	1,010	75,676	346	19,068	38	4,491	328,166
1970													
Sources of Pollution	460	112	15			4,702		821	300	380			6,790
Transportation & Fate	5,495	14,725	90		1,000	6,771		2,423	0	0	0	230	30,734
Measurement & Monitoring	1,115	9,265	422		115	6,945		2,287	0	1,375	0	89	21,613
Evaluation of Effects	9,500	44,302	230		135	28,625	40	12,222	150	885			96,089
Prevention & Control Technology	42,665	4,518	85		1,610	37,919	220	38,579	50	15,029	39	1,156	141,870
Standards & Regulations	135		42		95	16,888	150	1,539				2,919	21,568
Total	59,370	72,122	884		2,955	101,850	410	57,871	500	17,669	39	4,194	318,664

223

TABLE II – RESEARCH, DEVELOPMENT & DEMONSTRATION NOT CONDUCTED DIRECTLY FOR POLLUTION RELATED PURPOSES, BUT CONTRIBUTES TO UNDERSTANDING & CONTROLLING POLLUTION
(costs in thousands of dollars)

	(1) USDA	(2) AEC	(3) COMM	(4) FPC	(5) DOD	(6) DHEW	(7) HUD	(8) USDI	(9) NSF	(10) NASA	(11) State	(12) Trans.	Total
1969													
Sources of Pollution	2,525		216	39		98		15	136	110	2,210		5,349
Transportation & Fate	6,280	840	562		347			425	3,413	1,482			13,349
Measurement & Monitoring	180		2,156		184			326	642	5,555			9,043
Evaluation of Effects	3,175	16,360	460		340	350		246	1,423	1,434		269	24,057
Prevention & Control Technology	9,755		289			170		4,328	57	2,526		105	17,230
Standards & Regulations								222					222
Total	21,915	17,200	3,683	39	871	618		5,562	5,671	11,107	2,210	374	69,250
1970													
Sources of Pollution	2,535		226	42		115		15	150	65	3,050		6,188
Transportation & Fate	6,255	850	616		415			431	4,567	1,431			14,555
Measurement & Monitoring	210		2,234		190			337	1,100	6,350			10,421
Evaluation of Effects	5,885	16,280	461		340	375		241	2,010	1,396		230	27,218
Prevention & Control Technology	9,855		289			185		4,522	60	2,229		165	17,305
Standards & Regulations								222					222
Total	24,740	17,130	3,826	42	955	665							

TABLE III – POLLUTION RESEARCH, DEVELOPMENT & DEMONSTRATION CONDUCTED OR SUPPORTED BY THE U.S. FEDERAL GOVERNMENT

(costs in thousands of dollars)

	(1) Air Pollution	(2) Water Pollution	(3) Land Pollution	(4) Solid Wastes	(5) Pesticides	(6) Radiation	(7) Thermal	(8) Noise	(9) Food*	(10) Other	Total
1969											
Sources of Pollution	3,438	998		476		212		1,545	461		7,130
Transportation & Fate	6,656	4,177	590		4,066	14,406	77	50	156		30,178
Measurement & Monitoring	5,124	2,071	161	189	1,269	9,652	69	638	244	992	20,447
Evaluation of Effects	10,600	9,286	856	120	12,109	47,208	621	895	179	9,796	91,676
Prevention & Control Technology	26,298	60,642	1,309	12,347	33,953	6,917	100	15,760	560	31	157,917
Standards & Regulations	1,768	1,810			8,233	755		2,603	1,214	4,435	20,818
Total	53,840	78,992	2,911	13,132	59,638	79,180	867	21,491	2,814	15,254	328,166
1970											
Sources of Pollution	3,716	1,176		540		217		380	461	300	6,790
Transportation & Fate	7,177	4,377	590		3,502	14,700	2	230	156		30,734
Measurement & Monitoring	5,871	2,739	100	445	945	9,690	31	375	244	1,153	21,613
Evaluation of Effects	12,363	9,829	989	125	11,105	47,673	816	947	179	11,263	96,089
Prevention & Control Technology	28,712	43,962	1,560	12,169	33,636	6,037		15,149	560	85	141,870
Standards & Regulations	2,305	1,599			8,194	650		2,715	1,350	4,755	21,568
Total	60,144	63,682	3,239	13,279	58,182	78,967	849	19,816	2,950	14,556	318,664

*USDA not included

TABLE IV – RESEARCH, DEVELOPMENT & DEMONSTRATION NOT CONDUCTED DIRECTLY FOR POLLUTION RELATED BUT CONTRIBUTES TO UNDERSTANDING & CONTROLLING POLLUTION

(costs in thousands of dollars)

	(1) Air Pollution	(2) Water Pollution	(3) Land Pollution	(4) Solid Wastes	(5) Pesticides	(6) Radiation	(7) Thermal	(8) Noise	(9) Food*	(10) Other	Total
1969											
Sources of Pollution	303	1,634	1,307		1,894	100	13			98	5,349
Transportation & Fate	2,856	7,105	1,914	50	17	840	90			477	13,349
Measurement & Monitoring	4,427	1,464	557	1,638		114	145	53		645	9,043
Evaluation of Effects	1,520	1,597	1,376	25	201	17,400	75	78		1,785	24,057
Prevention & Control Technology	3,803	4,538	3,687	643	300		10	139		4,100	17,230
Standards & Regulations		221	1								222
Total	12,909	16,559	8,842	2,350	2,412	18,454	333	270		7,115	69,250
1970											
Sources of Pollution	175	2,026	1,363		2,300	55	14			255	6,185
Transportation & Fate	1,689	6,209	928	70	12	850	90			4,707	14,555
Measurement & Monitoring	4,520	1,553	608	1,658	204	114	175	53		1,740	10,421
Evaluation of Effects	1,096	501	4,091	10	300	17,345	75	81		3,815	27,218
Prevention & Control Technology	4,094	4,200	3,790	587			10	139		4,185	17,305
Standards & Regulations		221	1								222
Total	11,574	14,710	10,781	2,325	2,816	18,364	364	273		14,702	75,909

*USDA not included

TABLE V – POLLUTION RESEARCH, DEVELOPMENT & DEMONSTRATION CONDUCTED OR SUPPORTED BY THE U.S. FEDERAL GOVERNMENT

(costs in thousands of dollars)

	(1) Air Pollution	(2) Water Pollution	(3) Land Pollution	(4) Solid Wastes	(5) Pesticides	(6) Radiation	(7) Thermal	(8) Noise	(9) Food*	(10) Other	Total
1969											
USDA	2,595	7,595	2,700		46,130						59,020
AEC	258	319			79	70,555	471				71,682
Commun.	554	177		10							741
FPC											
DOD	1,125	532	20	80				93			1,850
DHEW	45,942	1,145	76	10,639	10,399	8,625	22	22	2,814	14,960	94,644
HUD				100			100	410			610
USDI	1,605	68,218	70	2,268	2,347		274			294	75,676
USF	85	136	50		75						346
NASA	340	280		35				18,413			19,068
State	18	20									38
Trans.	1,568	570						2,356			4,491
Total	55,890	78,992	2,916	13,132	59,630	79,180	867	21,491	2,814	15,254	328,166
1970											
USDA	2,585	7,955	3,110		47,720						59,370
AEC	10	420			61	71,542	589				72,922
Commun.	454	125		25							884
FPC											
DOD	1,155	1,220	20	425				155			2,955
DHEW	53,466	1,300	99	10,290	9,454	7,425	22	22	2,950	16,762	101,850
HUD				100				310			410
USDI	1,431	50,787	10	2,164	2,947		238			294	57,871
USF										510	500
NASA	250	550		275				16,594			17,669
State	19	20									39
Trans.	214	1,245						2,735			4,194
Total	60,144	63,682	3,239	13,279	58,182	78,967	849	19,816	2,950	17,556	318,664

* USDA not included

227

TABLE VI – RESEARCH, DEVELOPMENT, & DEMONSTRATION NOT CONDUCTED DIRECTLY FOR POLLUTION RELATED PURPOSES, BUT CONTRIBUTES TO UNDERSTANDING & CONTROLLING POLLUTION

(costs in thousands of dollars)

	(1) Air Pollution	(2) Water Pollution	(3) Land Pollution	(4) Solid Wastes	(5) Pesticides	(6) Radiation	(7) Thermal	(8) Noise	(9) Food*	(10) Other	Total
1969											
USDA	690	9,780	5,790							5,655	21,915
AEC						17,200					17,200
Commerce	1,682	977	181	50		114		223		456	3,683
FPC	13	13					13				39
DOD	531					340					871
DHEW										618	618
HUD											
USDI	2,218	1,377	1,378	268	346		85				5,562
USF	2,213	2,101	971							386	5,671
NASA	5,517	1,996	421	2,138		800	235				11,107
State		215	101		1,894						2,210
Trans.	55	100			172			47			374
Total	12,909	16,559	8,842	2,356	2,412	18,454	333	270		7,115	69,250
1970											
USDA	775	9,820	8,495							5,650	24,740
AEC						17,130					17,130
Commerce	1,705	1,024	190	70		114		223		500	3,826
FPC	14	14					14				42
DOD	595					340					935
DHEW										660	665
HUD											
USDI	2,299	1,394	1,481	168	341		85				5,768
NSF										7,887	7,887
NASA	6,116	1,728	465	2,087		780	265				11,471
State		600	150		2,300						3,050
Trans.	70	100			175			50			395
Total	11,574	14,710	10,781	2,325	2,816	18,364	364	273		14,702	75,909

APPENDIX R:

Government Advisory Groups in the Environmental Quality Field

Councils

Advisory Council on Historic Preservation
Council on Environmental Quality
Domestic Affairs Council
Federal Radiation Council
National Council on Marine Resources and Engineering Development
National Industrial Pollution Control Council
President's Council on Recreation and Natural Beauty
President's Consumer Advisory Council
Water Resources Council

Boards

Advisory Board on National Parks, Historic Sites, Buildings and
    Monuments
Air Quality Advisory Board
Water Pollution Control Advisory Board

Commissions (Foundation)

Appalachia Regional Commission
Commission on Marine Science, Engineering and Resources
Commission on Population Growth and the American Future
Migratory Bird Conservation Commission
Lewis and Clark Trail Commission
National Capital Planning Commission
National Forest Preservation Commission
National Park Foundation
National Water Commission
Public Land Law Review Commission

Committees

Citizens' Advisory Committee on Environmental Quality
Committee on Populations and Family Planning
President's Committee on Consumer Interests

Task Forces

Task Force on Oceanography
Task Force on Air Pollution

APPENDIX S:

Text of UN General Assembly Resolution Calling for a 1972 Conference on the Human Environment

GENERAL ASSEMBLY RESOLUTIONS
TWENTY-FOURTH REGULAR SESSION

SUBJECT: *United Nations Conference on the Human Environment*

DATE AND MEETING: *15 December 1969, 1834th plenary meeting*

VOTE: *Adopted unanimously*

DOCUMENT NUMBERS
    REPORT TO ASSEMBLY: *Second Committee report A/7866*
    RESOLUTION ADOPTED: *2581 (XXIV)*

TEXT OF RESOLUTION

The General Assembly

In pursuance of its decision in resolution 2398 (XXIII) of 3 December 1968 to convene in 1972 a United Nations Conference on the Human Environment and to begin immediately preparations for the Conference,

Having considered with appreciation the report of the Secretary-General called for in the above-mentioned resolution,

Having considered the relevant chapter of the report of the Economic and Social Council,

Taking into account the recommendations of the Economic and Social Council in the matter,

Having taken cognizance of the note by the Secretary-General of 21 October 1969,

Reaffirming the importance and urgency of the problems of the human environment and underlining the necessity for complete preparatory arrangements for the 1972 United Nations Conference on the Human Environment to become operative as soon as possible,

Recognizing the important work on the problems of the human environment that is at present being undertaken and planned by the organizations in the United Nations system, other intergovernmental organizations, non-governmental organizations and national Governments,

1. *Endorses* in general the proposals contained in the report of the Secretary-General regarding the purposes and objectives of the United Nations Conference on the Human Environment;

2. *Affirms* that it should be the main purpose of the Conference to see as a practical means to encourage, and to provide guidelines for, action by Governments and international organizations designed to protect and improve the human environment, and to remedy and prevent its impairment, by means of international co-operation, bearing in mind the particular importance of enabling developing countries to forestall the occurrence of such problems;

3. *Entrusts* to the Secretary-General the over-all responsibility for organizing and preparing for the Conference, bearing in mind the views expressed during the debates of the forty-seventh session of the Economic and Social Council and the twenty-fourth session of the General Assembly;

4. *Establishes* a Preparatory Committee for the United Nations Conference on the Human Environment—consisting of highly qualified representatives nominated by the Governments of Argentina, Brazil, Canada, Costa Rica, Cyprus, Czechoslovakia, France, Ghana, Guinea, India, Iran, Italy, Jamaica, Japan, Mauritius, Mexico, the Netherlands, Nigeria, Singapore, Sweden, Togo, the Union of Soviet Socialist Republics, the United Arab Republic, the United Kingdom of Great Britain and Northern Ireland, the United States of America, Yugoslavia and Zambia—to advise the Secretary-General;

5. *Requests* the Secretary-General to set up immediately a small conference secretariat, by drawing, with the agreement of the specialized agencies concerned, particularly upon regular staff of the United Nations system, and to appoint, at the appropriate time, a Secretary-General of the Conference;

6. *Further requests* the Secretary-General to pursue the consultations on the preparations for the Conference, undertaken by him in accordance with General Assembly resolution 2398 (XXIII), to take account of the results of other international conferences such as the Conference on the Problems of Environment organized by the Economic Commission for Europe and scheduled to take place at Prague in 1971, and to draw on contributions from appropriate intergovernmental and non-governmental organizations;

7. *Invites* the specialized agencies, the International Atomic Energy

Agency and the Advisory Committee on the Application of Science and Technology to development to collaborate closely with the Secretary-General in the preparations for the Conference and to assist, as appropriate, in the work of the Preparatory Committee;

8. *Invites* the intergovernmental and non-governmental organizations concerned to lend every possible assistance in the preparations for the Conference;

9. *Requests* the Secretary-General, in collaboration with the Preparatory Committee, to take the necessary steps, as part of the preparations for the Conference, to bring to public attention the nature and importance of the problems of the human environment;

10. *Believes it essential* that all participating countries be enabled to take an active part in the preparations for the Conference and the Conference itself, and requests the Secretary-General to investigate what concrete steps could be taken to this end;

11. *Notes* the outline of the range of the possible financial implications for the United Nations of the holding of the Conference presented in the Secretary-General's reports and requests the Secretary-General, in the light of the views expressed during the debates of the forty-seventh session of the Economic and Social Council and the twenty-fourth session of the General Assembly, to make all efforts to reduce the costs of the Conference;

12. *Decides* that the Conference should be of two weeks' duration and requests the Secretary-General to take full account of this fact in preparing for the Conference;

13. *Believes* that, in order for the Conference to achieve its objectives, it is essential that its agenda be selective, its organizational structure be simple and efficient, and that the documentation be kept reasonably limited;

14. *Accepts with appreciation* the invitation of the Government of Sweden to hold the Conference in Sweden in June 1972;

15. *Requests* the Secretary-General to submit a brief progress report to the General Assembly at its twenty-fifth session through the Economic and Social Council at its forty-ninth session;

16. *Decides* to consider the progress of the preparatory work and to the necessary further decisions at its twenty-fifth and twenty-sixth sessions.

Also on 15 December 1969 at the 1834th plenary meeting, the General Assembly, without objection, adopted the following decision on the recommendation of the Second Committee (A/7866):

"The General Assembly decides that any interested Member State not appointed to the Preparatory Committee for the United Nations Conference on the Human Environment may designate highly qualified representatives to act as accredited observers at sessions of the Committee, with the right to participate in its discussions."

E/4667.

Official Records of the General Assembly, Twenty-fourth Session, Supplement No. 3 (A/7603), chapter V, section D.

A/7707.

APPENDIX T:

Senate Resolution 399 Relating to the Creating of a World Environmental Institute

The resolution *(S. Res. 399)*, with its preamble, reads as follows:

Relating to the creation of a World Environmental Institute to aid all the nations of the world in solving common environmental problems of both national and international scope.

Whereas human ecology is global in nature and human survival depends ultimately upon the cooperative effort of the entire human species; and

Whereas worldwide pollution of man's common resources—the air, the water, and the soil—poses a threat to all peoples; and

Whereas environmental problems caused by technological and population growth are common to all nations alike, and knowledge of such problems must be shared among all nations to insure the survival and well-being of the human species; and

Whereas an international institution open to all nations of the world is needed to provide technical information and scientific knowledge to each nation and to international organizations dealing with environmental problems; and

Whereas a forum for advocating such an institution exists in the International Conference on the Human Environment to be held under the sponsorship of the United Nations at Stockholm in 1972: Now, therefore, be it

Resolved, That the Senate recommends, urges, and supports the creation of a World Environmental Institute to act as a global research center and to disseminate knowledge of environmental problems and their solution to all nations of the world upon request; and be it further

Resolved, That such a World Environmental Institute, while coordinating its activities with existing international organizations, should be open to membership for all nations of the world, with its location and funding to be agreed upon by representatives of said nations assembled; and be it further

Resolved, That the Senate recommends and urges that the United States representatives to the International Conference on the Human Environment prepare to propose consideration of a World Environmental Institute to the Conference; and be it further

Resolved, That in furtherance of a World Environmental Institute concept, the Senate recommends, urges, and supports the invitation to the Conference of all nations not presently members of the General Assembly of the United Nations; and be it further *Resolved,* That the Senate recommends, urges, and supports creation of a World Environmental Institute as an official policy of the United States Government, to be pursued with other nations both formally and informally, at Stockholm and in other appropriate forums where the cause of the Institute can be furthered.

APPENDIX U:

Current International Study Projects Sponsored by the Committee on the Challenges of Modern Society

Air Pollution (Pilot country: United States; Co-pilots: Turkey and the Federal Republic of Germany) This study aims to make short- and long-term projections as to potential national and regional impact of air pollution on the air quality, formulate air quality criteria from which adequate air quality standards may be developed, and assess the control strategies required to meet the air quality standards. The United States, as pilot country, and Turkey and Germany, as co-pilots, organized a meeting in Ankara in March 1970, which was attended by representatives from six member countries. As a result of the meeting, it has been decided to carry out a two-pronged study: on the one hand, an assessment of air pollution in the Ankara and Frankfurt urban areas will be made, and, on the other hand, expert panels will review the air quality criteria and control techniques for sulfur oxides and particulate pollutants. The program of work will stretch over a period of 12 months, and it is expected that a report on the first phase of the overall air pollution project will be submitted to the CCMS in 1971.

Open-Water Pollution (Pilot country: Belgium; Co-pilots: Portugal, Canada, and France) The study will attempt to define international standards and criteria of pollution of open waters in order to make international anti-pollution measures more effective. Special attention will also be given to the pollution of the sea by oil spillage. It is intended to develop ways and means of detection of oil spillage and of its elimination through chemical, biological and physical processes. The project would attempt to coordinate national plans on an operational basis. A Conference on Oil Spills was held in Brussels in October, 1970.

Inland Water Pollution (Pilot country: Canada; Co-pilots: France, United States, and Belgium) This study will develop comprehensive basin plans for inland water pollution control, as well as concepts and techniques to provide more effective control programs in basins with divided jurisdiction. The physical dimensions of the pollution problem will be evaluated and technical solutions proposed.

Scientific Knowledge and Decision-Making (Pilot country: Federal Republic of Germany) The study aims at carrying out an investigation in three main areas: organization of internal coordination within each country as regards the handling of environmental problems; ways and means of implementing recommendations arising out of the CCMS studies and chronological synchronization between national and international projects; investigation of how scientific knowledge is translated into political decisions.

Work Satisfaction in a Technological Era (Pilot country: United Kingdom) This study concerns essentially the relationship in a changing environment between job satisfaction and proficiency at all levels.

Environment in the Strategy of Regional Development (Pilot country: France) This study will examine the inter-connection between environmental problems in the framework of regional development. It is intended to devote efforts to the elaboration of mathematical models which would allow a better understanding of the complex phenomena which modify the environment.

Road Safety (Pilot country: United States) The study goals are to exchange information on road safety decision-making practices and experience of member countries; to aid each member nation in deciding how to upgrade its road safety program with optimum use of available resources; and to develop, by means of demonstration and trial field programs in member countries, the application of modern technology to selected areas of road safety.

Disaster Assistance Project (Pilot country: United States; Co-pilot: Italy) This study aims at examination of mechanisms to coordinate relief assistance in the event of a disaster, the exchange of information on preparedness activites, disaster research, and scientific advances related to disasters. It is hoped to revamp and revitalize NATO capabilities for coordinating disaster assistance.

238

APPENDIX V:

Institutions for Effective Management of the Environment

Summary of Conclusions and Recommendations

Report of the
Environmental Study Group
to the
Environmental Studies Board
of the
National Academy of Sciences
National Academy of Engineering

PART I

NATIONAL ACADEMY OF SCIENCES
NATIONAL ACADEMY OF ENGINEERING
Washington, D.C.   January 1970

The quality of our lives is directly related to the quality of our environment, and the quality of that environment has deteriorated as our national affluence has increased. Unwise and thoughtless use of the environment can create, and in reality is now creating, an onerous national debt that will increasingly burden future generations. As our population increases, demands on the environment grow correspondingly. Rapidly growing population and the industrial economy that underlies our high standard of living have created vast problems that call for extraordinary steps to repair the damage already done and to prevent future destruction of our most valuable resource—our environment.

I. In order to reverse the trend of haphazard destruction we need effective mechanisms for the management of our environment at the highest levels of government; we therefore *recommend* the establishment of a Board of Environmental Affairs within the Office of the President.* This Board should have the strongest possible mandate for

*Since this recommendation was decided upon by the study group, the Congress has passed and the President has signed S.1075, National Environmental Policy Act of 1969.

action from the President and the Congress. It should recommend and assist the President in formulating policies; evaluate programs and activities of departments and agencies and consider how they will affect the environment, making their judgments fully known to the President, the Congress, and the public; analyze, interpret, and provide assistance in generating needed data concerning environmental matters; serve as coordinator on a working level for interdepartmental activities relating to the environment; and assist state and local governments in dealing with environmental problems. The Board should submit an annual report to the President for submission to the Congress. This report should contain evaluations of the state of the environment and the effectiveness of relevant ongoing policies, programs, and activities supported or carried out by other federal agencies, and should suggest to the Congress effective legislation bearing upon environmental problems.

The new Board would effectively augment the impact of the existing President's Council of Environmental Quality, established by Executive Order last May. Under the new arrangement, the President's Council would continue to provide strong coordinative, review, and oversight functions. Additionally, of course, as a Cabinet-level council it would attract critical public attention, marshaling significant public support for vigorous policies for the management of the environment.

The Board, of course, would differ from the President's Council in several important ways: 1) Deriving its existence from positive legislative action by the Congress, it would enjoy special Congressional interest and, indeed, a Congressional mandate. 2) It would be comprised of an interdisciplinary team of experts, staffed by highly professional, full-time personnel drawn from the relevant disciplines. At present, the Office of Science and Technology, already undermanned, provides only part-time staff backup, among its other duties; moreover, by definition of its legislated numerical limitations, it cannot effectively perform additional work, particularly insofar as the Board would exist outside of the OST hierarchy. 3) It would operate on a full-time basis, in contrast to the President's Council, which is comprised of the Secretaries of several agencies, chaired by the President, and which meets irregularly, giving only episodic attention to the problems within its purview. 4) It would be obligated to prepare an annual report on the condition of our environment which the President would submit to the Congress. The present Council has no mandated responsibilities of this kind to the Congress. 5) It would have an annual operating budget of its own. The existing Council has no regularly appropriated operating funds and is reliant on small inputs from other budgets. 6) It would be administratively separate from operating, mission-oriented agencies and therefore more capable of objective analysis of programs and policies, at least internally.

The Board that we recommend requires a highly professional staff, experienced not only in matters relating to the environment, but also in public-policy matters, science policies, Congressional affairs, federal, state, and local relations, information gathering and dispersal, and the broad range of disciplines related to the environment and its effective management.

II. The activities of the Executive Branch in establishing environmental policies, evaluating and overseeing their implementation, and in general managing environmental affairs should, we believe, relate to a more broadly effective Congressional organization than now exists. At present several committees of both Houses of the Congress have jurisdictions that relate to environmental matters. And while we would not presume to suggest a reorganization of Congressional committees, we do *recommend* that a joint committee of the Congress, comprised of the chairmen and ranking minority members of the relevant committees of both Houses, would provide a much needed focal point for the informed discussion of environmental affairs.

Such a joint committee would provide an open forum for annual hearings relating to the President's report, in which the important issues would be discussed and debated in public. This would, of course, in no way infringe upon existing jurisdictions relating to appropriations or other Congressional activities, though careful consideration should be given to organizational realignments in the future.

III. We cannot effectively manage the environment without knowing what it is, what it was, and what it can be. At present, we do not systematically, comprehensively, or regularly measure environmental quality, nor do we know how and to what extent it is changing and has already changed. We *recommend,* then, that a comprehensive federal program for the monitoring of the environment be initiated and assigned high priority. Though we have not made detailed organizational recommendations, it is clear to us that the present inordinately dispersed structure is inadequate to meet the pressing need for continuous and systematic environmental monitoring programs. The new Board of Environmental Affairs should develop and recommend for legislative action appropriate mechanisms for dealing with environmental problems.

Most of the data now obtained under the aegis of such agencies as the Environmental Science Services Administration, U.S. Geological Survey, Bureau of Commercial Fisheries, National Air Pollution Control Administration, and the Federal Water Pollution Control Administration, are obtained for limited special purposes and not for an overall, ecological evaluation of the quality of the environment. No single agency now assumes direct and specific responsibility for performing this vital function, nor is any common, interchangeable, or comparable sampling method now being used, though the quality of one aspect of the environment (e.g., air) obviously affects the quality of another (e.g., water).

Effective monitoring must be based on a carefully planned, integrated program of widespread and repeated observation. It is clear, moreover, that such a monitoring effort must include at least the following:

1. Physical and chemical properties of land, air, and water
2. Distribution of plants and animals in land, air, and water
3. Land use, including diversity of purpose
4. Construction
5. Noise
6. Epidemiology of man, animals, and plants
7. Evidence of environmental stress, such as tranquilizer consumption and asocial behavior
8. Aesthetic qualities

Once an effective, well-designed monitoring program has been established, it will become possible to set environmental quality goals, create policing mechanisms, and evaluate performance.

IV. Environmental matters involve values that are either difficult or impossible to measure in economic terms. Alternate means of defining these values are imperative. The management of environmental affairs would be greatly aided by the development of appropriate Environmental Quality Indices. We *recommend* that the research required to develop and maintain these indices be encouraged and supported to the fullest extent possible by the Board of Environmental Affairs and other interested government agencies.

Some quantitative measure of what is happening at regional and national levels is essential as an evaluation and management tool. The following are examples of such indices:

1. Transparency of the air
2. Purity of water

3. The ratio of area of open ground to population
4. Noise level
5. Ratio of wild animals to human population
6. Ratio of area of parks to area of parking lots
7. Fraction of utility wires above ground

The various individual indices would be combined and weighted into an overall Environmental Quality Index, which could become a powerful tool in developing priorities among programs affecting the environment. A similar index would need to be developed against which changes in the environment could be compared. The composition and weighting of this index or of its components will require careful analysis; we do not attempt even an outline of it. We do emphasize that the program of monitoring must be designed from the beginning to yield appropriate indices.

V. There is no laboratory in the federal government that now carries out systematic research on the environment as a whole. Present efforts are specialized and atomistic, and the overall ecological systems approach has not been adopted by any single federal agency. We *recommend* the establishment of a National Laboratory for the Environmental Sciences, which might well be contractor-operated as other national laboratories are, and funded by the several federal agencies with environmental responsibilities. Its research goal should be the development of knowledge and techniques that will lead to effective management of the environment. Its prime missions would be to carry out research in the environmental sciences and to develop a quick-reaction field function that would call attention to potential threats to the environment. It would perform research in monitoring but should not have operational responsibility for a monitoring program. It would conduct analysis of its research results but not be as policy-oriented as the Institute of Environmental Studies (cf. VI below).

A National Laboratory is one of the essential components of the institutional framework we believe necessary to meet the nation's needs for environmental research. An arrangement outside the government has the advantage of flexibility and a minimum of extra-bureaucratic constraints. It would encourage the relatively free interchange of research staff among universities, private research institutes, the National Laboratory, and other federal laboratories. An independent laboratory has the further advantage of providing diversity of talent and viewpoints necessary to cope with environmental problems. These characteristics have been partially responsible for the success of national laboratories in other fields, notably Brookhaven, Oak Ridge, Los Alamos, and Livermore. Many of the major oceanographic laboratories such as Woods Hole and Scripps behave as and consider themselves national laboratories although they are operated by private institutions. We have the successful experiences of these laboratories in mind in proposing yet another.

Activities of a National Laboratory

The National Laboratory for the Environmental Sciences should be responsible for basic and applied research with the following objectives:
1. Analysis of the interaction of environmental factors, leading to
2. Development of the capacity to predict environmental changes, and thus
3. Development of the capacity to maintain, modify, restore, improve, and generally control the environment.

In order to move effectively toward these objectives the laboratory will need a sizable research staff, laboratory facilities, and special supporting staff and equipment for environmental expeditions and field experiments. Part of the analysis of environmental factors would be based on the vast body of monitoring data to be acquired through the activities of the federal government.

Quick-Reaction Field Function

The capacity of the National Laboratory to conduct environmental expeditions will also permit it to carry out quick-reaction field studies pertinent to potential environmental crises. Quick reactions might involve the rapid deployment of a field force for a period of a few weeks or months. This requires a pool of experienced scientists and technicians familiar with field-operational needs, equipment, and instruments. The pool could function like a fire department, with members on standby, in training, or doing research when not in the field. Alternatively, a team might well be assembled from a sufficiently large group of experienced field environmentalists from outside the Laboratory, as was the case following the earthquake in Alaska in 1964. A similar quick-reaction mechanism may be anticipated in the environmental sciences once the flexible and diverse institutions we propose are operational. Such a team would respond to an early-warning signal from the monitoring and indexing system, or from a research laboratory, or from the Institute of Environmental Studies. The necessary components for building a National Laboratory, the scientists, supporting staff, and facilities, might well come from existing laboratories whose missions have been accomplished or whose original usefulness has diminished. Biologists, physicists, computer scientists, and other specialists could serve in the new laboratory and after a time serve as well as they did in the various old ones. The growing concern for the environment that we sense among scientists and other professionals, and the need for new kinds of research, might well serve to reinvigorate many professionals who seek new opportunities to assume useful social roles. Such a pool of talent would be useful in building environmental laboratories and should be enthusiastically tapped.

VI. Decision-making in environmental matters at all levels of government has been hampered by lack of adequate analyses of what is now taking place and alternative options. We *recommend* the establishment of an Institute for Environmental Studies. The Institute would carry out the following functions: 1) do long-range planning for the enhancement of the environment; 2) provide early warning on potential threats to the environment; 3) conduct rapid analytical studies in response to emergencies; 4) carry out rapid field analysis; and 5) systematically study and analyze the social, political, economic, administrative, legislative, and other factors that influence environmental decisions and the management of the environment. In order to achieve and maintain objectivity and independence, the Institute should be funded largely by the private sector, though it would, as well, accept grants and contracts from government agencies. The Institute would probably need a staff of approximately 200 professional researchers and analysts, including ecologists, biologists, economists, sociologists, physicians, lawyers, engineers, physicists, chemists, architects, social phychologists, and political scientists, particularly specialists in public administration and international relations, as well as information specialists and others. An institution of this size would require a sizable budget, a substantial portion of which, we believe, should come from the private sector— foundations, industry, and conservation groups—the remainder from contracts with federal, state, and local governments.

An effective Institute would:

1. Need to be financially independent of any department or agency of government and of industry and special-interest groups
2. Need to build confidence in its integrity among clients and sup-

porters as well as among the public

3. Need a talented and highly professional and dedicated staff, broadly representative of a suitable blend of the various relevant disciplines but well disposed toward interdisciplinary efforts

4. Need experienced and insightful public-policy specialists and, at least on an *ad hoc* basis, participation of administrators and other governmental officials

5. Need sufficient financial resources, with reasonable expectations of continuity of support

6. Need to make widely available to the public all studies and research findings

7. Need a conscious and conscientious recruitment policy aimed at attracting young people and placing them in positions of responsibility and influence.

VII. In the long term, efforts to conserve national resources and manage the environment depend on educating the public and their representatives and developing needed specialists with broad interdisciplinary backgrounds in problems of the environment. Adequately federally financed (National Science Foundation) curriculum efforts already exist at the elementary school level, but programs in junior and senior high schools are grossly deficient, and many of our children complete school without meaningful exposure to the values of the environment and knowledge about the dangers to it. We *recommend* that the National Science Foundation undertake to develop and sponsor a Junior Environmental Education Program at secondary school level designed to involve teenage youngsters with the whole range of environmental problems. We need to generate "environmental consciousness" through broadly based educational programs in the schools and for the public in general. No matter how rational, well informed, and sober the advice given to governments by science, and how alarming the consequences of inaction, there is little likelihood of effective action unless pressure for reform is generated by public opinion. This, we believe, can best be achieved by inclusion of environmental education in the secondary schools and by encouraging the media to carry the message to the public as broadly as possible.

VIII. The traditions of the university, with its established discipline-oriented structure and its system of rewarding excellence for research in traditional academic fields, may make development of the broad multidisciplinary efforts required for environmental studies difficult to achieve. Therefore, to promote such efforts, we *recommend* two approaches:

1. Creation of multidisciplinary programs of environmental affairs within existing universities, to be funded in part by federal grants
2. Establishment of an experimental problem-oriented graduate school to be supported in part by a proposed Environmental Coalition.

There is a great need for the universities to train the manpower essential to cope with environmental problems in the future, at both the undergraduate and graduate levels. At the undergraduate level, the problem is one of providing broad interdisciplinary, problem-oriented education to students who will, at the same time, acquire proficiency in one of the standard academic disciplines.

At the graduate level, the program would consist of advanced training in the student's speciality, together with group efforts guided by multidisciplinary groups of faculty, to study real environmental problems. For example, a physics student might work with students and faculty on meteorology, marine biology, physiology, and agriculture to study the partition of CO_2 among the atmosphere, the biosphere, and the sea. The results of the investigation might well constitute a group thesis.

The following difficulties must be overcome if successful multidisciplinary programs of environmental affairs are to be established:
1. Prestige value must somehow be attached to environmental problems of an applied nature, so that some of the best students and faculty will be attracted to work on such problems.
2. Universities must allocate substantial funds of their own for the development of new programs in environmental affairs precisely at a time when unprecedented demands are being made on their limited financial resources. These difficulties can be alleviated by provision of money from the federal government.
3. Faculty members must learn to work with colleagues from other disciplines in new, unfamiliar, and perhaps awkward ways. Summer workshops, seminars, and symposia can be of considerable help in this regard.

We believe this is best accomplished through multidisciplinary problem-oriented programs of environmental affairs. A typical undergraduate program of studies would include a conventional major program in a discipline but with substantial additional exposure to related environmental curricula. For example, a physics major would also study ecology, meteorology, and geology, as well as the usual mathematics. Regular seminars would be held on environmental problems from the points of view of different disciplines.

IX. Several avenues of approach to informing the public on environmental problems should be developed and implemented. Among these are: 1) displays and demonstrations in museums, schools, and similar public places about the environment, the demands being placed on it, and the effects, dangerous and otherwise; 2) the development of semipopular literature about the environment, its despoliation, and the need for restoring it as our most important resource and legacy; 3) the use of commercial and educational television and radio as means of creating "environmental consciousness"; 4) the development of curricula for adult education relating to the environment; 5) the encouragement of popular magazine articles about the environment; 6) the encouragement of public discussion groups and organization, such as the League of Women Voters, foreign affairs associations, P.T.A.'s and others, to adopt environmental discussion topics for their organizations. It will be necessary to develop materials and curricula for distribution to and by such groups.

To facilitate the Process of public education, we *recommend* the establishment of a National Environmental Coalition, which would be supported by foundations, conservation groups, population organizations, philanthropists, industry, commercial broadcasters, publishers, and the journalistic media. The Coalition would encourage and support the formation of local environmental coalitions all over the country and provide all possible support and encouragement for the formation of similar groups abroad. Such coalitions could well serve as viable mechanisms through which public action programs might be organized, channeled, and implemented.

APPENDIX W:

Statement by The President on Establishing the National Industrial Pollution Control Council

It is widely acknowledged that our productive economy and our advancing technology have helped to create many of our environmental problems. Now the same energy and skills which have produced quantitative gains in our economy must be used to improve the environment and to enhance the quality of life.

I have today signed an executive order creating the National Industrial Pollution Control Council and have called on a number of industrial leaders to serve as its members. I am pleased that Mr. Bert S. Cross and Mr. Willard F. Rockwell, Jr., have agreed to serve, respectively, as its Chairman and Vice Chairman.

The effort to restore and renew our environment cannot be successful unless the public and the private sector are both intensively involved in this work—with their efforts closely coordinated. The new Industrial Council will provide an important mechanism for achieving this coordination. It will provide a means by which the business community can help chart the route which our cooperative ventures will follow.

The new Council will allow businessmen to communicate regularly with the President, the Council on Environmental Quality and other government officials and private organizations which are working to improve the quality of the environment. It will also provide a direct opportunity for business and industry to actively and visibly support the drive to abate pollution from industrial sources. Both government and industrial leaders can use this mechanism to stimulate efforts toward the achievement of our environmental goals.

As we give more and more attention to the causes of industrial pollution, we must also recognize that many American industries have begun to face this problem squarely and to undertake significant pollution abatement activities. It would be unrealistic, of course, to think that private enterprise can meet this problem alone. The problem of the environment is one area where private enterprise can do the job only if government plays its proper role. For unless there are fair standards which are vigorously enforced, the responsible firms which take on the extra expense of pollution control will be at a competitive disadvantage with those who are less responsible.

At an early date, the new Industrial Council will submit to me and to the Chairman of the Council on Environmental Quality, through the Secretary of Commerce, a series of specific recommendations for further action. As a part of its report, the Council will consider the role it can play in helping to implement the nation's environmental protection program.

The challenge which faces this new Industrial Council and the entire business community is complex and demanding. But I have no doubt that it can and will be met.

Ellison L. Hazard, of New York, New York
Chairman and President, Continental Can Company, Inc.

Edwin D. Dodd, of Toledo, Ohio
President and Chief Executive Office, Owens-Illinois, Inc.

John L. Gushman, of Lancaster, Ohio
President, Anchor Hocking Corporation

Leo H. Schoenhofen, of Chicago, Illinois
Chairman and Chief Executive Officer,
Container Corporation of America

C. Raymond Dahl, of San Francisco, California
President and Chief Executive Officer,
Crown-Zellerbach Corporation

Edmund F. Martin, of Bethlehem, Pennsylvania
Chairman and Chief Executive Officer,
Bethlehem Steel Corporation

Thomas F. Patton, of Cleveland, Ohio
Chairman, Republic Steel Company

J. K. Jamieson, of New York, New York
President, Standard Oil Company of New Jersey

Robert O. Anderson, of New York, New York
Chairman and Chief Executive Officer, Atlantic-Richfield

Frank R. Milliken, of New York, New York
Chairman, Kennecott Copper Corporation

Gilbert W. Humphrey, of Cleveland, Ohio
Chairman, Hanna Mining Company

George H. Love, of Pittsburgh, Pennsylvania
Chairman, Consolidation Coal Company

Thomas C. Mullins, of St. Louis, Missouri
President, Peabody Coal Company

Russell DeYoung, of Akron, Ohio
Chairman, Goodyear Tire and Rubber Company

J. Ward Keener, of Akron, Ohio
Chairman, B. F. Goodrich Company

Karl R. Bendetsen, of New York, New York
Chairman and Chief Executive Officer,
U.S. Plywood – Champion Papers, Inc.

Norton Clapp, of Tacoma, Washington
Chairman, Weyerhaeuser Company

Chris Dobbins, of Denver, Colorado
Chairman and President, Ideal Basic Industries, Inc.

Robinson F. Barker, of Pittsburgh, Pennsylvania
Chairman, PPG Industries, Inc.

Edward N. Cole, of Detroit, Michigan
President, General Motors Corporation

Lido Anthony Iacocca, of Dearborn, Michigan
Senior Vice President, Ford Motor Company

Benjamin F. Biaggini, of San Francisco, California
President, Sothern Pacific Company

John M. Budd, of St. Paul, Minnesota
President, Great Northern Railway

George E. Keck, of Chicago, Illinois
President and Chief Executive Officer, United Airlines, Inc.

Charles C. Tillinghast, Jr. of New York, New York
Chairman, Trans-World Airlines

Frank A. Nemec, of New Orleans, Louisiana
President and Chief Operating Officer,
Lykes-Youngstown Corporation

Shermer L. Sibley, of San Francisco, California
President and Chief Executive Officer,
Pacific Gas and Electric Company

Lelan F. Sillin, Jr, of Weathersfield, Connecticut
President, Northeast Utilities

Fred J. Borch, of New York, New York
Chairman and Chief Executive Officer, General Electric Company

Donald C. Burnham, of Pittsburgh, Pennsylvania
Chairman, Westinghouse Electric Corporation

Paul L. Davies, of New York, New York
Senior Director, FMC Corporation

Arthur J. Santry, Jr, of New York, New York
President, Combustion Engineering, Inc.

H. Chandlee Turner, Jr, of New York, New York
Chairman, Turner Construction Company

Stephen D. Bechtel, Jr., of San Francisco, California
President, Bechtel Corporation

Ralph Evinrude, of Jensen Beach, Florida
Chairman, Outboard Marine

Rodney C. Gott, of New York, New York
Chairman and President, American Machine and Foundry Company

Arch Booth, of Washington, D.C.
President, U.S. Chamber of Commerce

William P. Gullander, of New York, New York
President, National Association of Manufacturers

H. Bruce Palmer, of New York, New York
President, National Industrial Conference Board

APPENDIX X:

Executive Order 11523 Establishing the National Industrial Pollution Control Council

By virtue of the authority vested in me as President of the United States, and in furtherance of the purpose and policy of the National Environmental Policy Act of 1969 (Public Law 91-190, approved January 1, 1970), it is ordered as follows:

Section 1. *Establishment of the Council.* a. There is hereby established the National Industrial Pollution Control Council (hereinafter referred to as "the Industrial Council") which shall be composed of a Chairman, a Vice-chairman, and other representatives of business and industry appointed by the Secretary of Commerce (hereinafter referred to as "the Secretary").

b. The Secretary, with the concurrence of the Chairman, shall appoint an Executive Director of the Industrial Council.

Sec. 2. *Functions of the Industrial Council.* The Industrial Council shall advise the President and the Chairman of the Council on Environmental Quality, through the Secretary, on programs of industry relating to the quality of the environment. In particular, the Industrial Council may –

1. Survey and evaluate the plans and actions of industry in the field of environmental quality.

2. Identify and examine problems of the effects on the environment of industrial practices and the needs of industry for improvements in the quality of the environment, and recommend solutions to those problems.

3. Provide liaison among members of the business and industrial community on environmental quality matters.

4. Encourage the business and industrial community to improve the quality of the environment.

5. Advise on plans and actions of Federal, State, and local agencies involving environmental quality policies affecting industry which are referred to it by the Secretary, or by the Chairman of the Council on Environmental Quality through the Secretary.

Sec. 3. *Subordinate Committees.* The Industrial Council may establish, with the concurrence of the Secretary, such subordinate committees as it may deem appropriate to assist in the performance of its functions. Each subordinate committee shall be headed by a chairman appointed by the Chairman of the Industrial Council with the concurrence of the Secretary.

Sec. 4. *Assistance for the Industrial Council.* In compliance with applicable law, and as necessary to serve the purposes of this order, the Secretary shall provide or arrange for administrative and staff services, support, and facilities for the Industrial Council and any of its subordinate committees.

Sec. 5. *Expenses.* Members of the Industrial Council or any of its subordinate committees shall receive no compensation from the United States by reason of their services hereunder, but may be allowed travel expenses, including per diem in lieu of subsistence, as authorized by law (5 U.S.C. 5703) for persons in the Government service employed intermittently.

Sec. 6. *Regulations.* The provisions of Executive Order No. 11007 of February 26, 1962 (3 CFR 573), prescribing regulations for the formation and use of advisory committees, are hereby made applicable to the Industrial Council and each of its subordinate committees. The Secretary may exercise the discretionary powers set forth in that order.

Sec. 7. *Construction.* Nothing in this order shall be construed as subjecting any Federal agency, or any function vested by law in, or assigned pursuant to law to, any Federal agency to the authority of any other Federal agency or of the Industrial Council or of any of its subordinate committees, or as abrogating or restricting any such function in any manner.

RICHARD NIXON

THE WHITE HOUSE,
April 9, 1970

APPENDIX Y:

White House Press Conference Introducing National Industrial Pollution Control Council

April 9, 1970

THE WHITE HOUSE

PRESS CONFERENCE
OF
MAURICE H. STANS, SECRETARY OF COMMERCE;
RUSSELL E. TRAIN, CHAIRMAN, COUNCIL ON
ENVIRONMENTAL QUALITY; BERT S. CROSS,
CHAIRMAN, NATIONAL INDUSTRIAL POLLUTION
CONTROL COUNCIL, AND WILLARD F. ROCKWELL, JR.,
VICE CHAIRMAN, NATIONAL INDUSTRIAL
POLLUTION CONTROL COUNCIL
THE BRIEFING ROOM

AT 11:40 A.M.   EST.

MR. WARREN: The President met this morning with Mr. Bert Cross and Mr. Willard Rockwell, who have accepted the positions of Chairman and Vice Chairman, respectively, of the National Industrial Pollution Control Council.

As you remember, the President said in his February 10 Message on the Environment, that he would create this Council to work with the Council on Environmental Quality and the Citizens Advisory Commitee on Environmental Quality and the Secretary of Commerce in the development of effective policies for the curbing of air, water, noise and waste pollution from industrial sources.

Secretary Stans and Chairman Russell Train of the Council on Environmental Quality are here.

You have the President's statement, the Executive Order and a release which lists most of the members of the Council. The Secretary will name other members of this Council in the near future.

Mr. Secretary.

SECRETARY STANS: The President this morning signed the Executive Order creating the National Industrial Pollution Control Council. The purpose of the Council is to draw together the talents of the business community to help the Government in resolving the problems of the environment.

You will observe that the members of the Council appointed thus far are 53 top executives of major United States corporations. These are Chairmen of the Board of their respective companies. They are the policy-making officers and not the scientists or the technical people.

The purpose is to enlist the help of the major corporations of the country—others beyond those whose officers have been appointed—in dealing with the pollution problems of their particular industries, as well as overall pollution problems in the whole environment.

Additional members will be appointed very soon. In addition, there will be subcouncils created within this organization for specific industry groups—a subcouncil for the steel industry, a subcouncil for the paper industry, one for the utilities industry, and so forth—so that we can get the specialization of the industry groups on their own particular pollution problems and the measures that are being taken.

The first meeting of the Council will be held next Tuesday. It will proceed immediately to organize itself along the lines that I have mentioned and to begin to collect the information dealing with the problems of pollution. This will include the efforts that have been made up to now, the steps that are currently being taken in the respective industries to deal with the environmental problems, the programs ahead, and the matters which could be done to accelerate these programs.

The total objective is to get the maximum input from the business community in coordination with the Government's effort to resolve the environmental problems and to urge the industries, solicit their support in developing the technology required to eliminate them.

On my left is Mr. Bert Cross of the 3-M Company, who is Chairman, and here is Al Rockwell, of the North American Rockwell Company, who is Vice Chairman of the group.

I will ask Mr. Train if he has anything he would like to add to that statement, and we will submit ourselves for your questions.

MR. TRAIN: I think it would be appropriate to say I am glad to see the press has a new environment, and I would like to think our Council could claim credit for it.

Seriously, we are delighted to see this group established. It is terribly important to engage the energy and the enthusiastic cooperation of the business and industry community in this job of providing a high quality environment.

I think this gives us a good mechanism to be working with and I anticipate that our Council will have good communication with this group and work closely with it along with a number of other groups representing all segments of the country.

SECRETARY STANS: Do you have any questions?

Q Mr. Stans, are you planning to put any members on the Council representing the Union Oil Company or the oil companies involved in the Louisiana incident?

SECRETARY STANS: There is not presently a member representing the Union Oil Company. There are two members of the Council who are from the oil industry, and they will select additional people on their subcouncil for the oil industry. I am sure that whatever input Union and the other companies have will be brought into play, but I cannot tell you who will be selected on the subcouncil as of yet, because I don't know.

Q Could you, by way of giving us an idea of what the Council is going to do, tell us how the Council might be effective in dealing with the off-shore oil problem?

SECRETARY STANS: I don't like to anticipate how the Council will operate on any one specific problem. I am certain that at a very early stage it will address itself to it, first through the subcouncil of the oil industry, and then through the Council itself, but I am not in a position to anticipate any solutions to any of the problems.

Q Have you selected an Executive Director yet, sir?

SECRETARY STANS: No, but he is in the process of being selected, and I would believe we would have him on board within ten days.

Q Is the concept of this that a public representation in these problems comes from Mr. Train's group and that, therefore, this group will be entirely an industry and business group?

SECRETARY STANS: This group is entirely an industry and business group enlisted to help the Government and to help the public in dealing with matters of the environment.

Q   Sir, how critical do you expect the Council to be? What will be the nature of their reports on things such as the off-shore oil problem?

SECRETARY STANS: We expect the Council to be totally constructive in analyzing the problems and measuring their size and significant in selecting alternative means of dealing with them and in recommending courses of action to the Administration.

Q   Do you anticipate any problems in getting all these top executives together to meet?

SECRETARY STANS: We hope not, and I don't think we will.

Q   How often are they likely to meet?

SECRETARY STANS: Their willingness to serve is indicated by the fact that of all the people who have been approached in this particular case, only one found it impossible to serve.

Q   How often are they likely to meet?

SECRETARY STANS: I would expect that the council itself might meet once every 60 days or so, but that the subcouncils would be meeting in the interim and probably more often.

MR. TRAIN: Could I supplement one thing that Secretary Stans said and simply remind you that there is a President's Citizens' Advisory Committee headed by Laurence Rockefeller on environmental quality which is also advisory to the President and to the Council and that has, of course, a very broad membership. I think Mr. Rockwell is a member of that committee.

Q   Could Mr. Cross address himself to what he sees as his own immediate problems as head of this council?

MR. CROSS: Well, I have felt for a long time that there was a void between industry and government and it seems to me as though this new council, being set up the way it is, gives us every opportunity to communicate with each other very well.

Secondly, on that same subject, without a shadow of a doubt, getting these top people together, obviously some industries have done a better job than others and I think that just being able to pass this technology back and forth between the separate members is going to have a good effect.

In other words, in my opinion this is going to be a very well-organized plan of actually getting some action that ordinarily would not take place simply because we have improved communications.

Q   Will you deal with the business of penalties for not cleaning up your own pollution or incentives, if you will, for doing it?

MR. CROSS: I certainly would hope, sir, that we show enough activity that penalties are not going to be a part of the problem. I think that your interest and our interest are identical. We are just trying to get something done that makes an awful lot of sense for all of us.

Q   Let me put the question a little differently: Do you foresee the possibility that out of this group will come a greater willingness on the part of industry to spend its own resources for dealing with the problems of pollution?

MR. CROSS: I think at a very early stage you are going to find that industry cooperates very well.

THE PRESS: Thank you very much.

END   (AT 11:52 A.M.   EST)

APPENDIX Z:

Summary Minutes of First Meeting of the National Industrial Pollution Control Council, April 14, 1970

The Secretary of Commerce, Maurice H. Stans, welcomed the attendees to the Council's first meeting and briefly outlined for them the purpose of the Council. He then administered to the Council members the oath of office and turned the meeting over to Mr. Bert Cross, Council Chairman. Mr. Cross briefed the members on the tasks before the Council.

Mr. James T. Lynn, General Counsel for the Department of Commerce, explained the legal aspects of the Council organization to the members and emphasized particularly the antitrust guideposts for this type of organization. He noted that the agenda for each Council and Sub-Council meeting must be submitted to the Department in advance for approval, that minutes will be kept of every meeting and that a Department of Commerce representative must be present at each such meeting.

Mr. Russell E. Train, Chairman of the President's Council on Environmental Quality, discussed with the Council the burgeoning interest in environmental quality, the purpose and responsibilities of the Council on Environmental Quality and the expected cooperation between both Councils. Mr. Train noted that the advisory function of the NIPCC should be coordinated through the Secretary of Commerce.

Following Mr. Train's presentation, Council members asked if the establishment of the NIPCC meant that industry groups were not to work directly with other Government departments. Secretary Stans explained that the Council was not intended to disrupt existing lines of communication between Government and industry, but generally the Council should provide the most effective link between industry and Government.

Mr. William D. Lee, Administrator of the Business and Defense Services Administration of the Department of Commerce, listed the activities within the Department relating to the quality of the environment. He further explained that these Department resources are available for support to the Council in its work.

In the discussion following Mr. Lee's presentation, the Council members were notified that the summary minutes of Council and Sub-Council meetings would be made available to the public if requested. Secretary Stans also suggested that each Sub-Council Chairman would be asked to approve the summary minutes before they are released.

Following a brief break in the proceedings, Chairman Cross reiterated that the object of the Council is to determine how and to what extent industry is responsible for the Nation's total pollution problem, to strive to eliminate the causes of industrial pollution and to cooperate with other elements in seeking overall solutions. He called for a concentrated effort by Government and private industry on the pollution problem and emphasized the need for total public awareness of the major causes of the overall problem as well as the need to win support for a multi-phased attack on the problem.

This Council, Chairman Cross explained, will be divided into industry Sub-Councils of which twenty-nine have been identified to date. The Chairman of each Sub-Council should give serious consideration to the appointment of a full-time representative who can give day-to-day attention to the workings of the Sub-Council. The Sub-Council chairmen were further asked to submit the names of nominees from their industry group for membership in their Sub-Councils. It was recommended that the Sub-Councils have no more than eight members including the chairman and vice-chairman, that every Sub-Council member be the chief executive of his company, and that the Sub-Councils reflect geographic distribution, as well as representation from small, medium, and large size firms. The names of nominees should be submitted to the Executive Director, Deputy Assistant Secretary Walter A. Hamilton, for clearance no later than April 29, 1970. Sub-Council chairmen were cautioned that governmental clearance is a prerequisite for membership on a Sub-Council.

Chairman Cross closed by describing the two basic functions of the Council. (1) to provide a group of high industry executives to give advice and counsel on the formulation of public policy as it relates to industrial pollution control and (2) by the broad nature of the organization to generate the backing and support essential to the success of voluntary efforts on a problem of this proportion.

During the discussion period, Chairman Cross noted that he anticipated some cross-over of responsibilities between Sub-Councils. He also noted that there was a need for a more precise definition of several of the Sub-Council categories.

One Council member asked if a Sub-Council member's deputy needed clearance if he were to sit in at a meeting for his chief executive. Secretary Stans said they would have to be cleared and cautioned Council members that it was most important that the high level of

Council and Sub-Council membership be maintained; he discouraged the attendance of substitutes at meetings. He added that the Council had been set up so that there would be a Chairman and Vice-Chairman from each industry group. In the absence of the Chairman, the Vice-Chairman would be able to take over.

Chairman Cross then read the names of the Sub-Council chairmen and vice-chairmen.

Secretary Stans then introduced the Under Secretary of Commerce, Rocco Siciliano, who will serve as the Secretary's alternate at Council meetings. He also introduced Mr. Walter Hamilton, Deputy Assistant Secretary of Commerce, who will serve as Executive Director of the NIPCC, and Mr. John L. Sullivan, Special Assistant to the Administrator of the Business and Defense Services Administration, who was appointed Council Administrator.

Chairman Cross noted that recommendations advanced by the Sub-Councils need not be unanimous. Alternative solutions may be submitted. Recommendations may be made by the Sub-Councils at any time and they should not feel that they must wait until everything is completed before making recommendations.

Chairman Cross noted that one immediate activity of the Sub-Councils would be to find out what has been and is being done by way of pollution control. Mr. Hamilton added that one function of the Government staff would be to make sure that the Sub-Council members are aware of what is going on in Government in the pollution area.

In reply to Council inquiries, Secretary Stans explained that funds are available for travel expenses for Council and Sub-Council members, but beyond that, financing is quite limited. Should the need for additional funds arise, the subject will be discussed further at that time.

Secretary Stans also explained that noise pollution and the esthetics of pollution were subjects for consideration by the Council. He added that the Council had been set up by industry groups rather than by source or type of pollution so that each group would have input to the total solution.

In response to questioning, Chairman Cross noted that the Sub-Councils may call upon Council members to draw on all possible technical and other information sources in working out Sub-Council programs. He reiterated, however, that the actual membership of the Sub-Councils must be restricted to a small number of chief executives.

Secretary Stans was asked if the Council would seek clarification of the jurisdiction of various local State and Federal authorities as to industry pollution problems. He replied that he felt recommendations regarding jurisdictional issues was a proper point of discussion for the Council.

Chairman Cross announced that the next meeting of the Council will be in Washington, D.C., on July 14, 1970.

NATIONAL INDUSTRIAL POLLUTION CONTROL COUNCIL

MEMBERS

*Bert S. Cross, Chairman
Willard F. Rockwell, Jr., Vice Chairman

Sub-Council Chairmen and Vice Chairmen

Airlines

George E. Keck, Chairman
Charles C. Tillinghast, Jr., Vice Chairman

Automobiles

*Edward N. Cole, Chairman
Lee Iacocca, Vice Chairman

Beverages

Donald M. Kendall, Chairman

Building Materials

*Cris Dobbins, Chairman
*Robinson F. Barker, Vice Chairman

Business Organizations

*Arch Booth, Chairman
*William P. Gullander, Chairman
*H. Bruce Palmer, Chairman

* indicates attendance at April 14, 1970 Meeting

264

Chemicals

Birny Mason, Jr., Chairman
*Charles H. Sommer, Vice Chairman

Coal

George H. Love, Chairman
*Thomas C. Mullins, Vice Chairman

Construction

Bertram L. Perkins, Chairman
H. Chandlee Turner, Jr., Vice Chairman

Containers

Cans:
*William F. May, Chairman
Ellison L. Hazard, Vice Chairman

Glass:
Edwin D. Dodd, Chairman
John L. Gushman, Vice Chairman

Paper:
*Leo H. Schoenhofen, Chairman
*C. Raymond Dahl, Vice Chairman

Detergents

*Howard J. Morgens, Chairman
*Milton Mumford, Vice Chairman

Electrical and Nuclear

*Donald C. Burnham, Chairman
Fred J. Borch, Vice Chairman

* indicates attendance at April 14, 1970 Meeting

Fertilizer and Agricultural Chemicals

>   *Clifford D. Siverd, Chairman
>   *Herbert Tomasek, Vice Chairman

Food

>   *C. William W. Cook, Chairman
>   Howard C. Harder, Vice Chairman

General Manufacturing

>   *Paul L. Davies, Vice Chairman

Grain Milling

>   *James P. McFarland, Chairman
>   *Robert J. Keith, Vice Chairman

Heavy Equipment

>   Arthur J. Santry, Jr., Chairman

Leisure

>   *Ralph Evinrude, Chairman
>   Rodney C. Gott, Vice Chairman

Lumber

>   Norton Clapp, Chairman

Meat Packing and Livestock

>   *Robert W. Reneker, Chairman
>   *Charles R. Orem, Vice Chairman

* indicates attendance at April 14, 1970 Meeting

Mining

   *Frank R. Milliken, Chairman
   *Gilbert W. Humphrey, Vice Chairman

Paper

   *Karl R. Bendetsen, Chairman

Petroleum

    J. K. Jamieson, Chairman
    Robert O. Anderson, Vice Chairman

Process and System Engineering

   **Stephen D. Bechtel, Jr., Chairman

Railroads

    Benjamin F. Biaggini, Chairman
    John M. Budd, Vice Chairman

Rubber

    Russell DeYoung, Chairman
   *J. Ward Keener, Vice Chairman

Shipping

    Frank A. Nemec, Chairman
   *Adolph Kurz, Vice Chairman

Steel

   *Edmund F. Martin, Chairman
   *Thomas F. Patton, Vice Chairman

* indicates attendance at April 14, 1970 Meeting
** Mr. Bechtel was represented by Mr. W. Eastman

Utilities

    *Shermer L. Sibley, Chairman
    Lelan F. Sillin, Jr., Vice Chairman

OTHER ATTENDEES

(April 14 Meeting)

Council On Environmental Quality

    Russell E. Train, Chairman

U.S. Department of Commerce

    Maurice H. Stans, Secretary of Commerce
    Rocco Siciliano, Under Secretary of Commerce
    James T. Lynn, General Counsel
    William D. Lee, Administrator, B.D.S.A.
    Walter A. Hamilton, Deputy Assistant Secretary of
        Commerce and Executive Director, N.I.P.C.C.
    John L. Sullivan, Council Administrator

* indicates attendance at April 14, 1970 Meeting

APPENDIX AA:

The Johns Hopkins University Department of Geography and Environmental Engineering Program Description

Operational Objectives: (1) Study the operation and interrelationships of the environment; (2) study man-environment in social and cultural terms, and impacts on the environment of technological and economic activities; (3) develop solutions to be translated into engineering and administrative actions.

Scholastic scope, requirements, enrollment: Graduate with opportunities for undergraduate and post-doctoral study, and supplemental professional training. 60 graduate students.

Interdisciplinary research activities (a), major areas (b): Broad range based on basic natural sciences, systems engineering, hydrology, social psychology (a) environmental biology, engineering science and technology; human spacial location (b).

Additional dimensions planned: Better capacity to plan statistical aspects of sampling and data gathering systems. Improve ability to apply advanced engineering technology to design of waste treatment system.

Special materials and instruction techniques: Labs for chemical and biological analyses. Additional sophisticated equipment is needed. Seminars and group attack on major problems is characteristic technique.

Sources: University, Ford Foundation, National Council, Edison Electric Institute, Westvaco, Department of the Interior, Department of Health, Education and Welfare.

Form of funding: Under 30 percent of support from University income. Bulk from multiple grants. No single source predominates.

Potential untapped sources: City, county, State governments

Annual budget: Approximately $1,000,000

Respondent: John C. Geyer, Chairman, Department of Geography and Environmental Engineering.

APPENDIX BB:

The University of Maryland Natural Resources Institute Program Description

Operational Objectives: Conduct a comprehensive research and educational program covering the non-agricultural and forestry natural resources of the State of Maryland: (1) advance knowledge of the resources of Maryland and their best uses with emphasis on the tidewater and inland resources and organisms, including forests, fish and wildlife, and the surface water of the State through a continuing program of research; (2) support and participate in education of the public and of individuals in the problems and potentials of natural resources; (3) aid in training of students and specialists for future service in the field of natural resources.

Scholastic scope, requirements, enrollment: Counselling and instructing undergraduates and graduates in the University; assistance to teachers-in-training; cooperation with professional colleagues and other University departments in presenting summer workshop sessions and other programs in fields of natural resources education. Summer program at major facility, Chesapeake Biological Laboratory, Solomons, Md., embraces courses for credit in Marine Botany an Marine Zoology, and NSF-sponsored undergraduate research participation program for 6 students, and availability of student assistant positions—total summer complement of students from all over U.S. approximately 40. In addition, staff members serve as visiting lecturers in U.S. and abroad.

Interdisciplinary research activities (a), major areas (b): Broad range based on natural sciences (a); fisheries research, estuarine ecology, pollution ecology, estuarine geology, forest genetics, forest entomology, wildlife research, molluscan ecology and culture, parasitology, crustacean ecology, seafood processing.

Additional dimensions planned: Broaden all programs and, especially, environmental studies.

Special materials and instruction techniques: Labs for chemical and biological analyses. Some sophisticated equipment in use. Techniques include team and interdisciplinary effort in meeting major estuarine problems, and interchange with other key individuals and groups in and outside the University. Seminars are encouraged for exchange of new information and research techniques.

Sources: State of Maryland through the University; contracts with State agencies, Federal agencies, private industry, foundations.

Form of funding: Major support from University income. About 15%-25% from research grants.

Potential untapped sources: Private foundations.

Annual budget: Approximately $1,000,000

Respondent: William W. Bergoffen, Editor, Natural Resources Institute

APPENDIX CC:

Resolution of Maryland State Board of Education on Environmental Studies, January 28, 1970

Resolution No. 1970—15

RE: Institution of a planned program of environmental education in all Maryland elementary and secondary schools.

WHEREAS, Education is a process through which citizens understand their responsibilities for the conservation of the human environment; and

WHEREAS, Understanding and respect for the natural world and its complex balances must be developed and sustained; and

WHEREAS, Each student needs to develop an understanding of the ecological relationship of man to his environment; and

WHEREAS, The public schools have a responsibility for developing in each student an awareness of his environment; now, therefore, be it

RESOLVED, That the State Board of Education supports the initiation of a program of environmental studies in all public schools of Maryland; and be it further

RESOLVED, That the State Board of Education urges the establishment of a program of environmental studies as a planned part of the curriculum in all elementary and secondary schools in Maryland.

APPENDIX DD:

The President's Message on the Environment
February 8, 1971

To The Congress of the United States:

Last August I sent to the Congress the first annual report on the state of the nation's environment. In my message of transmittal, I declared that the report "describes the principal problems we face now and can expect to face in the future, and it provides us with perceptive guidelines for meeting them.... They point the directions in which we must move as rapidly as circumstances permit."

The comprehensive and wide-ranging action program I propose today builds upon the 37-point program I submitted to the Congress a year ago. It builds upon the progress made in the past year, and draws upon the experience gained in the past year. It gives us the means to ensure that, as a nation, we maintain the initiative so vigorously begun in our shared campaign to save and enhance our surroundings. This program includes:

Measures to strengthen pollution control programs

Charges on sulfur oxides and a tax on lead in gasoline to supplement regulatory controls on air pollution
More effective control of water pollution through a $12 billion national program and strengthened standard-setting and enforcement authorities
Comprehensive improvement in pesticide control authority
A Federal procurement program to encourage recycling of paper

Measures to control emerging problems

Regulation of toxic substances
Regulation of noise pollution
Controls on ocean dumping

Measures to promote environmental quality in land use decisions

A national land use policy

A new and greatly expanded open space and recreation program, bringing parks to the people in urban areas

Preservation of historic buildings through tax policy and other incentives

Substantial expansion of the wilderness areas preservation system

Advance public agency approval of power plant sites and transmission line routes

Regulation of environmental effects of surface and underground mining

Further institutional improvement

Establishment of an Environmental Institute to conduct studies and recommend policy alternatives

Toward a better world environment

Expanded international cooperation

A World Heritage Trust to preserve parks and areas of unique cultural value throughout the world

1970 — A Year of Progress

The course of events in 1970 has intensified awareness of and concern about environmental problems. The news of more widespread mercury pollution, late summer smog alerts over much of the East Coast, repeated episodes of ocean dumping and oil spills, and unresolved controversy about important land use questions have dramatized with disturbing regularity the reality and extent of these problems. No part of the United States has been free from them, and all levels of government — Federal, State and local — have joined in the search for solutions. Indeed, there is a growing trend in other countries to view the severity and complexity of environmental problems much as we do.

There can be no doubt about our growing national commitment to find solutions. Last November voters approved several billion dollars in State and local bond issues for environmental purposes, and Federal funds for these purposes are at an all time high.

The program I am proposing today will require some adjustments by governments at all levels, by our industrial and business community, and by the public in order to meet this national commitment. But as we strive to expand our national effort, we must also keep in mind the greater cost of *not* pressing ahead. The battle for a better environment can be won, and we are winning it. With the program I am outlining in this message we can obtain new victories and prevent problems from reaching the crisis stage.

During 1970, two new organizations were established to provide Federal leadership for the Nation's campaign to improve the environment. The Council on Environmental Quality in the Executive Office of the President has provided essential policy analysis and advice on a broad range of environmental problems, developing many of our environmental initiatives and furnishing guidance in carrying out the National Environmental Policy Act, which requires all Federal agencies to devote specific attention to the environmental impact of their actions and proposals. Federal pollution control programs have been consolidated in the new Environmental Protection Agency. This new agency is already taking strong action to combat pollution in air and water and on land.

I have requested in my 1972 budget $2.45 billion for the programs of the Environmental Protection Agency – nearly double the funds appropriated for these programs in 1971. These funds will provide for the expansion of air and water pollution, solid waste, radiation and pesticide control programs and for carrying out new programs.

In my special message on the Environment last February, I set forth a comprehensive program to improve existing laws on air and water pollution, to encourage recycling of materials and to provide greater recreational opportunities for our people. We have been able to institute some of these measures by executive branch action. While unfortunately there was no action on my water quality proposals, we moved ahead to make effective use of existing authorities through the Refuse Act water quality permit program announced in December. New air pollution control legislation, which I signed on the last day of 1970, embodies all of my recommendations and reflects strong bipartisan teamwork between the administration and the Congress – teamwork which will be needed again this year to permit action on the urgent environmental problems discussed in this message.

We must have action to meet the needs of today if we would have the kind of environment the nation demands for tomorrow.

I. *STRENGTHENING POLLUTION CONTROL PROGRAMS*

The Clean Air Amendments of 1970 have greatly strengthened the

Federal-State air quality program. We shall vigorously administer the new program, but propose to supplement it with measures designed to provide a strong economic stimulus to achieve the pollution reduction sought by the program.

Air Pollution

Sulfur Oxides Emissions Charge

Sulfur oxides are among the most damaging air pollutants. High levels of sulfur oxides have been linked to increased incidence of diseases such as bronchitis and lung cancer. In terms of damage to human health, vegetation and property, sulfur oxide emissions cost society billions of dollars annually.

Last year in my State of the Union message I urged that the price of goods "should be made to include the cost of producing and disposing of them without damage to the environment." A charge on sulfur emitted into the atmosphere would be a major step in applying the principle that the costs of pollution should be included in the price of the product. A staff study underway indicates the feasibility of such a charge system.

— Accordingly, I have asked the Chairman of the Council on Environmental Quality and the Secretary of the Treasury to develop a Clean Air Emissions Charge on emissions of sulfur oxides. Legislation will be submitted to the Congress upon completion of the studies currently underway.

The funds generated by this charge would enable the Federal Government to expand programs to improve the quality of the environment. Special emphasis would be given to developing and demonstrating technology to reduce sulfur oxides emissions and programs to develop adequate clean energy supplies. My 1972 budget provides increased funds for these activities. They will continue to be emphasized in subsequent years.

These two measures — the sulfur oxides emissions charge and expanded environmental programs — provide both the incentive for improving the quality of our environment and the means of doing so.

Leaded Gasoline

Leaded gasolines interfere with effective emission control. Moreover, the lead particles are, themselves, a source of potentially harmful lead concentrations in the environment. The new air quality legislation provides authority, which I requested, to regulate fuel additives, and I have recently initiated a policy of using unleaded or low-lead gasoline in Federal vehicles whenever possible. But further incentives are needed. In 1970, I recommended a tax on lead used in gasoline to bring about a gradual transition to the use of unleaded gasoline. This transition is essential if the automobile emission control standards scheduled to come into effect for the 1975 model automobiles are to be met at reasonable cost.

I shall again propose a special tax to make the price of unleaded gasoline lower than the price of leaded gasoline. Legislation will be submitted to the Congress upon completion of studies currently underway.

Water Quality

We have the technology now to deal with most forms of water pollution. We must make sure that it is used.

In my February 1970 special message to the Congress on the Environment, I discussed our most important needs in the effort to control water pollution: adequate funds to ensure construction of municipal waste treatment facilities needed to meet water quality standards; more explicit standards, applicable to all navigable waters; more effective Federal enforcement authority to back up State efforts; and funds to help States build the necessary capability to participate in this joint endeavor.

Municipal Wastes

Adequate treatment of the large volume of commercial, industrial and domestic wastes that are discharged through municipal systems requires a great expenditure of funds for construction of necessary facilities. A thorough study by the Environmental Protection Agency completed in December 1970 revealed that $12 billion will be required by 1974 to correct the national waste treatment backlog. The urgency of this need, and the severe financial problems that face many communities, require that construction of waste treatment facilities be jointly funded by Federal, State, and local governments. We must also assure that adequate Federal funds are available to reimburse States that advanced the

Federal share of project costs.

I propose that $6 billion in Federal funds be authorized and appropriated over the next three years to provide the full Federal share of a $12 billion program of waste treatment facilities.

Some municipalities need help in overcoming the difficulties they face in selling bonds on reasonable terms to finance their share of construction costs. The availability of funds to finance a community's pollution control facilities should depend not on its credit rating or the vagaries of the municipal bond market, but on its waste disposal needs.

I again propose the creation of an Environmental Financing Authority so that every municipality has an opportunity to sell its waste treatment plant construction bonds.

A number of administrative reforms which I announced last year to ensure that Federal construction grant funds are well invested have been initiated. To further this objective:

I again propose that the present, rigid allocation formula be revised, so that special emphasis can be given to those areas where facilities are most needed and where the greatest improvements in water quality would result.

I propose that provisions be added to the present law to induce communities to provide for expansion and replacement of treatment facilities on a reasonably self-sufficient basis.

I propose that municipalities receiving Federal assistance in constructing treatment facilities be required to recover from industrial users the portion of project costs allocable to treatment of their wastes.

Standards and Enforcement

While no action was taken in the 91st Congress on my proposals to strengthen water pollution standard setting and enforcement, I initiated a program under the Refuse Act of 1899 to require permits for all industrial discharges into navigable waters, making maximum use of present authorities to secure compliance with water quality standards. However, the reforms I proposed in our water quality laws last year are still urgently needed.

Water quality standards now are often imprecise and unrelated to specific water quality needs. Even more important, they provide a poor basis for enforcement: without a precise effluent standard, it is often difficult to prove violations in court. Also, Federal-State water quality standards presently do not apply to many important waters.

I again propose that the Federal-State water quality program be extended to cover all navigable waters and their tributaries, ground waters and waters of the contiguous zone.

I again propose that Federal-State water quality standards be revised to impose precise effluent limitations on both industrial and municipal sources.

I also propose Federal standards to regulate the discharge of hazardous substances similar to those which I proposed and the Congress adopted in the Clean Air Amendments of 1970.

I propose that standards require that the best practicable technology be used in new industrial facilities to ensure that water quality is preserved or enhanced.

I propose that the Administrator of the Environmental Protection Agency be empowered to require prompt revision of standards when necessary.

We should strengthen and streamline Federal enforcement authority, to permit swift action against municipal as well as industrial and other violators of water quality standards. Existing authority under the Refuse Act generally does not apply to municipalities.

I propose that the Administrator of EPA be authorized to issue abatement orders swiftly and to impose administrative fines of up to $25,000 per day for violation of water quality standards.

I propose that violations of standards and abatement orders be made subject to court-imposed fines of up to $25,000 per day and up to $50,000 per day for repeated violations.

I again propose that the Administrator be authorized to seek immediate injunctive relief in emergency situations in which severe water pollution constitutes an imminent danger to health, or threatens irreversible damage to water quality.

I propose that the cumbersome and time-consuming enforcement conference and hearing mechanism in the current law be replaced by a provision for swift public hearings as a prelude to issuance of abatement orders or requiring a revision of standards.

I propose an authorization for legal actions against violations of standards by private citizens, as in the new air quality legislation, in order to bolster State and Federal enforcement efforts.

I propose that the Administrator be empowered to require reports by any person responsible for discharging effluents covered by water quality standards.

I again propose that Federal grants to State pollution control enforcement agencies be tripled over the next four years – from $10 million to $30 million – to assist these agencies in meeting their expanded' pollution control responsibilities.

Control of Oil Spills

Last May I outlined to the Congress a number of measures that should be taken to reduce the risks of pollution from oil spills. Recent events have underlined the urgency of action on these proposals. At the outset of this present Congress I resubmitted the Ports and Waterways Safety Act and the legislation requiring the use of bridge-to-bridge radiotelephones for safety of navigation. Such legislation would have decreased the chances of the oil spill which occurred as a result of a tanker collision in San Francisco Bay.

I have provided $25 million in next year's budget for development of better techniques to prevent and clean up oil spills and to provide more effective surveillance. I am asking the Council on Environmental Quality in conjunction with the Department of Transportation and the Environmental Protection Agency to review what further measures can be developed to deal with the problem.

I also am renewing my request that the Senate give its advice and consent on the two new international conventions on oil spills and the pending amendments to the 1954 Oil Spills Convention for the Prevention of Pollution of the Sea by Oil.

The Intergovernmental Maritime Consultative Organization (IMCO) is presently preparing a convention to establish an International Compensation Fund to supplement the 1969 Civil Liability Convention. Our ratification of the 1969 convention will be withheld until this supplementary convention can also be brought into force because both conventions are part of a comprehensive plan to provide compensation for damages caused by oil spills. In addition, we have taken the initiative in NATO's Committee on the Challenges of Modern Society and achieved wide international support for terminating all intentional discharges of oil and oily wastes from ships into the oceans by 1975, if possible, and no later than the end of this decade. We will continue to work on this matter to establish through IMCO an international convention on this subject.

Pesticides

Pesticides have provided important benefits by protecting man from disease and increasing his ability to produce food and fiber. However, the use and misuse of pesticides has become one of the major concerns of all who are interested in a better environment. The decline in numbers of several of our bird species is a signal of the potential hazards of pesticides to the environment. We are continuing a major research effort to develop nonchemical methods of pest control, but we must continue to rely on pesticides for the foreseeable future. The challenge is to institute the necessary mechanisms to prevent pesticides from harming human health and the environment.

Currently, Federal controls over pesticides consist of the registration and labeling requirements in the Federal Insecticide, Fungicide, and Rodenticide Act. The administrative processes contained in the law are inordinately cumbersome and time-consuming, and there is no authority to deal with the actual *use* of pesticides. The labels approved under the Act specify the uses to which a pesticide may be put, but there is no way to insure that the label will be read or obeyed. A comprehensive strengthening of our pesticide control laws is needed.

I propose that the use of pesticides be subject to control in appropriate circumstances, through a registration procedure which provides for designation of a pesticide for "general use," "restricted use," or "use by permit only." Pesticides designated for restricted use would be applied only by an approved pest control applicator. Pesticides designated for "use by permit only" would be made available only with the approval of an approved pest control consultant. This will help to ensure that pesticides which are safe when properly used will not be misused or applied in excessive quantities.

I propose that the Administrator of the Environmental Protection Agency be authorized to permit the experimental use of pesticides under strict controls, when he needs additional information concerning a pesticide before deciding whether it should be registered.

I propose that the procedures for cancellation of a registration be streamlined to permit more expeditious action.

I propose that the Administrator be authorized to stop the sale or use of, and to seize, pesticides being distributed or held in violation of Federal law.

Recycling of Wastes

The Nation's solid waste problem is both costly and damaging to the environment. Paper, which accounts for about one-half of all municipal solid waste, can be reprocessed to produce a high quality product. Yet the percentage the Nation recycles has been declining steadily.

To reverse this trend, the General Services Administration, working with the Council on Environmental Quality, has reviewed the Federal Government's purchasing policies. It found a substantial number of prohibitions against using paper with recycled content. Such prohibitions are no longer reasonable in light of the need to encourage recycling.

As a result of this review, the GSA has already changed its specifications to require a minimum of 3 to 50 percent recycled content, depending on the product, in over $35 million per year of paper purchases. GSA is currently revising other specifications to require recycled content in an additional $25 million of annual paper purchases. In total, this will amount to more than one-half of GSA's total paper products purchases. All remaining specifications will be reviewed to require recycled content in as many other paper products as possible. The regulations will be reviewed continually to increase the percentage of recycled paper required in each.

I have directed that the Chairman of the Council on Environmental Quality suggest to the Governors that they review State purchasing policies and where possible revise them to require recycled paper. To assist them, I have directed the Administrator of GSA to set up a technical liaison to provide States with the federally revised specifications as well as other important information on this new Federal program, which represents a significant first step toward a much broader use of Federal procurement policies to encourage recycling.

II. *CONTROLLING EMERGING PROBLEMS*

Environmental control efforts too often have been limited to cleaning up problems that have accumulated in the past. We must concentrate more on preventing the creation of new environmental problems and on dealing with emerging problems. We must, for example, prevent the harmful dumping of wastes into the ocean and the buildup of toxic materials throughout our environment. We must roll back increasingly annoying and hazardous levels of noise in our environment, particularly in the urban environment. Our goal in dealing with emerging environmental problems must be to ward them off before they become acute, not merely to undo the damage after it is done.

Toxic Substances

As we have become increasingly dependent on many chemicals and metals, we have become acutely aware of the potential toxicity of the materials entering our environment. Each year hundreds of new chemicals are commercially marketed and some of these chemicals may pose serious potential threats. Many existing chemicals and metals, such as PCB's (polychlorinated biphenyls) and mercury, also represent a hazard.

It is essential that we take steps to prevent chemical substances from becoming environmental hazards. Unless we develop better methods to assure adequate testing of chemicals, we will be inviting the environmental crises of the future.

I propose that the Administrator of EPA be empowered to restrict the use or distribution of any substance which he finds is a hazard to human health or the environment.

I propose that the Administrator be authorized to stop the sale or use of any substance that violates the provisions of the legislation and to seek immediate injunctive relief when use or distribution of a substance presents an imminent hazard to health or the environment.

I propose that the Administrator be authorized to prescribe minimum standard tests to be performed on substances.

This legislation, coupled with the proposal on pesticides and other existing laws, will provide greater protection to humans and wildlife from introduction of toxic substances into the environment. What I propose is not to ban beneficial uses of chemicals, but rather to control the use of those that may be harmful.

Ocean Dumping

Last year, at my direction, the Council on Environmental Quality extensively examined the problem of ocean dumping. Its study indicated that ocean dumping is not a critical problem now, but it predicted that as municipalities and industries increasingly turned to the oceans as a convenient dumping ground, a vast new influx of wastes would occur.

Once this happened, it would be difficult and costly to shift to land-based disposal.

Wastes dumped in the oceans have a number of harmful effects. Many are toxic to marine life, reduce populations of fish and other economic resources, jeopardize marine ecosystems, and impair aesthetic values. In most cases, feasible, economic, and more beneficial methods of disposal are available. Our national policy should be to ban unregulated ocean dumping of all wastes and to place strict limits on ocean disposal of harmful materials. Legislation is needed to assure that our oceans do not suffer the fate of so many of our inland waters, and to provide the authority needed to protect our coastal waters, beaches, and estuaries.

I recommend a national policy banning unregulated ocean dumping of all materials and placing strict limits on ocean disposal of any materials harmful to the environment.

I recommend legislation that will require a permit from the Administrator of the Environmental Protection Agency for any materials to be dumped into the oceans, estuaries, or Great Lakes and that will authorize the Administrator to ban dumping of wastes which are dangerous to the marine ecosystem.

The legislation would permit the Administrator to begin phasing out ocean dumping of harmful materials. It would provide the controls necessary to prevent further degradation of the oceans.

This would go far toward remedying this problem off our own shores. However, protection of the total marine environment from such pollution can only be assured if other nations adopt similar measures and enforce them.

I am instructing the Secretary of State, in coordination with the Council on Environmental Quality, to develop and pursue international initiatives directed toward this objective.

Noise

The American people have rightly become increasingly annoyed by the growing level of noise that assails them. Airplanes, trucks, construction equipment, and many other sources of noise interrupt sleep, disturb communication, create stress, and can produce deafness and other adverse health effects. The urban environment in particular is being degraded by steadily rising noise levels. The Federal Government has set and enforces standards for noise from aircraft, but it is now time that our efforts to deal with many other sources of noise be strengthened and expanded.

The primary responsibility for dealing with levels of noise in the general environment rests upon local governments. However, the products which produce the noise are usually marketed nationally, and it is by regulating the noise-generating characteristics of such products that the Federal Government can best assist the State and local government in achieving a quieter environment.

I propose comprehensive noise pollution control legislation that will authorize the Administrator of EPA to set noise standards on transportation, construction and other equipment and require labeling of noise characteristics of certain products.

Before establishing standards, the Administrator would be required to publish a report on the effects of noise on man, the major sources, and the control techniques available. The legislation would provide a method for measurably reducing major noise sources, while preserving to State and local governments the authority to deal with their particular noise problems.

III. *PROMOTING ENVIRONMENTAL QUALITY IN OUR LAND USE DECISIONS*

The use of our land not only affects the natural environment but shapes the pattern of our daily lives. Unfortunately, the sensible use of our land is often thwarted by the inability of the many competing and overlapping local units of government to control land use decisions which have regional significance.

While most land use decisions will continue to be made at the local level, we must draw upon the basic authority of State government to deal with land use issues which spill over local jurisdictional boundaries. The States are uniquely qualified to effect the institutional reform that is so badly needed, for they are closer to the local problems than is the Federal Government and yet removed enough from local tax and other pressures to represent the broader regional interests of the public. Federal programs which influence major land use decisions can thereby fit into a coherent pattern. In addition, we must begin to restructure economic incentives bearing upon land use to encourage wise and orderly decisions for preservation and development of the land.

I am calling upon the Congress to adopt a national land use policy. In addition, I am proposing other major initiatives on land use to bring "parks to the people", to expand our wilderness system, to restore and preserve historic and older buildings, to provide an orderly system for power plant siting, and to prevent environmental degradation from mining.

A National Land Use Policy

We must reform the institutional framework in which land use decisions are made.

I propose legislation to establish a National Land Use Policy which will encourage the States, in cooperation with local government, to plan for and regulate major developments affecting growth and the use of critical land areas. This should be done by establishing methods for protecting lands of critical environmental concern, methods for controlling large-scale development, and improving use of lands around key facilities and new communities.

One hundred million dollars in new funds would be authorized to assist the States in this effort – $20 million in each of the next five years – with priority given to the States of the coastal zone. Accordingly, this proposal will replace and expand my proposal submitted to the last Congress for coastal zone management, while still giving priority attention to this area of the country which is especially sensitive to development pressures. Steps will be taken to assure that federally-assisted programs are consistent with the approved State land use programs.

Public Lands Management

The Federal public lands comprise approximately one-third of the Nation's land area. This vast domain contains land with spectacular scenery, mineral and timber resources, major wildlife habitat, ecological significance, and tremendous recreational importance. In a sense, it is the "breathing space" of the Nation.

The public lands belong to all Americans. They are part of the heritage and the birthright of every citizen. It is important, therefore, that these Lands be managed wisely, that their environmental values be carefully safeguarded, and that we deal with these lands as trustees for the future. They have an important place in national land use considerations.

The Public Land Law Review Commission recently completed a

study and report on Federal public land policy. This Administration will work closely with the Congress in evaluating the Commission's recommendations and in developing legislative and administrative programs to improve public land management.

The largest single block of Federal public land lies in the State of Alaska. Recent major oil discoveries suggest that the State is on the threshold of a major economic development. Such development can bring great benefits both to the State and to the Nation. It could also – if unplanned and unguided – despoil the last and greatest American wilderness.

We should act now, in close cooperation with the State of Alaska, to develop a comprehensive lan; use plan for the Federal lands in Alaska, giving priority to those north of the Yukon River. Such a plan should take account of the needs and aspirations of the native peoples, the importance of balanced economic development, and the special need for maintaining and protecting the unique natural heritage of Alaska. This can be accomplished through a system of parks, wilderness, recreation, and wildlife areas and through wise management of the Federal lands generally. I am asking the Secretary of the Interior to take the lead in this task, calling upon other Federal agencies as appropriate.

Preserving Our Natural Environment

The demand for urban open space, recreation, wilderness and other natural areas continues to accelerate. In the face of rapid urban development, the acquisition and development of open space, recreation lands and natural areas accessible to urban centers is often thwarted by escalating land values and development pressures. I am submitting to the Congress several bills that will be part of a comprehensive effort to preserve our natural environment and to provide more open spaces and parks in urban areas where today they are often so scarce. In addition, I will be taking steps within the executive branch to assure that all agencies are using fully their existing legislative authority to these ends.

"Legacy of Parks"

Merely acquiring land for open space and recreation is not enough. We must bring parks to where the people are so that everyone has access to nearby recreational areas. In my budget for 1972, I have proposed a new "Legacy of Parks" program which will help States and local governments provide parks and recreation areas, not just for today's Americans but for tomorrow's as well. Only if we set aside and develop such recreation areas now can we ensure that they will be available for future generations.

As part of this legacy, I have requested a $200 million appropriation to begin a new program for the acquisition and development of additional park lands in urban areas. To be administered by the Department of Housing and Urban Development, this would include provision for facilities such as swimming pools to add to the use and enjoyment of these parks.

Also, I have recommended in my 1972 budget that the appropriation for the Land and Water Conservation Fund be increased to $380 million, permitting the continued acquisition of Federal parks and recreation areas as well as an expanded State grant program. However, because of the way in which these State grant funds were allocated over the past five years, a relatively small percentage has been used for the purchase and development of recreational facilities in and near urban areas. The allocation formula should be changed to ensure that more parks will be developed in and near our urban areas.

I am submitting legislation to reform the State grant program so that Federal grants for the purchase and development of recreation lands bear a closer relationship to the population distribution.

I am also proposing amendments to the Internal Revenue Code which should greatly expand the use of charitable land transfers for conservation purposes and thereby enlarge the role of private citizens in preserving the best of America's landscape.

Additional public parks will be created as a result of my program for examining the need for retention of real property owned by the Government. The Property Review Board, which I established last year, is continuing its review of individual properties as well as its evaluation of the Government's overall Federal real property program. Properties identified as suitable for park use and determined to be surplus can be conveyed to States and political subdivisions for park purposes without cost. The State or other political subdivision must prepare an acceptable park use plan and must agree to use the property as a park in perpetuity. More than 40 properties with high potential for park use have already been identified.

Five such properties are now available for conversion to public park use. One, Border Field, California, will be developed as a recreation area with the assistance of the Department of the Interior. The other four will be conveyed to States or local units of government as soon as adequate guarantees can be obtained for their proper maintenance and operation. These four are: (1) part of the former Naval Training Devices Center on Long Island Sound, New York; (2) land at a Clinical Research Center in Fort Worth, Texas; (3) about ten miles of sand dunes and beach along the Atlantic Coast and Sandy Hook Bay, a part of Fort Hancock, New Jersey; and (4) a portion of Fort Lawton, Washington, a wooded, hilly area near the heart of Seattle. In addition, efforts are underway to open a significant stretch of Pacific Ocean Beach Front and Coastal Bluffs at Camp Pendleton, California.

Many parcels of federal real property are currently under-utilized because of the budgetary and procedural difficulties that are involved in transferring a Federal operation from the current site to a more suitable location.

I am again proposing legislation to simplify relocation of federal installations that occupy properties that could better be used for other purposes.

This will allow conversion of many additional Federal real properties to a more beneficial public use. Lands now used for Federal operations but more suited to park and recreational uses will be given priority consideration for relocation procedures. The program will be self-financing and will provide new opportunities for improving the utilization of Federal lands.

Wilderness Areas

While there is clearly a need for greater efforts to provide neighborhood parks and other public recreation areas, there must still be places where nature thrives and man enters only as a visitor. These wilderness areas are an important part of a comprehensive open space system. We must continue to expand our wilderness preservation system, in order to save for all time those magnificent areas of America where nature still predominates. Accordingly, in August last year I expressed my intention to improve our performance in the study and presentation of recommendations for new wilderness areas.

I will soon be recommending to the Congress a number of specific proposals for a major enlargement of our wilderness preservation system by the addition of a wide spectrum of natural areas spread across the entire continent.

National Parks

While placing much greater emphasis on parks in urban areas and the designation of new wilderness areas, we must continue to expand our national park system. We are currently obligating substantial sums to acquire the privately owned lands in units of the National Park System which have already been authorized by the Congress.

Last year, joint efforts of the administration and the Congress resulted in authorization of ten areas in the National Park System, including such outstanding sites as Voyageurs National Park in Minnesota, Apostle Islands National Lakeshore in Wisconsin, Sleeping Bear Dunes National Lakeshore in Michigan, Gulf Islands National Seashore in Mississippi and Florida, and the Chesapeake and Ohio Canal National Historical Park in the District of Columbia, Maryland and West Virginia.

However, the job of filling out the National Park System is not complete. Other unique areas must still be preserved. Despite all our wealth and scientific knowledge, we cannot recreate these unspoiled areas once they are lost to the onrush of development. I am directing the Secretary of the Interior to review the outstanding opportunities for setting aside nationally significant natural and historic areas, and to develop priorities for their possible addition to the National Park System.

Power Plant Siting

The power shortage last summer and continuing disputes across the country over the siting of power plants and the routing of transmission lines highlight the need for longer-range planning by the producers of electric power to project their future needs and identify environmental concerns well in advance of construction deadlines. The growing number of confrontations also suggest the need for the establishment of public agencies to assure public discussion of plans, proper resolution of environmental issues, and timely construction of facilities. Last fall, the Office of Science and Technology sponsored a study entitled "Electric Power and the Environment," which identified many of these issues. Only through involving the environmental protection agencies early in the planning of future power facilities can we avoid disputes which delay construction timetables. I believe that these two goals of adequacy of power supply and environmental protection are compatible if the proper framework is available.

I propose a power plant siting law to provide for establishment within each State or region of a single agency with responsibility for assuring that environmental concerns are properly considered in the certification of specific power plant sites and transmission line routes.

Under this law, utilities would be required to identify needed power supply facilities ten years prior to construction of the required facilities. They would be required to identify the power plant sites and general transmission routes under consideration five years before construction and apply for certification for specific sites, facilities, and routes two years in advance of construction. Public hearings at which all interested parties could be heard without delaying construction timetables would be required.

Mined Area Protection

Surface and underground mining have scarred millions of acres of land and have caused environmental damages such as air and water pollution. Burning coal fires, subsidence, acid mine drainage which pollutes our streams and rivers and the destruction of aesthetic and recreational values frequently but unnecessarily accompany mining activities. These problems will worsen as the demand for fossil fuels and other raw materials continues to grow, unless such mining is subject to regulation requiring both preventive and restorative measures.

I propose a Mined Area Protection Act to establish Federal requirements and guidelines for State programs to regulate the environmental consequences of surface and underground mining. In any State which does not enact the necessary regulations or enforce them properly, the Federal Government would be authorized to do so.

Preserving Our Architectural and Historic Heritage

Too often we think of environment only as our natural surroundings. But for most of us, the urban environment is the one in which we spend our daily lives. America's cities, from Boston and Washington to Charleston, New Orleans, San Antonio, Denver, and San Francisco, reflect in the architecture of their buildings a uniqueness and character that is too rapidly disappearing under the bulldozer. Unfortunately, present Federal income tax policies provide much stronger incentives for demolition of older buildings than for their rehabilitation.

Particularly acute is the continued loss of many buildings of historic value. Since 1933 an estimated one-quarter of the buildings recorded by the Historic American Building Survey have been destroyed. Most lending institutions are unwilling to loan funds for the restoration and rehabilitation of historic buildings because of the age and often the location of such buildings. Finally, there are many historic buildings under Federal ownership for which inadequate provision has been made for restoration and preservation.

I shall propose tax measures designed to overcome these present distortions and particularly to encourage the restoration of historic buildings.

I shall propose new legislation to permit Federal insurance of home improvement loans for historic residential properties to a maximum of $15,000 per dwelling unit.

I am recommending legislation to permit State and local governments more easily to maintain transferred Federal historic sites by allowing their use for revenue purposes and I am taking action to insure that no federally-owned property is demolished until its historic significance has first been reviewed.

IV. *TOWARD A BETTER WORLD ENVIRONMENT*

Environmental problems have a unique global dimension, for they afflict every nation, irrespective of its political institutions, economic system, or state of development. The United States stands ready to work and cooperate with all nations, individually or through international institutions, in the great task of building a better environment for man. A number of the proposals which I am submitting to Congress today have important international aspects, as in the case of ocean dumping. I hope that other nations will see the merit of the environmental goals which we have set for ourselves and will choose to share them with us.

At the same time, we need to develop more effective environmental efforts through appropriate regional and global organizations. The United States is participating closely in the initiatives of the Organization for Economic Cooperation and Development (OECD), with its emphasis on the complex economic aspects of environmental controls, and of the Economic Commission for Europe (ECE), a U.N. regional organization which is the major forum for East-West cooperation on environmental problems.

Following a United States initiative in 1969, the North Atlantic Treaty Organization has added a new dimension to its cooperative activities through its Committee on the Challenges of Modern Society. CCMS has served to stimulate national and international action on many problems common to a modern technological society. For example, an important agreement was reached in Brussels recently to eliminate intentional discharges of oil and oily wastes by ships into the oceans by 1975 if possible or, at the latest, by the end of the decade. CCMS is functioning as an effective forum for reaching agreements on the development of pollution-free and safe automobiles. Work on mitigating the effects of floods and earthquakes is in progress. These innovative and specific actions are good examples of how efforts of many nations can be focused and coordinated in addressing serious environmental problems facing all nations.

The United Nations, whose specialized agencies have long done valuable work on many aspects of the environment, is sponsoring a landmark Conference on the Human Environment to be held in Stockholm in June 1972. This will, for the first time, bring together all member nations of the world community to discuss those environmental issues of most pressing common concern and to agree on a world-wide strategy and the basis for a cooperative program to reverse the fearful trend toward environmental degradation. I have pledged full support for this Conference, and the United States is actively participating in the preparatory work.

Direct bilateral consultations in this field are also most useful in jointly meeting the challenges of environmental problems. Thus, the United States and Canada have been working closely together preparing plans for action directed to the urgent task of cleaning up the Great Lakes, that priceless resource our two nations share. Over the past few months, ministerial level discussions with Japan have laid the basis for an expanded program of cooperation and technological exchange from which both nations will benefit.

It is my intention that we will develop a firm and effective fabric of cooperation among the nations of the world on these environmental issues.

World Heritage Trust

As the United States approaches the centennial celebration in 1972 of the establishment of Yellowstone National Park, it would be appropriate to mark this historic event by a new international initiative in the general field of parks. Yellowstone is the first national park to have been created in the modern world, and the national park concept has represented a major contribution to world culture. Similar systems have now been established throughout the world. The United Nations lists over 1,200 parks in 93 nations.

The national park concept is based upon the recognition that certain areas of natural, historical, or cultural significance have such unique and outstanding characteristics that they must be treated as belonging to the nation as a whole, as part of the nation's heritage.

It would be fitting by 1972 for the nations of the world to agree to the principle that there are certain areas of such unique worldwide value that they should be treated as part of the heritage of all mankind and accorded special recognition as part of a World Heritage Trust. Such an arrangement would impose no limitations on the sovereignty of those nations which choose to participate, but would extend special international recognition to the areas which qualify and would make available technical and other assistance where appropriate to assist in their protection and management. I believe that such an initiative can add a new dimension to international cooperation.

I am directing the Secretary of the Interior, in coordination with the Council on Environmental Quality, and under the foreign policy guidance of the Secretary of State, to develop initiatives for presentation in appropriate international forums to further the objective of a World Heritage Trust.

Confronted with the pressures of population and development, and with the world's tremendously increased capacity for environmental modification, we must act together now to save for future generations the most outstanding natural areas as well as places of unique historical, archeological, architectural, and cultural value to mankind.

V. *FURTHER INSTITUTIONAL IMPROVEMENT*

The solutions to environmental and ecological problems are often complex and costly. If we are to develop sound policies and programs in the future and receive early warning on problems, we need to refine our analytical techniques and use the best intellectual talent that is available.

After thorough discussions with a number of private foundations, the Federal Government through the National Science Foundation and the

Council on Environmental Quality will support the establishment of an Environmental Institute. I hope that this nonprofit institute will be supported not only by the Federal Government but also by private foundations. The Institute would conduct policy studies and analyses drawing upon the capabilities of our universities and experts in other sectors. It would provide new and alternative strategies for dealing with the whole spectrum of environmental problems.

VI. *TOWARD A BETTER LIFE*

Adoption of the proposals in this message will help us to clean up the problems of the past, to reduce the amount of waste which is disposed, and to deal creatively with problems of the future before they become critical. But action by government alone can never achieve the high quality environment we are seeking.

We must better understand how economic forces induce some forms of environmental degradation, and how we can create and change economic incentives to improve rather than degrade environmental quality. Economic incentives, such as the sulfur oxides charge and the lead tax, can create a strong impetus to reduce pollution levels. We must experiment with other economic incentives as a supplement to our regulatory efforts. Our goal must be to harness the powerful mechanisms of the marketplace, with its automatic incentives and restraints, to encourage improvement in the quality of life.

We must also recognize that the technological, regulatory, and economic measures we adopt to solve our environmental problems cannot succeed unless we enlist the active participation of the American people. Far beyond any legislative or administrative programs that may be suggested, the direct involvement of our citizens will be the critical test of whether we can indeed have the kind of environment we want for ourselves and for our children.

All across the country, our people are concerned about the environment — the quality of the air, of the water, of the open spaces that their children need. The question I hear everywhere is "What can *I* do?"

Fortunately, there is a great deal that each of us can do. The businessman in his every day decisions can take into account the effects on the environment of his alternatives and act in an environmentally responsible way. The housewife can make choices in the marketplace that will help discourage pollution. Young people can undertake projects in their schools and through other organizations to help build a better environment for their communities. Parents can work with the schools to help develop sound environmental teaching throughout our education system. Every community in the nation can encourage and promote concerned and responsible citizen involvement in environmental issues, an involvement which should be broadly representative of the life-styles and leadership of the community. Each of us can resolve to help keep his own neighborhood clean and attractive and to avoid careless, needless littering and polluting of his surroundings. These are examples of effective citizen participation; there are many others.

The building of a better environment will require in the long term a citizenry that is both deeply concerned and fully informed. Thus, I believe that our educational system, at all levels, has a critical role to play.

As our nation comes to grips with our environmental problems, we will find that difficult choices have to be made, that substantial costs have to be met, and that sacrifices have to be made. Environmental quality cannot be achieved cheaply or easily. But, I believe the American people are ready to do what is necessary.

This nation has met great challenges before. I believe we shall meet this challenge. I call upon all Americans to dedicate themselves during the decade of the seventies to the goal of restoring the environment and reclaiming the earth for ourselves and our posterity. And I invite all peoples everywhere to join us in this great endeavor. Together, we hold this good earth in trust. We must — and together we can — prove ourselves worthy of that trust.

RICHARD NIXON

THE WHITE HOUSE,
February 8, 1971.

Part 7

Annotated
Bibliography

Introduction

The fast-growing literature on the environment has made the bibliographic problem one of exclusion. Mindful of the purposes of the study we have tried to locate materials dealing with policy issues primarily, rather than with the scope of the problem or technical means for its solution. Governmental materials on all levels have been emphasized. Works of popularization and most of the scientific literature have been excluded, regardless of their importance.

However, we have made a particular effort to offset our omissions by including bibliographies and secondary sources through which the broader literature of the field can be identified. Actually, familiar library reference tools lead readily to the more popular publications. The book trade has been quick to see the demand. *Paperbound Books in Print* for March 1970 was able to include a useful critical essay and an annotated bibliography of several dozen inexpensive books reflecting concern for the environment. Some good lists have been published by the Conservation Library Center, Denver, Colorado, and by the American Library Association. Environmental topics are prominent in such sources as *Books in Print* and *Library Journal,* which should serve to guide acquisition in this area.

For the reader's convenience, the bibliography has been divided into three parts: (A.) General Bibliography, (B.) Bibliographies and Other Secondary Sources, and (C.) Periodicals Dealing With the Environment.

Periodicals

Where there is rapid recognition of problems, with much political involvement and popular participation, the best insights and the freshest news will be in the periodical literature. The publications here included are either substantially devoted to environmental concerns, or can be counted on to make regular contributions. As with the general bibliography, we have excluded most of the scientific and technical and a good part of the popular, preferring to concentrate on policy-conscious publications. Considerations of space and time lead us to rule out the standard learned journals accessible through such indexing services as *Biological Abstracts, Public Affairs Information Service,* or *Index Medicus.*

The newsletters of private associations and "pressure groups" have been included about as we found them, with the exception of a few that didn't seem viable. Some are professional, others are grass-roots, regional, or student groups. Here a phone book is about equivalent to a bibliography; an association without a newsletter is poor indeed. Also in this group are the commercially-published and often rather expensive news services catering to planners, lawyers, researchers, and other special client groups.

Recently a number of popular magazines have launched regular features on the environment; a notable example is the *Saturday Review*. Since these are well known and readily available, they have been excluded along with many excellent articles in the news magazines and the press.

Obviously, these publications differ in quality, scope, and sophistication. This is more a study of the range of the literature than a list of recommended acquisitions; however, our annotations should indicate which subscriptions might be the most useful.

A. General Bibliography

Books, articles, reports and government documents on environmental policy and action.

Agency for International Development. "International Aspects of Man's Effect Upon the Environment." Summary report to AID Bureau for Technical Assistance, prepared by the Ad Hoc Committee of the National Academy of Sciences on Environmental Aspects for Foreign Assistance Programs. Washington, D.C.: National Academy of Sciences, January 1970. 28 p., mimeo. The Committee considers problems created by AID programs and recommends ways of helping less-developed countries deal with environmental problems.

Albert, Rep. Carl. Remarks upon introduction of H. J. Res. 1117, to establish a Joint Committee on Environment and Technology. *Congressional Record,* XVI 35 (March 9, 1970), H. 1586-1587.

Allen, James E., Jr. "Education for Survival." Address by U.S. Commissionar of Education before 1970 Annual Meeting of the American Council of Learned Societies, Washington, D.C., January 23, 1970. Asserts need for widespread environmental education and awareness, indicates policy directions for Office of Education.

The American Assembly, Columbia University. Clifford N. Hardin, ed. *Overcoming World Hunger.* Englewood Cliffs, N.J.: Prentice-Hall, Inc., Spectrum Books, 1969. 177 p., paperback, $1.95. Papers dealing with the problem of feeding a growing world population.

American Association of University Women. *A Resource Guide on Pollution Control.* Washington, D.C.: The Association, 1970. 100 p., no price given. For each major environmental problem (including population), briefly states problem, indicates available resources, suggests action. Strong on bibliographic and directory information.

American Chemical Society. *Cleaning Our Environment: The Chemical Basis for Action.* Washington, D.C.: ACS, 1969. 249 p., price $2.75. Concise solid waste bibliography.

American Society for Engineering Education. *Interdisciplinary Re-*

search Topics in Urban Engineering. A report by the Society's Urban Engineering Study Committee. Washington, D.C.: The Society, October 1969. 312 p., mimeo., price $5.00. Major sections on urban transportation, housing, and environment (including health care systems). In each instance, states problem, outlines research topics, indicates concerned agencies and officials, provides bibliographic references.

"Asia's Effluent Societies." A set of articles and an editorial in *Far Eastern Economic Review,* LXVIII, 17 (April 23, 1970). Industrialization combines with population pressure to produce environmental degradation in developing Asian nations.

Ames, Edward A. "Schools and The Environment." A Ford Foundation Reprint. New York: Ford Foundation, Office of Reports, 1970. Paper prepared for American Nature Study Society, December 27, 1969. Deals with schooling and values, community involvement, curriculum change. Birefly describes five Foundation grants in environmental education.

Ayres, Robert U. and Allen V. Kneese. "Environmental Pollution." A paper submitted to the Subcommittee on Economic Progress of the Joint Economic Committee, U.S. Congress. Reprinted from *Federal Programs for the Development of Human Resources,* Vol. 2. Washington, D.C.: Government Printing Office, 1968. 60 p. Elaborates on "materials balance" concept of waste disposal, taking full cognizance of the "closed" nature of our environment.

Baker, Sen. Howard H. Remarks upon introduction of S. 3410, the National Environmental Laboratory Act of 1970. *Congressional Record,* CXVI 16 (February 6, 1970).

Barnett, Harold J. and Chandler Morse. *Scarcity and Growth: The Economics of Natural Resource Availability.* Baltimore: Johns Hopkins Press, 1965. xv + 288 p.

Berelson, Bernard et al. *Family Planning and Population Programs: A Review of World Developments.* Chicago: University of Chicago Press, 1966.

Bethlehem Steel Corporation. *Keep It Clean.* Bethlehem, Pa.: The Corporation n.d. 32 p. Subtitled "Highlights of Bethlehem's Pollution Control Program." Typical of well-illustrated institutional releases describing the effectiveness–and costliness– of industry's efforts against pollution.

"The Biosphere." *Scientific American,* September 1970. Single-topic issue containing twelve articles on technology and the environment. The concept of earth as a closed system provides the unifying theme.

Boulding, Kenneth E. "A Data-Collecting Network for the Sociosphere." Impact of Science on Society, XVIII, 2 (1968), 97-101. The technology now permits the collection and display of current world political, social, and economic data for international decision-making.

Business and the Urban Crisis. A McGraw-Hill Special Report. New York: McGraw-Hill, Inc., 1968. 16 p. Responsibilities and opportunities facing business in the wake of the urban riots.

Caldwell, Lynton K. "Environment: A New Focus for Public Policy." *Public Administration Review*, XXIII, 3 (September 1963), 132-139. In this prophetic article, the author asks whether "environment" as a generic concept might not give us a new perspective, so that we could see our society as an integrated whole. Provision of an optimal environment, rather than isolated and fragmented functions and services, should be the objective of public policy.

Calhoun, John B. "Population Density and Social Pathology." *Scientific American* CCVI, 2 (February 1962), 139-148. When a rat population is allowed to increase in a limited space, abnormal patterns of behavior can lead to the extinction of the population. A popularized statement of Calhoun's now-classic reaearch.

"Can Law Reclaim Man's Environment?" *Trial,* V 5, (August/September 1969), 10-28. A variety of articles on the uses of legislation and litigation.

Carter, Luther J. "Conservation Law I: Seeking a Breakthrough in the

Courts," *Science*, CLXVI (December 19, 1969), 1487-1491; "Conservation Law II: Scientists Play a Key Role in Court Suits," (December 26, 1969), 1601-1605.

Center for Political Research. *Federal Environmental Programs: A Summary*. Washington, D.C.: CPR, May 9, 1970. 34 p., mimeo. Current Federal agency roles and responsibilities in several basic environmental categories.

Center for Urban Studies, University of Chicago. *Metropolitan Water Resource Management*. Chicago: University of Chicago, 1969. 124 p. A state-of-the-art and literature review.

Chamber of Commerce of the United States. *Business and the Consumer – A Program for the Seventies*. A report of the Council on Trends and Perspectives. Washington, D.C.: Chamber of Commerce of the United States, 1970. 14 p., price $1.00. Origins and meaning of the new consumerism, legislation and policy, recommendations to business.

Chamber of Commerce of the United States. *Improving Environmental Quality: Business-Led Action to Improve Water and Air Quality*. Washington, D.C.: Chamber of Commerce of the United States, 1970. 24 p.

"The Chesapeake at Bay." A 12-part illustrated report on water pollution, reprinted from the *Baltimore Evening Sun*. By staff members William J. Perkinson, Bill Burton and Dean Mills. Baltimore: The Sunpapers, 1969. 20 p. Detailed series covers background, current status, political problems, and regulatory efforts in relation to the deterioration of the Chesapeake. A good example of popular education through the press.

Citizens' Advisory Committee on Environmental Quality. *Community Action for Environmental Quality*. Washington, D.C.: Government Printing Office, 1970. 42 p. A simple but comprehensive how-to-do-it book for citizens' groups interested in making their communities more livable.

Citizens' Advisory Committee on Environmental Quality. *A New Ap-

proach to the Disposal of Liquid Waste. New York: The Committee, n.d. 24 p. Recommends establishment of large public corporations to centralize administration and funding of disposal operations.

Citizens' Advisory Committee on Environmental Quality. *Report to the President and to the President's Council on Environmental Quality.* Washington, D.C.: The Committee, August 1969. 36 p. Committee chaired by Laurance S. Rockefeller noted and made recommendations on a wide range of problems, urged population control, emphasized funding and education.

Clawson, Marion. *Land and Water for Recreation.* Resources for the Future Policy Background Series. Chicago: Rand-McNally and Company for Resources for the Future, Inc., 1963. 144 p., paperback, price $2.25. Demand for space will increase; this book attempts to place outdoor recreation accurately in the national framework: economic, cultural, and political.

Commission on Marine Science, Engineering and Resources. *Our Nation and the Sea: A Plan for National Action.* Washington, D.C.: Government Printing Office, January 1969. 305 p., paper cover, price $2.75. Report of the "Stratton Committee," recommending a National Oceanic and Atmospheric Agency with centralized responsibility.

The Conservation Foundation. *Marine Parks for Tanzania.* Washington, D.C.: The Foundation, 1968. 47 p., price $2.00. Results of a survey of the Coast of Tanzania for the Tanzania National Parks, sponsored by the Foundation and the New York Zoological Society. Protection of marine ecosystem and promotion of both tourism and sustained-yield fisheries in a developing nation.

The Conservation Foundation. *Pollution by Pesticides.* Washington, D.C.: The Foundation, reprinted from *CF Letter,* April 25 and May 5, 1969. 32 p., price 50 cents. Subtitled "Some Not Very Well Calculated Risks and Some Alternatives for Better Regulation." Account of Congressional response particularly interesting.

The Conservation Foundation. *Rookery Bay Area Report.* Washington, D.C.: The Foundation, 1968. 61 p., price $2.50. A demonstration study in conservation and development, to determine whether profit-making development could be compatible with a wildlife sanctuary.

Council of Economic Advisers. *Economic Report of the President,* February 1970, Chapter 3. Washington, D.C.: Government Printing Office, 1970. In this chapter the Council presents a 5-year projection of the nation's resources and the demands made against them. Offers a quantitative rendering of the consequences of choices on available resources.

Council on Evironmental Quality. *Environmental Quality: The First Annual Report of the Council on Environmental Quality.* Washington, D.C.: Government Printing Office, August 1970. 326 p., price $1.75. Outlines major problem areas, describes current Federal organization and activity, points to present and future environmental needs. Includes President Nixon's February 10, 1970 Message on the Environment; other relevant statutes, Executive Orders, reorganization plans, and Presidential documents.

Council on Environmental Quality. *Ocean Dumping; A National Policy.* Washington, D.C.: Government Printing Office, 1970. 45 p., price 55 cents. A report to the President, October 1970. Notes that the use of the seas as a receptacle for human wastes will increase, places emphasis on the international aspects of ocean disposal. Includes text of President Nixon's April 15, 1970 Message on Waste Disposal.

The Council of State Government. *1970 Suggested State Legislation.* Vol. XXIX of series. Lexington: The Council, August 1969. xxii + 190 p. Contains drafts of suggested constitutional provisions and statutes for assistance to interested state legislatures. Analytical index 1941-1970 reveals persisting concern with environment. Outstanding item in this volume is proposed model interstate air pollution agreement.

Darling, F. Fraser. "A Wider Environment of Ecology and Conservation." *Daedalus.* XCVI, 4 (Fall 1967), pp. 1003-1019, Development of ecology as a science.

Darling, F. Fraser. and Noel D. Eichorn. *Man and Nature in the National Parks: Reflections on Policy.* 2d ed. Washington, D.C.: The Conservation Foundation, 1969. 86 p., price $1.50. A report into the socio-political-ecological problems of the national parks in the United States; notes new dangers arising from population growth, affluence, and the automobile.

Darling, F. Fraser and John P. Milton (eds.). *Future Environments of North America.* Garden City, N.Y. Natural History Press. 1966.

Davis, Kingsley. "Population Policy: Will Current Programs Succeed?" *Science,* CLVIII 3801 (November 10, 1967). The entire spectrum of possible population control strategies, arranged in order of increasing stringency and decreasing acceptability.

Degler, Stanley E. and Sandra C. Bloom. *Federal Pollution Control Programs: Water, Air, and Solid Wastes.* Washington, D.C.: Bureau of National Affairs, Inc., 1969. 111 p. BNA's Environmental Management Series.

Delafons, John. *Land-Use Controls in the United States.* Cambridge, Mass.: The M.I.T. Press, 2d ed., 1969. 203 p. A clear introductory account of the objectives, techniques, and innovations in public control of private development with social, legal, political, and historical context.

Department of Defense. *Environmental Pollution Control Committee: 1969 Annual Report.* Washington, D.C.: DOD Environmental Pollution Control Committee, 1969. 52 p., mimeo., no price given. Defense Department's control of its own pollutants, relationships with other agencies.

Dingell, Rep. John D. Remarks upon introduction of H,R. 16848, a bill to create a National Environmental Data Bank within the Smithsonian Institution. *Congressional Record.* CXVI 55 (April 8, 1970), H. 2754-2755.

"Education for Survival." Article by Commissioner of Education James E. Allen, Jr., reprinted from *American Education,* VI, 2 (March 1970). Washington, D.C.: Government Printing Office, 1970. 8 p., price 20 cents. Based on speech by Commissioner Allen just prior to announcement of U.S. Office of Education's programs of Environmental Education.

The Environment: A National Mission for the Seventies. 220 p., paperback, price $1.25. Chapters in this book originally appeared in *Fortune* magazine for October 1969 and February 1970. New York and London: Harper and Row, Publishers, Perennial Library No. P-189, 1970.

Ewald, William R., Jr. (ed.). *Environment and Change: The Next Fifty Years.* Papers commissioned for the American Institute of Planners' Two Year Consultation, Part II Bloomington: Indiana University Press, 1968. xvii + 397 p., paperback, price $4.95. These papers were intended to articulate the philosophy and values required for the creative development of our environment; a companion volume (below) deals with the policies, programs, legislation, and bodies of information needed to the same end.

Ewald, William R., Jr. (ed.). *Environment and Policy: The Next Fifty Years.* Papers commissioned for the American Institute of Planners' Two Year Consultation, Part II. Bloomington: Indiana University Press, 1968. xiv + 459 p., paperback, price $4.95. These papers explore the policies, legislation, programs, resources, and specific adjustments needed for the creative development of our environment; a companion volume (above) deals with the requisite philosophy and values.

Ewald, William R., Jr. (ed.). *Environment for Man: The Next Fifty Years.* Based on papers commissioned for the American Institute of Planners' Two-Year Consultation, Part I, 1966. Bloomington: Indiana University Press, 1967. 308 p., price $2.95.

Farvar, M. Taghi and John Milton (eds.) "The Unforeseen International Ecologic Boomerang." Reprinted from *Natural History,* February 1969, pp. 42-70. Unexpected consequences of environmental tinkering, such as unstable ecosystems, milk intolerance, schistosomiasis, and some other things. Material will be expanded to 100 or more case histories in a book to be published by Doubleday in 1971.

Federal Council for Science and Technology. *Federal Expenditures on Research, Development, and Demonstration Related to Pollution for FY 1969 and FY 1970.* Washington, D.C.: FCST, April 2, 1970. 13 p., mimeo. Prepared by Research, Development, and Demonstration

Subcommittee on Environmental Quality of FCST in cooperation with the Bureau of the Budget. Expenditures categorized by functional area and by agency.

Federal Council for Science and Technology. *The Federal Program in Population Research.* Parts 1 and 2 of the report by the Ad Hoc Group on Population Research to the Council. Washington, D.C.: Government Printing Office, 1969. 115 p., price $1.25.

Federal Council for Science and and Technology. *Noise: Sound Without Value.* Committee on Environmental Quality. Washington, D.C.: Government Printing Office, 1968. 56 p., price 60 cents.

Federal Council for Science and Technology. *Population Research: The Federal Concern.* A report by the Ad Hoc Group on Population Research. Washington, D.C.: FCST, July 1969. Part I, 44 p., mimeo; Part II, 65 p., mimeo. First part surveys Federal activities and recommends improved coordination; the second part consists of a categorized citation list itemizing Federally-supported research.

Federal Power Commission. *Federal Power Commission Interests in Environmental Concerns Affecting the Electric Power and Natural Gas Industries.* Washington, D.C.: Federal Power Commission, 1969. 31 p., mimeo.

Federal Water Pollution Control Administration. *Lake Erie Report: A Plan for Water Pollution Control.* Washington, D.C.: FWPCA, August 1968. 107 p., A major study identifying sources, nature, and extent of pollution, recommending a plan of action.

Federal Water Pollution Control Administration. *Lake Ontario and St. Lawrence River Basins: Water Pollution Problems and Improvement Needs.* Chicago: Federal Water Pollution Control Administration, Great Lakes Region, June 1968. 125 p. Detailed survey of water pollution sources and treatment needs, done in cooperation with the Division of Pure Waters, New York State Department of Health.

Federal Water Pollution Control Administration. *Showdown.* Washington, D.C.: Government Printing Office, October 1968. 26 p., price 65 cents. Illustrated booklet describing FWPCA programs to show that the problem can be solved.

Federal Water Quality Administration. *Clean Water for the 1970's: A Status Report.* Washington, D.C.: Federal Water Quality Administration, Department of the Interior, April 1970. 221 p., mimeo., no price given. Water pollution programs of the FWQA through the decade.

The Ford Foundation, Division of National Affairs. "Resources and Environment: Excerpt from a Report to the Trustees." December 1969. 48 p., mimeo. Background paper for formulation of granting policy. Includes list of Ford environment and resources grants since 1963.

Freeman, Orville L. *World Without Hunger.* New York: Praeger, 1968. 190 p. Comments of former Secretary of Agriculture.

"General Clarke Enlarges Corps' Environmental Role." *Engineering News-Record,* CLXXXIV, 16 (April 16, 1970), 14. Army Corps of Engineers chief responds to rising criticism, asserts that problems will be solved when emotionalism recedes.

Goodell, Sen. Charles E. Remarks upon introduction of S. 3237, the Environmental Reclamation Education Act of 1969. *Congressional Record.* CXV, 206 (December 11, 1969), S. 16462-16465.

Great Lakes Basin Commission. *Annual Report, Fiscal Year Ending June 30, 1969.* Ann Arbor, Mich.: The Commission, 1969. 29 p. Report of a body engaged in coordinated planning of water resource use and development in the Great Lakes area.

Hardin, Garrett (ed.). *Population, Evolution and Birth Control, a Collage of Controversial Ideas.* San Francisco: W. H. Freeman and Company, 1964.

Hardin, Garrett. "The Tragedy of the Commons." *Science,* CLXII, 3859 (December 13, 1968), 1243-48. The population problem has no technical solution, only an unlikely moral one; voluntary relinquishment of the "right" to breed.

Hardin, Garrett. "To Trouble a Star: The Cost of Intervention in

Nature." *Bulletin of the Atomic Scientists,* January 1970. p. 17-20. Good statement of the "we can never do one thing" principle, with caustic cost-benefit analysis of the SST.

Harrison, Gordon. *Graduate Training for Environmental Scientists and Managers.* New York: The Ford Foundation, March 12, 1970. 16 p., mimeo. A major effort must be made to train managers and scientists for leadership roles in environmental management.

Harvard, University Program on Technology and Society, *Fifth Annual Report,* 1968-1969. Cambridge, Mass.: The Program, 1969. 82 p. Includes bibliography of publications growing out of the Program's research.

Hatfield, Sen. Mark O. "The Nixon Administration Environmental Protective Legislation." *Congressional Record,* March 6, 1970. pp. S 3163-3178. Summaries of bills (S.3466 through S.3472) on various aspects of environmental protection and quality.

Hoffman, Michael L. "Development Finance and the Environment." *Finance and Development,* VII, 3 (September 1970), 2-6. Must economic progress impose on underdeveloped economies the same bibliogical penalties now being suffered by the highly industralized countries? The author argues that development finance institutions should give immediate attention to the dangers.

Hogan, Rep. Lawrence J. Remarks upon introduction of H.R. 16847, a bill to create a National College of Ecological and Environmental Studies. *Congressional Record,* CXVI, 55 (April 8, 1970), H. 2758.

Hornig, Roberta and James Welsh. "A World in Danger." Articles appearing in *The Washington Star,* January 11 through 18, 1970.

Hoult, David P. (ed.). *Oil on the Sea: Proceedings of a Symposium on Oil Pollution of the Sea.* New York: Plenum Publishing Corp., 1969. 114 p.

International Atomic Energy Agency. *Nuclear Energy and the Environment.* Addendum to the agency's report to the Economic and Social Council of the United States for 1969-70. Austria. IAEA, 1969.

Discusses power plant siting and control on a rather elementary level, includes annexes dealing with the activities and publications of IAEA.

International Union for Conservation of Nature and Natural Resources. *First World Conference on National Parks.* Proceedings of a conference organized by IUCN and cosponsored by UNESCO, FAO, and the National Park Service, and the Natural Resources Council of America; Seattle, June 30-July 7, 1962. Washington, D.C.: Government Printing Office, 1962. 471 p., paper cover, price $1.75. The research, recreational, and resources values of park areas from an international perspective. Another similar conference will be held in 1972.

International Union for Conservation of Nature and Natural Resources. *Toward a New Relationship of Man and Nature in Temperate Lands.* Part I: "Ecological Impact on Recreation and Tourism on Temperate Environments." Proceedings and Papers. Tenth Technical Meeting, Lucerne, Switzerland, June 1966. Morges, Switzerland: UICN, 1967. UICN Publications nouvelle series, No. 7. French and English, with summaries in English.

Izaak, Walton League of America. *Clean Water: It's Up to You.* Glenview, Illinois: Izaak Walton League: n.d. 48 p., narrow format, free. Prepared for the League's Citizen Workshops for Clean Water for America; indicates possible channels for political action.

Jackson, Sen. Henry M. "Establishment of a Board of Environmental Quality Advisors." *Congressional Record,* CXV, 164 (October 8, 1969), p. S. 12124. Comment on S. 1075, bill to establish a national policy on environment and other purposes. Includes bibliography on environmental problems; a list of environmental legislation introduced in the 90th Congress; a list of concerned agencies, quasi-governmental bodies, and interagency committees; the text of the Congressional White Paper on a National Policy for the Environment; and an analysis of S. 1075.

Kneese, Allen V. *Approaches to Regional Water Quality Management.* Washington, D.C.: Resources for the Future, Inc., June 1967. 47 p., mimeo. Single copies free, additional 50 cents.

Kneese, Allen V. "The Problem Shed' as a Unit for Environmental Control." *Archives of Environmental Health,* XVI (January 1968), 124-127. Economic analysis in relation to the environment.

Kneese, Allen V. and Blair T. Bower. *Managing Water Quality: Economics, Technology, Institutions.* Baltimore: The Johns Hopkins Press, for Resources for the Future, Inc., 1968. 328 p., price $8.95. Discusses the level of water quality that should be maintained and the management, methods, and types of organization required; includes case studies.

Landsberg, Hans H. *Natural Resources for U.S. Growth: A Look Ahead to the Year 2000.* Baltimore: The Johns Hopkins Press, for Resources for the Future, Inc., 1965. 260 p., paperback, price $1.95. An examination of the adequacy of natural resources in the United States over the rest of the century; concludes that resources are available if we plan carefully.

Lankenau, Hospital. "Environmental Health." From *Health Education Curriculum Guide* prepared by Department of Health Education. Philadelphia: Lankenau Hospital, 1968. 10 p., no price given. A curriculum guide for grades K–12.

League of Women Voters Education Fund. *The Big Water Fight.* Brattleboro, Vermont: The Stephen Green Press, 1966. 246 p., $6.95. A good guidebook for action by citizens' groups.

The Library of Congress, Legislative Reference Service. *Environmental Policy and the Law.* Prepared by the Environmental Policy Division. Washington, D.C.: Library of Congress, January 1970. 48 p., mimeo. Contains a bibliography of reference works and government documents, and a bibliography of legal periodicals.

Library of Congress, Legislative Reference Service. *Selected Bills Recently Passed by the Congress on Environmental Quality and Productivity.* Prepared by the Environmental Policy Division. Washington, D.C.: Library of Congress, January 21, 1970. 4 p., mimeo. Covers 89th and 90th Congresses (1965-1968), and the 1st session of the 91st Congress (1969), through P.L. 91–190, the National Environmental Policy Act.

314

Ludwig, John H. "The U.S. Government Air Pollution Control Program." Paper prepared for the Conference on Air Pollution sponsored by the Department of Health, Republic of South Africa, October 15 and 16, 1970. 66 p., mimeo. A concise statement outlining the major Federal agencies and their missions in maintaining and enhancing air quality. Mr. Ludwig is Assistant Commissioner for Science and Technology, National Air Pollution Control Administration, U.S. Department of Health, Education, and Welfare.

Madden, Carl H. "Business and Tomorrow's Consumer." Substance of remarks at the annual meeting of the Grocery Manufacturers of America, Inc., New York City, November 11, 1969. Dr. Madden is Chief Economist, Chamber of Commerce of the United States. The new consumerism is more than a reaction to a few excesses in advertising; it is a response to the corporate state and the commercialization of life. Madden finds one dimension of consumerism in the "hippie" life style; pointedly contrasts this with the life style of business.

Man's Impact on the Global Environment: Assessment and Recommendations for Action. Report of the Study of Critical Environmental Problems (SCEP). Cambridge, Mass.: M.I.T. Press, 1970. 319 p., paperbound, price $2.95. Report of a month-long study by about 100 scientists and professionals concentrating on environmental problems of world-wide, rather than local, significance. Emphasis on consequences of pollution in terms of changes in climate, ocean ecology, and large eco-systems. Detailed information, findings, recommendations.

Mansfield, Sen. Michael. "Senator Magnuson's Plan for a World Environmental Institute." *Congressional Record.* CXVI, 64 (April 23, 1970), S. 6068-6070.

Marquis, Ralph W. (ed.). *Environmental Improvement: Air, Water, and Soil.* Washington, D.C.: The Graduate School, U.S. Department of Agriculture, Oct. 1966. 105 p., price $3.00, paperback $1.50. Lectures dealing with environmental pollution.

McElroy, William D. "Biomedical Aspects of Pollution Control." *Bio-*

Science, XIX, 1 (January 1969), 19-23. Numerous recommendations for achieving ultimate goal of zero growth.

McHale, John. "The Timetable Project." Outline draft of a proposal. Binghamton, N.Y.: February 1970. 14 p., mimeo. Problems must be evaluated, and our resources assessed, so as to establish the time and scale of possible solutions. When will specified problems come to crisis? When will appropriate solutions be at hand? A long-range predictive model is proposed. Dr. McHale is Director of the Center for Integrative Studies, State University of New York at Binghamton.

McHale, John. *World Facts and Trends.* Binghamton: Center for Integrative Studies, School of Advanced Technology, State University of New York at Binghamton, 1969. 66 p., mimeo. Facts and figures on the biosphere, environment systems, human systems; also selected comparative indicators.

Mishan, E.J. *Technology and Growth: The Price We Pay.* New York: Praeger. An overview of the basic economic issues involved in rescuing or improving the environment, in which the author argues for a diminution of economic growth as the only means of preventing the ruin of our planet in the long run.

National Academy of Sciences. *Eutrophication: Causes, Consequences, Correctives.* Proceedings of the International Symposium on Eutrophication, Madison, Wisconsin, June 11-15, 1967. Washington, D.C.: National Academy of Sciences, 1969. vii + 661 p. Exhaustive treatment of subject by international list of contributors.

National Academy of Sciences. *Institutions for Effective Management of the Environment.* A Report of the Environmental Study Group to the Environmental Studies Board of NAS, Part I. Washington, D.C.: NAS, 1970. viv + 62 p. Present institutions are inadequate for effective environmental management; greater emphasis is needed on education, monitoring, and planning. National Laboratory for Environmental Science advocated. Cabinet-level Department on the Environment recommended, also joint Congressional committee.

National Academy of Sciences. *The Growth of U.S. Population.* Washington, D.C.: NAS/NRC, 1965. Publication No. 1279.

National Academy of Sciences. *Report of the Ad Hoc Committee of ICSU on Problems of the Human Environment.* Washington, D.C.: National Academy of Sciences, August 1969. Pre-publication version, 30 p., mimeo. Urges establishment of an international Scientific Committee on Problems of the Environment, global environmental monitoring, other activities. References to international organization.

National Academy of Sciences/National Academy of Engineering. *Environmental Problems in South Florida.* Report of the Environmental Study Group to the Environmental Studies Board, Part II. Washington, D.C.: NAS/NRC, March 1970. A specific application (jet port near the Everglades) of the principles developed in Part I noted above, in which the general problem of anticipating and dealing with environmental effects was investigated.

National Academy of Sciences/National Research Council. *Waste Management and Control.* A report by the Committee on Pollution to the Federal Council on Science and Technology. Washington, D.C.: NAS/NRC, 1966. 257 p., paperback, $4.00. Findings and recommendations, with detailed appendixes.

National Aeronautics and Space Administration, Office of Space Science and Applications. *Earth Observations: Program Review, 4 and 5 November, 1969. Washington, D.C.: NASA Headquarters,* 1969. 90 p., no price given. This report prepared by the Earth Observations Division reviews NASA's current programs for the survey of Earth resources and the monitoring of its weather, and discusses the supporting research and technology. Points out that while meteorological satellites represent a proven and operational technology, Earth resource surveying remains in an early stage of development.

National Aeronautics and Space Administration. *Earth Resources Program: Synopsis of Activity, March 1970.* Houston, Texas: National Aeronautics and Space Administration, Manned Spacecraft Center, 1970. Approximately 200 pages, not paginated. Presents history and accomplishments of remote sensing program by means of color photographs, extensive charts and diagrams, brief text.

National Aeronautics and Space Administration. *Ecological Surveys From Space.* NASA SP-230. Washington, D.C.: Government Printing

Office, 1970. 75 p., paperbound, price $1.75. Outlines some of the possible use of satellite surveys by both optical cameras and remote sensing devices in seven different natural science disciplines: geography, agriculture, forestry, geology, hydrology, oceanography, and cartography.

National Commission on Product Safety. *Final Report* presented to the President and Congress, June 1970. Washington, D.C.: Government Printing Office, 1970. xiv + 167 p., paper cover, price $1.75. Presidential commission finds "intolerable conditions" in product safety, but names no villains: "Producers, sellers, and buyers have been trapped by complex economic forces..." Recommends independent Federal commission, extensive testing and research, enactment of Consumer Product Safety Act (model text included).

National Council on Marine Resources and Engineering Development. *Marine Science Affairs--Selecting Priority Programs.* Annual report of the President to the Congress on marine resources and engineering development, April 1970. Washington, D.C.: Government Printing Office, 1970. 284 p., price $1.50. The Council each year reviews the activities and accomplishments of all Federal agencies in marine science and engineering and recommends high priority programs for Federal support and emphasis in the coming year.

National Goals Research Staff. *Toward Balanced Growth: Quantity with Quality.* Washington, D.C.: Government Printing Office, July 4, 1970. v + 228 p., price $1.50. Report to the President. Attempts to define questions, analyze debates, and examine alternative sets of consequences with respect to such salient social problems as population, environment, education, basic science, technology assessment, consumerism, and economic policy. An unexciting book, somewhat uneven, conventional treatment of familiar questions; The Staff disavowed any intention to select or advocate specific goals.

National Park Service. *National Environmental Study Areas: A Guide.* Washington, D.C.: Government Printing Office, 1970. 103 p. Areas within the National Parks and other lands administered by the Department of the Interior have been identified as National Environmental Study Areas. These areas include natural, historical, cultural, or technological features which can be used to supplement environmental education programs on many levels. This publication is a handbook for the use of these areas, offering curriculum suggestions and outlining assistance and materials available from the National Park Service.

National Park Service. *NEED: National Environmental Education Development.* An environmental school program designed to provide an understanding of the values to be found in a visit to the National Park Service areas. Developed by Educational Consulting Service. Washington, D.C.: National Park Foundation, 1969. 24 p. Preliminary version for field test, contains pre-site and post-visit lesson materials and plans.

National Association of Counties/Research Foundation. *Community Action Program for Water Pollution Control.* Washington, D.C.: National Association of Counties, 1967. 182 p. Consists of ten Community Action Guides prepared for use of locally elected and appointed policy-making officials. Selected bibliographies with each Guide.

National Science Foundation. *Human Dimensions of the Atmosphere.* Washington, D.C.: Government Printing Office, 1968. 174 p., price $1.50. Articles by members of the Task Force on Human Dimensions of the Atmosphere. Atempts to cope with complex legal, economic, and social aspects of weather modification.

National Science Foundation. *Weather Modification: Tenth Annual Report for Fiscal Year Ended June 30, 1968.* Washington, D.C.: Government Printing Office, 1969. 141 p., price 65 cents. Detailed discussion of research and field testing; stresses need to understand weather processes before attempting to alter them substantially.

National Wildlife Federation. *Conservation Directory 1970.* Washington, D.C.: The Federation, 1970. ix + 140 p., price $1.50. An outstanding directory to organizations, agencies, and officials (in both private and public sectors) concerned with natural resource use and management.

National Wildlife Federation. "Our National EQ: The First National Wildlife Federation Index of Environmental Quality." Reprinted from *National Wildlife.* Washington, D.C.: The Federation, 1969. 16 p. An effort to develop and consolidate indexes of quality as indicators of progress or deterioration in major environmental categories.

Nelson, Sen. Gaylord A. Remarks upon introduction of S. 3151. The Environmental Quality Education Act. *Congressional Record.* CXV, 191 (November 19, 1969), S. 14600-14602.

(New York City). Mayor's Task Force on Noise Control. *Toward a Quieter City.* New York: New York Board of Trade, Inc., 1970. 55 p., price $1.75. Recommendations include strong enforcement agency, establishment of acoustical criteria, long-range programs of prevention.

Office of Economic Opportunity. *Need for Subsidized Family Planning Services in the United States.* Washington, D.C.: Office of Economic Opportunity Pamphlet 6130-6, 1968.

Office of Science and Technology, Executive Office of the President. *Alleviation of Jet Aircraft Noise Near Airports.* Report of Jet Aircraft Noise Panel. Washington, D.C.: Executive Office of the President, 1966. 167 p.

Office of Science and Technology, Executive Office of the President. *Electric Power and the Environment.* A report sponsored by the Energy Policy Staff, OST. Washington, D.C.: Government Printing Office, August 1970. 71 p., price 75 cents. Report developed by a study group of interested Federal agencies proposes a four-part program for resolving the apparent conflict between power needs and environmental protection that has emerged in the siting of nonnuclear power plants and their transmission lines. Emphasis is on long-range planning, state and local review of projects, advance notice and early public participation, and expanded research and development to minimize environmental damage.

Office of Science and Technology, Executive Office of the President. *The Universities and Environmental Quality: Commitment to Problem Focused Education.* A report to the President's Environmental Quality Council, prepared by J.S. Steinhart and S. Cherniack. Washington, D.C.: Government Printing Office, September 1969. 22

p., mimeo., price 70 cents. This study of environmental programs at six universities sees serious obstacles to the establishment of truly interdisciplinary effort, recommends formation of Schools of the Human Environment, with Federal support.

Perkinson, William J., Bill Burton and Dean Mills. "The Chesapeake at Bay." A 12-part illustrated report on water pollution reprinted from *The Baltimore Evening Sun.* Baltimore: The Sunpapers, 1969. 36 p. Well-prepared popularization of a regional problem.

Perloff, Harvey (ed.). *The Quality of the Urban Environment.* Baltimore: Johns Hopkins Press, for Resources for the Future, Inc., 1969. 344 p., paperbound, price $6.50. Essays on "new resources" in an urban age.

Platt, John. "What We Must Do." *Science,* CLXVI, 3909 (November 28, 1969), pp. 1115-1121. A large-scale mobilization of science may be the only way to meet the "crisis of transformation." Classifies problems by estimated crisis intensity and estimated time to crisis; shows that we may have very little time.

"Politics of Pollution." *Congressional Quarterly Weekly Report.* XXVIII, 17 (April 24, 1970), 1135-1138. Federal agencies, Congress, compete for roles in popular national issue.

Popkin, Roy. *Desalination: Water for the World's Future.* New York: Praeger, 1968. 235 p., price $6.50. Exhaustive investigation of present-day technology, its costs and values.

Potomac Basin Center. *The Potomac: A Summary of Basin Facts and Brief Review of Proposals of Recent Years.* Washington, D.C.: Potomac Basin Center, August 1969. 37 p. narrow format. Reviews 14 major natural resources management plans for the Potomac River Basin as presented between 1963 and 1969 by almost as many Federal agencies.

The President's Council on Recreation and Natural Beauty. *From Sea to Shining Sea.* Washington, D.C.: Government Printing Office, 1968. 304 p., paper cover, price $2.50. Subtitled "A Report on the American Environment—Our Natural Heritage." Proposals and goals for Federal, state and local action. Optimistic, little sense of crisis; emphasis on esthetic values and recreation already seems a little dated. Comprehensive and informative. Bibliography of "books and pamphlets which can help."

Public Land Law Review Commission. *One Third of the Nation's Land.* A report to the President and the Congress. Washington, D.C.: Government Printing Office, June 1970. xiii + 342 p., price $4.50. Recommendations for policy guidelines for the retention and management or disposition of the various types of federal lands. Extensive appendixes, large-scale map of public lands.

Rienow, Robert. "Manifesto for the Sea." *American Behavioral Scientist,* II, 6 (July/August, 1968), 34-37. Sovereign jurisdiction over rivers and estuaries must yield to prescriptive rights of the family of nations to a viable system of unpolluted seas.

Robinson, Nicholas A. "Columbia and the Emergence of Environmental Law." *Law Alumni Bulletin,* XII, 1 (Fall 1969), 7-12. Emergence of environmental law at Columbia Law School, Columbia University, appears to be typical of the movement as it has developed at various institutions throughout the nation.

Russett, Bruce M. "Licensing for Cars and Babies." *Bulletin of the Atomic Scientists,* XXII, 9 (November 1970), pp. 15-18. Proposes a general method of licensing which preserves free choice while avoiding certain undersirable consequences of other plans for controlling the consequences of technology.

San Francisco Bay Conservation and Development Commission. *Sedimentation,* November 1966; *Airports,* Sept. 1966; *Salt, Sand, Shells and Water,* Jan. 1967; *Flood Control,* Feb. 1967; *Geology,* Feb. 1967; *Fill,* May 1967; *Tidal Movement,* June 1966; *Public Facilities and Utilities,* June 1967; *Marshes and Mud Flats,* Oct. 1966. San Francisco: The Commission.

Senate Republican Policy Committee. "Our Poisoned Skies." *Republican Report No. 1-70,* January 1970. First of a series of reports by the Committee staff on various aspects of environmental pollution. Meant to be factual, not a policy statement.

Shulz, P. E. (ed.). *Public Use of Underwater Resources.* Proceedings and papers of the IUCN 10th Technical Meeting. IUCN Publication, New Series, No. 7, 1966. Develops concept of underwater parks and reserves.

The Sierra Club. *Ecotactics: The Sierra Club Handbook for Environmental Activists.* New York: Pocket Books, April 1970, 288 p., paperback, price 95 cents. Youth movement, use of the media, population control, innovative curricula. List of conservation organizations, bibliography, "activist's checklist."

Smithsonian Institution. *National and International Environmental Monitoring Activities: A Directory.* Cambridge, Mass.: Smithsonian Institution Center for Short-Lived Phenomena, October 1970. 292 p., mimeo. Result of a worldwide survey of existing and planned monitoring activities. Extensive but not entirely comprehensive, the directory contains information on 33 major international systems, both current and planned, and additional notes on some 2,000 other national and regional monitoring programs in almost every important area of environmental concern.

Smithsonian Institution, Science Information Exchange. "Notes on an Environmental Pollution Vocabulary." Washington, D.C.: SIE, 17 p., mimeo. An outline or authority list for the classification of research and other materials to facilitate retrieval.

Stakman, E. C., Richard Bradfield and Paul C. Mangelsdorf. *Campaigns Against Hunger.* Cambridge, Mass.: The Belknap Press of Harvard University Press, 1967.

Stapp, William B. et al. "The Concept of Environmental Education." *The Journal of Environmental Education.* I, 1 (Fall 1969), 30-31. Definition and main objectives.

Steiff, William L. and George N. Arnstein. "Environmental Degradation and Education." Chicago: Editors of College and University Business and Nation's Schools, 1970. 16 p., free.

Steinhart, John S. and Stacie Cherniak. *The Universities and Environmental Quality: Commitment to Problem Focused Education.* A report to the President's Environmental Quality Council, prepared by the Office of Science and Technology. Washington, D.C.: Government Printing Office, September 1969. 22 p., mimeo, price 70 cents.

Taylor, Theodore B. and Charles C. Humpstone. *Agenda for International Action to Preserve the Quality of the Earth's Natural Environment.* Washington, D.C.: International Research and Technology Corp.; contract with Harper's Magazine Press. Publication planned for Spring of 1970. Emphasis on pollutants that can cross international boundaries and may cause unacceptable changes in the biological and physical balance of nature.

Train, Hon. Russell E. Remarks before the North American Wildlife and Natural Resources Conference, Chicago, Illinois, March 23, 1970. As Chairman of the Council on Environmental Quality, Train's comments are indicative of the possible shape of Administration policy. Here proposes guidelines and a review process covering legislative and other Federal actions significantly impinging upon the environment.

United Nations. *Natural Resources of Developing Countries: Investigation, Development and Rational Utilization.* Report of the Advisory Committee on the Application of Science and Technology to Development, to the Department of Economic and Social Affairs. New York: United Nations, 1970. 174 p., price $2.00.

United Nations, Economic and Social Council. "Problems of the Human Environment: Report of the Secretary-General." New York: United Nations, May 26, 1969. Release E/4667. Forty-Seventh session, agenda item 10. 66 p., mimeo. Defines problems, cites current work. UN Conference on Human Environment outlined. Annexes describe activities of United Nations, International Labour Organization, Food and Agriculture Organization, and other bodies relevant to environment.

United Nations General Assembly. "United Nations Conference on the Human Environment." Resolution 2581 (XXIV) adopted December 15, 1969. Part IV, page 63, General Assembly Resolutions, Twenty-fourth Regular Session, 1969. Text of so-called "Swedish Resolution" calling for an International conference to be held in Stockholm in 1972.

University of California. *Project 70: A Clean Air Environment for California.* Berkeley: The University of California, January 2, 1970. 75 p., mimeo. Proposes an Air Environment Program that will mobilize the resources of all of the University's campuses.

The Urban Institute. "Quality of the Urban Environment: the Federal Role," and "Urban Waste Management: the Federal Role." Washington, D.C.: The Urban Institute, February 10, 1970. 83 p., 172 p., respectively, mimeo. Working papers prepared by Elizabeth Haskell. Final versions will be made available by mid-year. Problems defined, Federal programs described in some detail. Policy analyses and recommendations. (First paper revised May 1970).

"U.S. and UN Debate Man's Uses and Abuses of the Sea." *Congressional Quarterly Weekly Report,* XXVIII, 20 (May 15, 1970), 1303-06. Magnitude of problem, responses on national and international levels. A CQ Fact Sheet.

U.S. Army, Corps of Engineers. "Effects of Engineering Activities on Coastal Ecology." An interim report to the Corps by L. Eugene Cronin of the Natural Resources Institute, University of Maryland. September 1969, 40 p., mimeo. Reviews most probable ecological effects of major corps activities in the coastal zone, identifies areas for further study.

U.S. Army, Corps of Engineers. *Water Resources Development.* Washington, D.C.: Office of Chief of Engineers, August 1969. 42 p., mimeo., no price given. Civil Works Program of Corps, including navigation, recreation, water supply, coastal protection, flood control, and other activities.

U.S. Atomic Energy Commission. *Biological Implications of the Nuclear Age.* Proceedings of a symposium held at Lawrence Radiation Laboratory. Livermore, California, March 5-7, 1969. Washington, D.C.: AEC, 1969. 341 p. price $3.00. Available from Clearinghouse for Federal Scientific and Technical Information, Springfield, Virginia 22151. Problems of risk standards, dose estimation, observation and interpretation with respect to released radiation and radionuclides.

U.S. Atomic Energy Commission. *The Fusion Torch: Closing the Cycle from Use to Reuse.* By Bernard J. Eastlund and William C. Gough, Division of Research. Washington, D.C.: Government Printing Office, May 15, 1969. 22 p., price 35 cents. Advocates investigation of controlled fusion as a primary energy source, not merely as a basis for steam generation and other conventional heat applications. Fusion power is safe and inexpensive, offers solution to problems of resource depletion, waste disposal, and water desalination, among others.

U.S. Congress. *Nature and Control of Aircraft Engine Exhaust Emissions.* Report of the Secretary of Health, Education and Welfare to the Congress pursuant to the Air Quality Act of 1967. Document No. 91-9, 91st Cong., 1st Sess., Washington, D.C.: Government Printing Office, 1969. 32 p. References.

U.S. Congress, Joint Committee on Atomic Energy. *Environmental Effects of Producing Electric Power.* Hearings before the Committee on October 28-31, November 4-7, 1969. 91st Cong., 1st Sess. Washington, D.C.: Government Printing Office, 1969. 1108 p., price $4.50.

U.S. Department of Agriculture. *A National Program of Research for Environmental Quality: Pollution in Relation to Agriculture and Forestry.* Prepared by a joint task force of the U.S. Department of Agriculture and the State Universities and Land Grant Colleges, Washington, D.C.: USDA, September 1968. 111 p., mimeo. Available in limited quantities from Research Program and Evaluation Staff, USDA, Washington, D.C. 20250. Other titles in the National Program of Research report series include:

Forage, Range and Pasture, November 1968, 93 p.
Forestry, July 1967, 73 p.
Food Safety, November 1968, 30 p.
Plants to Enhance Man's Environment, November 1968, 30 p.
Remote Sensing, December 1967, 24 p.
Soil and Land Use, April 1969, 62 p.
Water and Watersheds, May 1969, 99 p.
Weather Modification, January 1968, 35 p.

U.S. Department of Agriculture. *Wastes in Relation to Agriculture and*

Forestry. USDA Miscellaneous Publication No. 1065. Washington, D.C.: Government Printing Office, March 1968. 112 p., price 60 cents. Prepared by Cecil H. Wadleigh, Director, Soil and Water Conservation Research Division, Agricultural Research Service. Considers 1) effects of wastes on agriculture and forestry, 2) wastes contributed by agriculture and forestry, 3) value of research to date, and 4) problems requiring attention.

U.S. Department of Agriculture and Office of Science and Technology. *Control of Agriculture – Related Pollution.* A report to the President, submitted by the Secretary of Agriculture and the Director of the Office of Science and Technology, January 1969. 102 p., with unpaginated tables. No price given. Federal agencies concerned with problems of agricultural wastes contributed to report in response to Presidential message of March 8, 1968, titled "To Serve a Nation." Defines agriculture broadly; includes runoff, sedimentation, pesticides, and processing wastes.

U.S. Department of Commerce. *Motor Vehicle Abandonment in Urban Areas.* Prepared by Gardner F. Derrickson, Washington, D.C.: Government Printing Office, 1967. 51 p., price 35 cents. Extent of problem, adequacy of methods for handling it.

U.S. Department of Commerce, Environmental Science Services Administration. *ESSA Research Laboratories: Programs and Services.* Boulder, Colo.: ESSA Research Laboratories, January 1970. iii + 164 p., no price given.

U.S. Department of Health, Education and Welfare. *A Compilation of Selected Air Pollution Emission Control Regulations and Ordinances.* Environmental Health Series, PHS Publication No. 999-AP-43. Washington, D.C.: Government Printing Office, 1968. 146 p., price 75 cents. Samples of many emission control measures, to provide guidance to state and local agencies and to industry.

U.S. Department of Health, Education and Welfare. *Interim Report of the National Survey of Community Solid Waste Practices.* Government Printing Office, 1969.

U.S. Department of Health, Education, and Welfare. Office of Education. *A New Role for American Education.* Washington, D.C.: DHEW, May 19, 1970. 46 p., mimeo., no price given. Outlines USOE's policy toward, and support for, environmental/ecological education in the period between President Nixon's Message to Congress on Environmental Quality and the subsequent enactment of the Environmental Quality Education Act in September 1970. Prepared by the Task Force on Environmental Education.

U.S. Department of Health, Education and Welfare. *Proceedings of a Symposium on Human Ecology,* Airlie House, Warrenton, Virginia, November 24-27, 1968. Sponsored by Consumer Protection and Environmental Health Service. Washington, D.C.: Government Printing Office, 1968. 123 p.

U.S. Department of Health, Education and Welfare. *Proceedings: The Surgeon General's Conference on Solid Waste Management for Metropolitan Washington,* July 19-20, 1967. PHS Publication No. 1729. Washington, D.C.: Government Printing Office, 1967. vi + 194 p., price 75 cents. Practices, needs, and technology in solid waste disposal.

U.S. Department of Health, Education and Welfare. Office of Education. *Readings in Environmental Awareness.* Washington, D.C.: DHEW, May 19, 1970. 66 p., mimeo., no price. A selection of concept papers supplementing *A New Role for American Education.*

U.S. Department of Health, Education and Welfare. *Solid Waste Handling in Metropolitan Areas.* Cincinnati: The Department, PHS Publication No. 1554, January 1968. 41 p., paperback, free. Discusses problems and approaches; see especially Policy Questions, p. 37.

U.S. Department of Health, Education and Welfare. *Strategy for a Livable Environment.* A report to the Secretary by the Task Force on Environmental Health and Related Problems. Washington, D.C.: Government Printing Office, 1967. 90 p., paper cover, price 60 cents. Task Force examined environmental quality in a broad context; evolved ten recommendations, some of which have been to some extent acted upon. One of the first governmental groups to deal frankly with the population threat. Bibliography.

U.S. Department of Health, Education and Welfare. *Toward a Social Report.* Washington, D.C.: Government Printing Office, 1969. 101 p., price 55 cents. Prepared under the direction of Mancur Olson, Deputy Assistant Secretary for Social Indicators. Identifies problem areas and indicates most of the conventional statistical and other indices; makes relatively little progress toward new means of evaluating social health.

U.S. Department of Health, Education and Welfare, Consumer Protection and Environmental Health Service. *Environmental Health Planning Guide.* Washington, D.C.: Government Printing Office, 1968. iv + 100 p., price $1.00. Designed to guide the preparation of the environmental health plan required as part of the comprehensive health plan prepared by each state and urban area pursuant to the Partnership for Health Act (PL 89-749) and the Demonstration Cities Act (PL 89-754).

U.S. Department of Health, Education and Welfare, Consumer Protection and Environmental Health Service. *Issue Study on Human Ecology.* CPEHS-OPD Program Analysis Series. Washington, D.C.: Office of Program Development, CPEHS, October 1968. 48 p., mimeo. Recommendations of Human Ecology Study Group.

U.S. Department of Health, Education and Welfare, Consumer Protection and Environmental Health Service. *Resource Book on Planning, Issues, Organization, Funding, and Program Strategy.* Washington, D.C.: CPEHS, October 1969. Briefing book on funding, organization, issues and program strategy of agency; it should be noted that recent reorganization has fragmented the agency, dividing the consumer and environmental missions.

U.S. Department of Housing and Urban Development. "Open Space and a Quality Environment: An Eight Year Report." Washington, D.C.: The Department, Office of the Assistant Secretary for Metropolitan Planning and Development, May 1970. 21 p., mimeo, no price given. The Open Space Land Program from its inception in 1962 through July 1969. Shows increased concern with inner city.

U.S. Department of Housing and Urban Development. *Tomorrow's Transportation: New System for the Urban Future.* Washington,

D.C.: Government Printing Office, 1968. 100 p., price $1.75. Imaginative solutions for the urban mass transportation problem.

U.S. Department of State. *The Potential Impact of Science and Technology on Future U.S. Foreign Policy.* Papers presented at a joint meeting of the Policy Planning Council, Department of State, and a special panel of the Committee on Science and Public Policy, National Academy of Sciences, June 16-17, 1968. Washington, D.C.: National Academy of Sciences, 1968. 171 p., No price given. Ten papers, largely environmental, including population, food, mineral resources, atmospheric sciences, the oceans, water resources, and pollution of the environment.

U.S. Department of the Interior. *Conservation Yearbook.* Washington, D.C.: Government Printing Office, 1965+. Well-illustrated, adequate text, semi-popular.

Quest for Quality, 1965. $1.00
The Population Challenge, 1966. $1.25 Deals with effect of population stress on resources, rather than with problem per se.
The Third Wave, 1967. $2.00. Third phase of conservationism, the ecological.
Man...an Endangered Species? 1968. $1.50. Useful for classrooms, discussion groups.
It's Your World, 1969. $2.00. Takes cognizance of environmental activism.
River of Life, 1970. $2.00.

U.S. Department of the Interior. *Economics of Clean Water.* Third Annual Report to the Congress under Federal Water Pollution Control Act. Four volumes. Washington, D.C.: Government Printing Office, 1970. Summary Report, 50 cents; Vol. I, $1.50; Vol. II, $1.00; Vol. III, $3.50. An exhaustive analysis of the sources, costs, and control of water pollution.

U.S. Department of the Interior. *The Nation's River: A Report on the Potomac From the U.S. Department of the Interior.* Includes recommendations for action by the Federal Interdepartmental Task Force on the Potomac.

U.S. Department of the Interior. *Quantitative Comparison of Some Aesthetic Factors Among Rivers.* Washington, D.C.: Government Printing Office, 1969. Geological Survey Circular 631, 15 p., free.

U.S. Department of the Interior. *Surface Mining and Our Environment: A Special Report to the Nation.* Washington, D.C.: Government Printing Office, second printing 1967. 124 p., price $2.00. Colorfully illustrated book arguing that strip-mining ravages can be undone.

U.S. Department of the Interior. Bureau of Mines. *Automobile Disposal: A National Problem.* Washington, D.C.: Government Printing Office, 1967. 569 p., price $4.50. Factors influencing accumulation and disposition of junked autos.

U.S. Department of the Interior, Bureau of Outdoor Recreation. *Federal Outdoor Recreation Programs.* Washington, D.C.: Government Printing Office, 1968. 224 p. price $1.75. Reference guide summarizing activities of 102 agencies and divisions.

U.S. Department of the Interior, National Park Service. *Public Use of the National Park System: 1872-2000.* By Ronald Lee. Washington, D.C.: National Park Service, 1968. 93 p., free. Notes heavy usage, recommends controls and additional study.

U.S. Department of the Interior, National Park Service. *Summer in the Parks.* Washington, D.C.: Park Service, 1969. 28 p., free. Available from Office of Information, National Park Service, Washington, D.C.: 20240. A fresh and vital venture in the use of city parks in Washington, D.C. Extensive community involvement has brought a degree of success to a program to revive park areas formerly considered obsolete.

U.S. House of Representatives, Committee on Education and Labor. *Environmental Education Act.* Report recommending passage of H.R. 18260. Report No. 91-1362. 91st Cong., 2d Sess., July 31, 1970. Washington, D.C.: Government Printing Office, 1970. 14 p. Analysis and background of bill, later enacted, to authorize support of environmental/ecological education programs by the Office of Education.

U.S. House of Representatives, Committee on Education and Labor. *Environmental Quality Education Act of 1970.* Hearing on H.R. 14753 before the Select Subcommittee on Education between March 24 and May 2, 1970, In Washington, New York, San Francisco, and Los Angeles. Hearings on a bill to authorize the support of environmental/ecological education programs by the Office of Education. An amended, but substantially similar, version subsequently was enacted.

U.S. House of Representatives, Committee on Government Operations. *Deficiencies in the Administration of Federal Insecticide, Fungicide, and Rodenticide Act.* Eleventh Report, 91st Cong., 1st Sess. Washington, D.C.: Government Printing Office, 1969.

U.S. House of Representatives, Committee on Government Operations. *The Environmental Decade (Action Proposals for the 1970's).* Twenty-fourth report by the Committee, 91st Cong., 2d Sess., May 13, 1970. House Report No. 91-1082, Union Calendar No. 502. Washington, D.C.: Government Printing Office, 1970. 38 p., price 20 cents. Summarizes proposals received in nine days of hearings before the Committee's Conservation and Natural Resources Subcommittee. Remarkable cross-section of opinion, no recommendations by the Committee.

U.S. House of Representatives, Committee on Government Operations. *Environmental Pollution: Discharge of Raw Human Wastes from Railroad Trains.* Thirty-second report by the Committee, 91st Cong., 2d Sess., October 8, 1970. House Report No. 91-1581, Union Calendar No. 755. Washington, D.C.: Government Printing Office, 1970. 27 p., price 20 cents. An example of the detailed attention that must be given to real problems that may seem trivial in themselves, but which contribute to the degradation of the larger environment.

U.S. House of Representatives, Committee on Government Operations. *The Nation's Estuaries: San Francisco Bay and Delta, Calif.* (Part 2). Hearings before the Subcommittee on Conservation and Natural Resources. 91st Cong., 1st Sess., August 20 and 21, 1969. Washington, D.C.: Government Printing Office, 1970. 564 p., price $2.50.

U.S. House of Representatives, Committee on Interstate and Foreign Commerce. *Clean Air Act Amendments of 1970.* Committee report recommending passage of H.R. 17255. Report No. 91-1146. 91st Cong., 2d Sess., June 3, 1970. Washington, D.C.: Government Printing Office, 1970. 53 p.

U.S. House of Representatives, Committee on Merchant Marine and Fisheries. *Environmental Quality.* Hearings before the Subcommittee on Fisheries and Wildlife Conservation on several bills to provide for the establishment of a Council on Environmental Quality. 91st Cong., 1st Sess., May and June, 1969. Serial No. 91-6. Washington, D.C.: Government Printing Office, 1969. 472 p.

U.S. House of Representatives. Committee on Public Works. *1970 National Highway Needs Report.* Prepared for the Committee by the Bureau of Public Roads, Federal Highway Administration, Department of Transportation pursuant to PL 90-495. 91st Cong., 2d Sess., December 1969. Washington, D.C.: Government Printing Office, 1970. 38 p. Biennial report on future highway needs. In this issue, the Transportation Department assumes as a major goal optimal use of environmental resources.

U.S. House of Representatives, Committee on Science and Astronautics. *Managing the Environment.* Report of the Subcommittee on Science, Research, and Development, June, 1968. Washington, D.C.: Government Printing Office, 1968. 59 p., committee print, no price given. Summarizes hearings on a variety of legislative proposals, makes recommendations affecting all branches of government. Includes index to hearings on environmental quality issues.

U.S. House of Representatives, Committee on Science and Astronautics. *Technology: Processes of Assessment and Choice.* A report of the National Academy of Sciences to the Committee. Washington, D.C.: Government Printing Office, July 1969. 163 p., price 75 cents.

U.S. National Commission for UNESCO. *Man and His Environment: A View Toward Survival.* Background book for the 13th National Conference of the U.S. National Commission for UNESCO, San Francisco, California, December 23-25, 1969. Place of publication not indicated. 102 p. Heterogeneous collection of papers and essays by conference panelists and others.

U.S. President (Nixon). "Coal Mine Safety." Message to the Congress. March 3, 1969. *Presidential Documents,* V 10 (Monday, March 10, 1969). 357-8.

U.S. President (Nixon). "Control of Air and Water Pollution at Federal Facilities." Executive Order 11507. February 4, 1970. *Presidential Documents,* VI 6 (February 9, 1970), 127-8; also statement, p. 126.

U.S. President (Nixon). "Environmental Quality." Message to the Congress, February 10, 1970. *Presidential Documents,* VI 6, No. 7 (Monday, February 16, 1970), 160-173. Also H. Doc. No. 91-225, 91st Cong., 2d Sess. Recommending 37-point administrative and legislative program.

U.S. President (Nixon). "Marine Pollution from Oil Spills." Message to the Congress, May 20, 1970. *Presidential Documents,* VI 21 (Monday, May 25, 1970), 660-663.

U.S. President (Nixon).*Problems of Population Growth.* Message to the Congress, July 18, 1969. H. Doc. 91-139. 91st Cong., 1st Sess. Also available as reprint from Population Crisis Committee, Washington, D.C.:

U.S. President (Nixon). *World Weather Program: Plan for Fiscal Year 1971.* Washington, D.C.: Government Printing Office, 1970. v + 30 p., price 50 cents. President's report (pursuant to Sen. Con. Res. 67, 90th Cong.) describing second annual plan for United States' participation in World Weather Program.

U.S. Senate. *Progress in the Prevention and Control of Air Pollution.* First report of the Secretary of Health, Education and Welfare to the Congress pursuant to PL 90-148, the Air Quality Act of 1967. S. Doc. No. 92, 90th Cong., 2d Sess. Washington, D.C.: Government Printing Office, 1968. 85 p., price 30 cents.

U.S. Senate, Committee on Commerce. *Effects of Pesticides on Sports and Commercial Fisheries.* (Part 2). Hearing before Subcommittee on Energy, Natural Resources, and the Environment. 91st Cong., 1st Sess., September 29 and 30, 1969. Washington, D.C.: Government Printing Office, 1969. 618 p.

U.S. Senate, Committee on Commerce. *The Search for a Low-Emission Vehicle.* Washington, D.C.: Government Printing Office, 1969. A staff report prepared for the Committee.

U.S. Senate, Committee on Government Operations. *Establish a Select Senate Committee on Technology and the Human Environment.* Hearings on S. Res. 78 before the Subcommittee on Intergovernmental Relations, March 4,5,6, April 24, and May 7, 1969, 91st Cong., 1st Sess. Washington, D.C.: Government Printing Office, 1969, 334 p., price $1.50.

U.S. Senate, Committee on Government Operations. *Federal Role in Traffic Safety.* Subcommittee on Executive Reorganization, 89th Cong., 2d Sess., March 1966. Washington, D.C.: Government Printing Office, 1966. Largely concerned with role of public agencies and coordination with private sector.

U.S. Senate, Committee on Government Operations. *Research in the Service of Man: Biomedical Knowledge, Development, and Use.* A conference sponsored by the Subcommittee on Government Research pursuant to S. Res. 218, 89th Cong. November 2, 1967, 90th Cong., 1st Sess. Washington, D.C.: Government Printing Office, 1967. 246 p., price 70 cents.

U.S. Senate, Committee on Interior and Insular Affairs. *A Definition of the Scope of Environmental Management.* Prepared by Staff Member Daniel A. Dreyfus for the use of the Committee, January 1970. 91st Cong., 2d Sess. Washington, D.C.: Government Printing Office, 1970. 27 p. Includes a compilation of Federal agencies which administer environmental management programs, arranged by activity classification.

U.S. Senate, Committee on Interior and Insular Affairs, and U.S. House of Representatives, Committee on Science and Astronautics. *A National Policy for the Environment.* Congressional White Paper, 90th Cong., 2d Sess., October 1968. Washington, D.C.: Government Printing Office, 1968. 19 p., price not given. Paper intended to broaden consideration of environmental policy, issued following informal joint House-Senate colloquium on July 17, 1968, on environmental policy planning.

U.S. Senate, Committee on Labor and Public Welfare. *Environmental Quality Education Act.* Hearings on S. 3151, S. 3237, and S. 3809 before the Subcommittee on Education, May 19 and 20, 1970. 91st Cong., 2d Sess. Washington, D.C.: Government Printing Office, 1970. 451 p. Hearings on bills to authorize support of environmental education programs, establish a national committee on technology and the environment, and to authorize fellowships for persons training for environmental careers.

U.S. Senate, Committee on Labor and Public Welfare. *The Environmental Quality Education Act.* Report recommending passage of H.R. 18260. Report No. 91-1164, Calendar No. 1181. 91st Cong., 2d Sess., September 9, 1970. Washington, D.C.: Government Printing Office, 1970. 11 p. Analysis and background of bill, later enacted, to authorize support of environmental/ecological education programs by the Office of Education.

U,S. Senate, Committee on Public Works. *Air Pollution -- 1969.* Hearings before the Subcommittee on Air and Water Pollution, October 27, 1969. 91st Cong. 1st Sess. Washington, D.C.: Government Printing Office, 1970. 244 p.

U.S. Senate, Committee on Public Works. *The Case for National Environmental Laboratories.* A report prepared by the Ad Hoc NEL Concept Committee, Oak Ridge National Laboratory, 91st Cong., 2d Sess. Washington, D.C.: Government Printing Office, 1970. 40 p. Includes text of S. 3410, the National Environmental Laboratory Act of 1970, introduced in February 1970, by Senators Howard H. Baker, Jr. and Edmund S. Muskie.

U.S. Senate, Committee on Public Works. *National Air Quality Standards Act of 1970.* Conference report and individual views on S. 4358. Report No. 91-1196. 91st Cong., 2d Sess., September 17, 1970. Washington, D.C.: Government Printing Office, 1970. 129 p.

U.S. Senate, Committee on Public Works. *Resource Recovery Act of 1969.* Hearings before the Subcommittee on Air and Water Pollution on S. 2005, a bill to amend the Solid Waste Disposal Act in order to support research, facilities construction, other purposes. Two parts, between April 10 and October 28, 1969. Serial No. 91-13, 91st

Cong., 1st Sess., 1969. Washington, D.C.: Government Printing Office, 1969. 1418 p. Out of print.

U.S. Senate, Committee on Public Works. *Thermal Pollution--1968.* Hearings before the Subcommittee on Air and Water Pollution. In four parts, between February 6 and April 19, 1968, 90th Cong., 2d Sess. Washington, D.C.: Government Printing Office, 1968. 1394 p. Part 4 includes extensive (110 p.) bibliography on the effects of heated effluents on aquatic life.

U.S. Senate, Committee on Public Works. *Toward a National Materials Policy.* A report on a proposed commission on national materials policy, prepared by the Legislative Reference Service, Library of Congress. 91st Cong., 1st Sess. Washington, D.C.: Government Printing Office, 1969. vii + 86 p.

U.S. Senate, Committee on Public Works. *Underground Uses of Nuclear Energy.* Hearings before the Subcommittee on Air and Water Pollution on S. 3042, a bill to provide for a study and evaluation of the environmental effects of underground uses of nuclear energy for excavation and other purposes. November 18, 19 and 20, 1969. Washington, D.C.: Government Printing Office, 1970. 519 p., price $2.25.

U.S. Senate, Committee on Public Works. *Water Pollution--1970.* Hearings before the Subcommittee on Air and Water Pollution on bills amending the Federal Water Pollution Control Act and other pending legislation relating to water pollution control, between April 20 and June 8, 1970. Washington, D.C.: Government Printing Office, 1970. Part 1, 401 p., price $1.50; Part 2, 501 p., price $2.00; Part 3, 878 p., price $1.75; Part 4, 230 p., price $1.00.

Wang, J.Y. and R.R. Balter. *Survey of Environmental Sciences Organizations in the United States.* Berkeley, California: Environmental Sciences Institute, San Jose College, 1969. 20 p. no price given.

"Water Pollution Control Efforts Will Cost Billions." *Congressional Quarterly Weekly Report.* XXVII, 20 (May 15, 1970), 1307-10. The rising price of arresting the continued deterioration of our water resources. A CQ Fact Sheet.

Water Resources Council. *The Nation's Water Resources,* Parts 1–7, Washington, D.C.: Government Printing Office, 1968. paper bound, price $4.25. First national assessment under the Water Resources Planning Act. Describes nation's water and related land resources and their use and management problems.

"Will Success Spoil the National Parks?" A series of 16 articles reprinted from *The Christian Science Monitor.* Boston, Mass.: The Christian Science Publishing Co., 1968. 56 p., no price given. Use and misuse of the National Parks, suggestions for coping with the problem of people.

Wilson, David G. *"Technology and the Solid-Waste Problem."* Technology Review. LXXI, 4 (February 1969), 29-33. Summarizes findings of a study group examining the management of solid wastes.

Wolozin, H. (ed.). *The Economics of Air Pollution.* New York: W.W. Norton, 1968. 318 p.

World Health Organization. *Noise, an Occupational Hazard and Public Nuisance.* Geneva, Switzerland: WHO, 1966. Public Health Paper No. 30.

B. Bibliographies and Other Secondary Sources.

As an indirect way of covering the proliferating literature of environmental concern, we have sought to discover other bibliographies and reading lists particularly those dealing with the two areas we tended to exclude: the popular and the technical literatures. Most of the items listed should be available without great difficulty.

American Association for the Advancement of Science, Commission on Science Education. *Science for Society: A Bibliography.* Preparation and publication supported by the National Science Foundation and Battelle Memorial Institute. Washington, D.C.: AAAS, 1970. 42 p. Excellent bibliography on the application of science and technology to human problems, with emphasis on environment and population. Prepared for students and teachers, but certainly useful to professionals. More than 1,500 references to relatively easy-to-obtain materials.

American Association of University Women. *A Resource Guide on Pollution Control.* Washington, D.C.: The Association, 1970. 100 p., no price given. For each environmental problem (including population), briefly states problem, indicates available resources, suggests action. Strong on bibliographic and directory information.

American Chemical Society. *Cleaning Our Environment: The Chemical Basis for Action.* Washington, D.C.: ACS, 1969. 249 p., price $2.75. Includes concise bibliography on solid waste problems, largely technical.

American Institute of Architects. *AIA Cope.* Washington, D.C.: The Association, March 1970. Approx. 100 p., mimeo. A collection of sources for environmental education on all levels, organized in two parts – one for the educator, the other for the design professional. Cover books, films and film strips, classroom kits, other sources of information.

American Society for Engineering Education. *Interdisciplinary Research Topics in Urban Engineering.* A report by the Society's Urban Engineering Study Committee. Washington, D.C.: The Society, October 1969. 312 p., mimeo., price $5.00. Major sections on urban transportation, housing, and environment include selected annotated bibliographies.

Arndt, Carol A. *Bibliography on Total Waste Management.* Washington, D.C.: Federal Water Pollution Control Administration, February 14, 1969. Unpaginated draft, approx. 25 p. May be published in completed form.

Battelle Memorial Institute. *Science Policy Bulletin.* Available from the Institute, 505 King Avenue, Columbus, Ohio 43201, without charge. Published bimonthly, the Bulletin offers an annotated bibliography of current books, reports, and articles on public policy issues associated with science and technology. Attentive to national goals and the allocation of resources, and, therefore, to environmental issues.

Bowker, R.R. Company. *The Environmental Crisis: A Paperback Library.* Reprinted from *Paperbound Books in Print,* March 1970. Available from R.R. Bowker Company, 1180 Avenue of the Americas, New York, N.Y. 10036. An extensive annotated bibliography covering popular and semi-technical works on environmental quality, pollution, and the population explosion.

Center for Urban Studies, University of Chicago. *Metropolitan Water Resources Management.* Chicago: University of Chicago, 1969. 124 p. A state-of-the-art and literature review.

Citizens Advisory Committee on Environmental Quality. *Community Action for Environmental Quality.* Washington, D.C.: Government Printing Office, 1970. 42 p. Brief listings of government agencies, private associations, and useful publications for citizen's groups about to tackle environmental and community problems.

Conservation Education Association. *Conservation Education: A Selected Bibliography.* Prepared for the Association by Joan Carvajal and Martha E. Munzer, Danville, Illinois: The Interstate Printers and Publishers, 1968. 98 p., paperbound, price $2.50. Bibliography of books, 1957-1966.

The Conservation Foundation. *State and Regional Conservation Councils.* Washington, D.C.: The Conservation Foundation, February 1969. 57 p., mimeo. Preliminary listing of clearinghouse, shared--service and joint action organizations formed by diverse environmental planning and conservation groups in the United States. Describes 36 organizations, identifies others.

Council of State Governments, The. *State Administrative Officials Classified by Function.* Lexington, Kentucky: The Council, July 1969. 78 p., price $3.00.

Dingell, Rep. John D. "Bibliographies on Ecology, Pollution Control, and Environmental Deterioration." *Congressional Record,* April 15, 1970. E 3211-E 3216. Reproduces annotated bibliographies prepared by Bureau of Library Services, Michigan State Department of Education. Both popular and semi-technical materials, largely books. Includes some "package" bibliographies of supplementary readings for school use, organized by grade, with prices.

Federal Council for Science and Technology, Committee on Environmental Quality. *Noise: Sound Without Value.* Washington, D.C.: Government Printing Office, September 1969. Bibliography includes references on physiological and other effects of sound, control of noise, agency programs and Federal standards.

Great Lakes Commission. *Great Lakes Research Checklist.* No. 16, April 1970. Ann Arbor, Mich.: The Commission, 1970. 11 p., mimeo. Articles theses, other publications on research in the area. Prepared by the Commission in cooperation with the Great Lakes Research Division, the University of Michigan.

Hammerman, Donald R. et al *Research in Outdoor Education.* Washington, D.C.: American Association for Health, Physical Education, and Recreation. 1960. 62 p., mimeo. Summaries of doctoral studies on the subject.

Harvard University Program on Technology and Society. *Fifth Annual Report.* 1968-69. Cambridge, Mass.: The Program, 1969. 82 p. Bibliography of publications growing out of the Program's research.

Jackson, Sen. Henry M. "Establishment of a Board of Environmental Quality Advisors." *Congressional Record,* CXV, 164 (October 8, 1969), p. S. 12124. Comment on S. 1075, a bill to establish a national policy on environment, includes extensive bibliography and reading lists on environmental problems particularly useful to teachers and librarians.

The Library of Congress, Legislative Reference Service. *Environmental Policy and the Law.* Prepared by the Environmental Policy Division. Washington, D.C.: Library of Congress, January 1970. 48 p., mimeo., no price given. Two annotated bibliographies (reference works and government documents; legal periodicals) limited to literature guides, digests and compilations of laws, summaries of legislation, congressional hearings, government reports, and relevant legal articles. Excellent. Will also appear in the proceedings of the Airlie House *Conference on Law and Environment,* edited by Malcolm Baldwin, Walker and Company (in press).

The Library of Congress, Legislative Reference Service. *Federal Programs Related to Environment.* Prepared by Elizabeth M. Boswell,

Analyst in Conservation and Natural Resources, Environmental Policy Division. Washington, D.C.: The Library of Congress, February 1, 1970. 72 p. mimeo. A compilation and brief description of all Federal agency programs related to environment. Selected boards, committees, and commissions are included, as well as quasi-official organizations.

National Academy of of Sciences. *A Directory of Oceanographers in the United States.* Compiled by Richard C. Vetter, Committee on Oceanography. Division of Earth Sciences. Washington, D.C.: National Academy of Sciences, 1969. 72 p. Alphabetical by name, gives institution and primary interests. Based on information collected for UNESCO Office of Oceanography for an international directory.

National Recreation and Park Association. *A Guide to Books on Recreation.* 13th annual edition, 1970. Washington, D.C.: the Association, 1970. 45 p., indexed. price $1.00 Emphasis on park, camp, and recreation area management and program; less on environment.

The National Wildlife Federation. *Conservation Directory 1970.* Washington, D.C.: the Federation, 1970. 140 p. paperbound, price $1.50. Subtitled "A Listing of Organizations, Agencies and Officials Concerned with Natural Resource Use and Management." Useful.

Ochs, Jack, Harold J. Barnett and G. Ault. *Environmental Social Scientists: An Annotated List.* St. Louis, Mo.: Institute for Regional and Urban Studies, Washington University, 1968. 48 p., mimeo. Incomplete but still extensive directory to social scientists working on environmental quality.

Planned Parenthood–World Population. *1969 Publications About Planned Parenthood.* New York: Planned Parenthood–World Population, 1969. Price 25 cents.

Planned Parenthood–World Population. *A Selected Bibliography: Family Planning, Population, Related Subjects.* New York: Planned Parenthood–World Population, 1968. Price 25 cents.

Population Council. Current Publications in Population/Family Planning published three or four times yearly by the Council, 245 Park

Avenue, New York, N.Y. 10017. No price given. Usual issue 4 p. An abstract bibliography, part of an information service provided by the Council and the International Institute for the Study of Human Reproduction, Columbia University. Books, articles, papers; detailed abstracts. Can provide reprints of articles.

Population Reference Bureau. *Population Bulletin: A Sourcebook on Population,* XXV, 5 (November 1969). Washington, D.C.: Population Reference Bureau, 1969.

The President's Council on Recreation and Natural Beauty. *From Sea to Shining Sea.* Washington, D.C.: Government Printing Office, 1968. 304 p., paper cover, price $2.50. Bibliography of "Books and organizations which can help."

The Research and Design Institute. *1969 Directory of Behavior and Environmental Design.* Providence, R.I.: Research and Design Institute, 1969. 210 p., narrow format. Persons exploring the relationships between human behavior and physical design. Indexed by discipline, useful as bibliography as well as directory.

The Sierra Club. *Ecotactics: The Sierra Club Handbook for Environmental Activists.* New York: Pocket Books, April 1970. 288 p., paperback, price 95 cents. Includes bibliography of popular and semi-popular books.

State University of New York College at Fredonia. *Directory of Organizations Concerned with Environmental Research.* Fredonia, New York: Lake Erie Environmental Studies, College at Fredonia, February 1970. 150 p., price $2.00. An international directory to organizations concerned with any aspect of environmental research or study. Pressure-sensitive mailing labels are available for circularizing institutions listed.

U.S. Department of Health, Education and Welfare. *Strategy for a Livable Environment.* A report to the Secretary by the Task Force on Environmental Health and Related Problems. Washington, D.C.: Government Printing Office, 1967. 90 p., paper cover, price 60 cents. Includes basic reference bibliography, strong on Federal and Congressional sources.

U.S. Department of Housing and Urban Development. *New Communities: A Bibliography.* Washington, D.C.: Government Printing Office, 1969. 84 p., price 75 cents. An annotated bibliography, including general and background material on the urban problem only where related to the new communities movement.

U.S. Department of the Interior. *A List of Publications on Conservation and Related Department of the Interior Subjects.* Washington, D.C.: Government Printing Office, 1970. Pamphlet, free. Title, price and annotation on conservation-related Department publications.

U.S. Department of the Interior. *Population Trends and National Policy: A Natural Resources Information Service* issued monthly by the Departmental Library. Available from Clearinghouse for Federal Scientific and Technical Information, Springfield, Virginia, 22151. Subscription $8.00 per year. Provides a monthly sample of comment and writing on population problems and the environment generally.

U.S. Department of the Interior. *Readings for the Eco-Activist: A Bibliography of Selected Environmental Publications of the Executive Branch of the Federal Government.* Task Force on Environmental Education and Youth Activities, Office of the Secretary. Washington, D.C.: the Department, 1970. 33 p., mimeo, No price given. Selected annotated list of Federal publications, ranging from popular to semi-technical; limited to recent and readily-available items.

U.S. Department of the Interior. *Selected Water Resources Abstracts* published semimonthly by the Water Resources Scientific Information Center (WRSIC), Office of Water Resources Research. Available from WRSIC, Department of the Interior, Washington, D.C. 20240. Subscription $22.00 per year. Abstracts current and earlier monographs, journal articles, reports, and other formats on all aspects of the water problem.

U.S. House of Representatives, Committee on Science and Astronautics. *Environmental Science Centers at Institutions of Higher Education.* A survey prepared for the Subcommittee on Science, Research, and Development by the Environmental Policy Division, Legislative Reference Service, Library of Congress. 91st Cong., 1st

Sess., December 1969. Washington, D.C.: Government Printing Office, 1969. 16 p. plus fold-out tables. Interdisciplinary studies at environmental science centers in more than 100 colleges and universities.

Western Electric Corporation. "A Topical Outline and Selected References on Applied Science and Environmental Management," prepared for Western Electric Seminar on environmental control, San Francisco, February 16-18, 1970. Available from Dr. Lynton K. Caldwell, Indiana University, Bloomington, Indiana. 16 p. A more extensive bibliography on environmental administration is being prepared by the Program in the Public Administration of Science and Technology, Indiana University, under Dr. Caldwell's direction.

"Who's Who in the Conservation Establishment." *The Washingtonian,* V, 7 (April 1970) 42-45, 93. "The People Who Protect Washington From Congress and Other Polluters." Organizations domiciled in Washington; their activities and policies.

C. Periodicals Dealing With The Environment

The periodicals and newsletters listed below are either substantially devoted to some aspect of the environmental problem, or can be counted upon to reveal a consistent and lasting interest in the maintenance of environmental quality. Necessarily, these publications differ in quality, scope, and sophistication. Some enjoy a high reputation for scientific, intellectual, or esthetic excellence; others are merely the ephemeral productions of concerned local groups. This is more of a study of the range of the literature than a list of recommended acquisitions; however, our annotations should indicate which subscriptions would be the most useful.

AIA Journal published monthly by the American Institute of Architects, the Octagon, 1735 New York Avenue, N.W., Washington, D.C. 20006. General library subscription rate $10 per year, less to organizations concerned with architecture. Official journal of AIA, comments on environment where related to design or education.

AIA Memo published monthly by the American Institute of Architects, 1735 New York Avenue, N.W., Washington, D.C. 20006. No subscription rate, free to members. A newsletter largely devoted to personalities and events within the organization; rather infrequent items of environmental relevance.

AIP Newsletter published monthly by the American Institute of Planners, 917 15th Street, N.W., Washington, D.C. 20005. Subscription $5 per year. Some environmental materials; see also the journal of the Association.

Air and Water News published weekly by McGraw-Hill Book Co., Inc., 330 West 42nd Street, New York, N.Y. 10036. Subscription $120 per year. News report on environmental problems: local, state, national, world-wide.

Air and Water Pollution Report published weekly by Business Publishers, Inc., P.O. Box 1067, Blair Station, Silver Spring, Maryland 20910. Subscription $90 per year. News, particularly governmental, about waste disposal, soil pollution, desalinization, noise, and conservation, as well as air and water.

Air Currents (formerly *Citizens for Clean Air*) published quarterly by Citizens for Clean Air, Inc., 40 West 57th Street, New York, N.Y. 10019. Free on request. Tabloid format. Centers on New York City, political and action oriented.

American Forest Institute Report published monthly by American Forest Institute, 1835 K Street, N.W., Washington, D.C. 20006. 4 p., no subscription rate given. Issues seen were attentive to Environmental Action (Earth Day), education, legislation.

American Forests published monthly by the American Forestry Association, 919 17th Street, N.W., Washington, D.C. 20006. Subscription $6 per year. Subtitled "The Magazine of Forests, Soil, Water, Wildlife, and Outdoor Recreation." Popular treatment, "seeks to promote an enlightened public appreciation of natural resources."

American Gas Association Monthly published eleven times a year by the Association, 605 Third Avenue, New York, N.Y. 10016. Subscription $5 per year. AGA promotes use of natural gas, seeks new applications and technology; has taken opportunity to urge gas as a relatively non-polluting fuel and as a raw material for production of protein. Rather typical of trade journals trying to bridge gap between the needs of their industry and the pressures beginning to arise in the larger society.

American Journal of Public Health and the Nation's Health published monthly by the American Public Health Association, 1749 Broadway, New York, N.Y. 10019. Subscription $15 per year. Entire public health field, including community and personal health protection; consistent attention to environmental pollution.

Appalachia published monthly by the Appalachian Regional Commission, 1666 Connecticut Avenue, N.W., Washington, D.C. 20235. Usual issue 30+p. Free on request. Devoted to special problems of regional development in an area where the natural environment has been damaged severely.

Architectural Forum published ten times a year by Urban America, Inc., 330 West 42nd Street, New York, N.Y. 10036. Subscription $6 per year. Construction industry orientation. Revealing of new technologies and advanced design concepts.

Architectural Record published monthly by McGraw-Hill Book Co., Inc., 330 West 42nd Street, New York, N.Y. 10036. Subscription $6 per year. Construction industry orientation. Revealing of new technologies and advanced design concepts.

Archives of Environmental Health published monthly by American Medical Association, 535 Dearborn Street, Chicago, Illinois 60610. Subscription $12 per year. Dissemination of information in preventive, occupational, and aerospace medicine. Typical medical journal in content and format.

Atmospheric Environment: An International Journal published every two months by Pergamon Press, Ltd., 44-01 21st Street, Long Island City, New York 11101. Institution, $40 per year; individuals $10. Both weather and pollution problems, largely technical and scientific.

Audubon published six times a year by the National Audubon Society,

1130 Fifth Avenue, New York, N.Y. 10028. Subscription $8.5C per year. Conservationist viewpoint, but more than bird-watching. Good popularizer of environmental concerns; well produced, high-level graphics.

Biology and Human Affairs published three times a year by the British Social Biology Council, 69 Eccleston Square, London S.W. 1, England. $3 per year. Genetics, eugenics, population, etc.

BioScience published twice monthly by the American Institute of Biological Sciences, 3900 Wisconsin Avenue, N.W., Washington, D.C. 20016. Institutional subscription $18 per year. Official publication of AIBS; gives major coverage to biological aspects of environment, including population. Style ranges from semi-popular to technical. Features and news sections attentive to legislative and governmental issues.

British Journal of Preventive and Social Medicine published quarterly by the British Medical Association, BMA House, Tavistock Square, London W.S.1, England. Subscription $10 per year. Public Health.

Bulletin of Environmental Contamination and Toxicology published every two months by Springer-Verlag, Heidelberger Platz 3, 1000 Berlin, West Germany. U.S. address Springer-Verlag, Inc., 175 Fifth Avenue, New York, N.Y. 10010. Subscription $20. International.

Bulletin of the Atomic Scientists published monthly ten times a year (except July and August) by Educational Foundation for Nuclear Science. Address inquiries to Bulletin of the Atomic Scientists, 935 East 60th Street, Chicago, Illinois 60637. Subscription $8.50 per year. In recent years has devoted increasing amounts of space to environmental issues, particularly in relation to atomic power and nuclear testing and fallout.

Bulletin of the Ecological Society of America published quarterly by the Society, 24 Wildwood Drive, Oak Ridge, Tennessee 37830. Subscription $4.00 per year. Abstracts of papers, reports, society activities.

Bulletin on Human Ecology published quarterly by the Human Ecological Society, Box 146, Elsah, Illinois 62028. Subscription $5.00 Not examined. Newsletter also available, published quarterly, subscription $1.00 per year.

The Canadian Scientist published quarterly by Pendragon House, Ltd., 71 Bathhurst Street, Toronto, Ontario. Subscription $2.00 per year. Equivalent to *Science.*

Catalyst for Environmental Quality published quarterly at 274 Madison Avenue, New York, N.Y. 10016. Subscription $5 per year. Prior to spring, 1970, entitled "Conservation Catalyst." High-level popularization; substantial articles on all aspects, including population control, "most basic of all." Review books and films suited to environmental education.

The Center Magazine published bimonthly by the Fund for the Republic, Inc., 2056 Eucalyptus Hill Road, Santa Barbara, California 93103, for the Center for the Study of Democratic Institutions. Membership only; annual dues (associate) $15 per year. Strong environmental concern, political and social science emphasis.

CF Letter published monthly by the Conservation Foundation, 1250 Connecticut Avenue, N.W., Washington, D.C. 20036. Subscription $6 per year. Usual issue 12 p., some specials. Recent issues attentive to Washington scene.

Chesapeake Science published quarterly by Natural Resources Institute, University of Maryland, Box 38, Solomons, Maryland 20688. Free to libraries and scientific institutions. Natural resources of Chesapeake Bay region.

City published every two months by Urban America, Inc., 1717 Massachusetts Avenue, N.W., Washington, D.C. 20036. Subscription $10 per year.

Clean Air and Water News published weekly by Commerce Clearing House, Inc., 4025 West Peterson Ave., Chicago, Illinois 60646. Subscription $80 per year. Usual issue 16 pages. Largely devoted to Federal legislation, rule-making, research and construction support, policy. Coverage broader than title suggests; includes noise, solid waste, industrial safety, disaster relief, and Other topics.

Clean Water Report published monthly by Business Publishers, Inc., P.O. Box 1067, Blair Station, Silver Spring, Maryland 20910. Subscription $18 per year. A related and less expensive version of *Air and Water Pollution Report,* which see.

Coal Research published quarterly by Bituminous Coal Research, Inc., 350 Hochberge Road, Monroeville, Pa., 15146. No price given. 8 p. Gives detailed attention to problems of mine drainage, waste disposal and pollution, more efficient utilization.

Commercial Fisheries Review published monthly by Bureau of Commercial Fisheries. U.S. Department of the Interior. Available from Government Printing Office, Washington, D.C. 20402. Subscription $7 per year. Technical and federal policy concerns.

Conservation Education Association Newsletter published quarterly by the Association, 1144 East 3rd South Street, Salt Lake City, Utah 84102. Free to membership and controlled circulation. Environmental education.

The Conservationist published every two months by the New York State Conservation Department, Albany, New York 12201. Subscription $2.00 per year. Problems and responses on the state level. Many state conservation agencies publish such periodicals.

Contamination Control published monthly by Blackwent Publication, Inc., 1605 Cahuenga Boulevard, Los Angeles, California 90028. Subscription $5 per year. An interesting aspect of the environmental problem: how to exclude technologically-generated contaminants from the sophisticated products and processes of our technology.

Contamination Newsletter published monthly by Ann Arbor Science Publishers, Inc., 2155 Jackson Road, Box 1425, Ann Arbor, Michigan 48106. Subscription $25 per year.

CUEBS News published six times yearly by the Commission on Undergraduate Education in the Biological Sciences, 3900 Wisconsin Avenue, N.W., Washington, D.C. 20016. Free on request. Usual issue 24 p. Recent emphasis on environmental awareness.

Current Publications in Population/Family Planning published quarterly by the Population Council, 245 Park Avenue, New York, N.Y. 10017. No price given. Usual issue 4 p. Detailed abstracts of books, articles, papers; reprints of articles available.

Defenders of Wildlife News published quarterly by Defenders of Wildlife, 731 DuPont Circle Building, Washington, D.C. 20036. Subscription $5 per year, free to members. Usual issue over 100 p. Organization is dedicated to the preservation of all forms of wildlife. Conservationist viewpoint; somewhat sentimental, particularly in children's section.

Demography published twice annually by Population Association of America, Box 14182 Benjamin Franklin Station, Washington, D.C. 20044. Subscription $12 per year, non-members. Major studies in demography and population policy. Bibliographies, references.

Design and Environment published quarterly by RC Publications, 6400 Goldsboro Road, N.W., Washington, D.C. 20034. Subscription $11 per year. A new journal devoted to the interaction between technology and environment and how this can be made constructive.

Design Methods Group Newsletter published by Sage Publications, Inc., 275 South Beverly Drive, Beverly Hills, California 90212.

Earth Science Newsletter published approximately six times a year by the Division of Earth Sciences, National Academy of Sciences/ National Research Council, Washington, D.C. 20418. Controlled circulation.

Ecology published every two months by Duke University Press, Box 6697 College Station, Durham, N.C. 27708. Publication of the Ecological Society of America. "All forms of life in relation to environment." Largely scientific, but cognizant of policy issues.

Ecological Society of America Bulletin published quarterly by the Society, c/o Editor, S.I. Auerbach, Oak Ridge National Laboratory, Oak Ridge, Tennessee 37830. Subscription $4 per year. News and abstracts.

Ekistics published monthly by the Athens Center of Ekistics, 24 Strat Syndesmou Street, Athens 136, Greece. Subscription $12 per year. "Reviews on the problems and science of human settlements." Reflects ideas of such planners as Constantine Doxiadis, R. Buckmaster Fuller, and John McHale.

Environment published twice yearly by Alan Wilson, 5 Cambridge Terrace, London N.W.1, England. Subscription $16 per year. Major studies, social science emphasis.

Environment published ten times a year by Committee for Environmental Information, 438 North Skinker Boulevard, St. Louis, Missouri 63130. Subscription $8.50 per year. An official publication of Scientists' Institute for Public Information. Entitled *Scientist and Citizen* prior to January/February 1969 issue. Seeks to put environmental information before the public.

Environment and Behavior published three times a year by Sage Publications, Inc., 275 South Beverly Drive, Beverly Hills, California 90212. Individuals $7 per year, institutions $10. Environmental and ecological studies, ethology. Effects of crowding, pollution, etc., on human and animal behavior.

Environment Improvement Case History Report Service published monthly by Freed Publishing Company, P.O. Box 1144, FDR Station, New York, N.Y. 10022. Subscription $35 per year. Provides 24 individual reports documenting successful efforts by private organizations or local governments to upgrade some aspect of the outdoor environment.

The Environment Monthly published by The Environment Monthly, 420 Lexington Avenue, New York, N.Y. 10017. Usual issue 12 p. Subscription $35 per year. "A report for professionals—and concerned non-professionals—who need to know what is happening in the field of environmental design." Picks up oddities other publications miss; somewhat flip in style.

Environment Reporter published weekly by Bureau of National Affairs, Inc., 1231 25th Street, N.W., Washington, D.C. 20037. Subscription $280 per year includes cumulative indexes, special monographs, set of binders. Covers legislative, administrative, and judicial developments in pollution and environmental control; detailed, legalistic, extensive full-text sections.

Environmental Action published every two weeks by Environmental Action, Inc., 2000 P Street, N.W. Washington, D.C. 20036. Subscription $4 per year. This is a successor to *Action: April 22,* the newsletter published by Environmental Teach-In, Inc. in preparation for the Earth Day programs.

Environmental Design published quarterly by U.S. Industrial Publications, Inc., 209 Dunn Avenue, Stamford, Connecticut 06905. Subscription $4 per year. Primarily interior environment; heating and air conditioning, related design.

Environmental Education published quarterly by Dembar Educational Research Services, Inc., Box 1605 Madison, Wisconsin 53701. Subscription $7.50 per year. "A journal of research and development in conservation communications." First issue (Fall 1969) devoted to "defining environmental education."

Environmental Health Letter published twice monthly by Gershon W. Fishbein, publisher, 1097 National Press Building, Washington, D.C. 20004. Subscription $50 per year. An independent publication in business since 1961, EHL tends to see environmental problems from a medical perspective, provides good coverage subject to this limitation.

Environmental Law Reporter published monthly by the Environmental Law Institute, Suite 620 Dupont Circle Building, 1346 Connecticut Avenue, N.W., Washington, D.C. 20036. A loose-leaf, cumulative service (about 1,000 pages in first year of publication) for lawyers representing environmental interests. A typical law reporter service, including seven sections: newsletter, court decisions, administrative proceedings, statutes and regulations, analytic comments, digest-bibliography, and index.

Environmental Science and Technology published monthly by the American Chemical Society, 1155 16th Street, N.W. Washington, D.C. 20036. Subscription $7 per year to nonmembers of ACS.

Emphasis on water, air, and waste chemistry. Aimed at technical and industrial readership.

Environmental Technology and Economics published bi-weekly by Technomic Publishing Company, Inc., 750 Summer Street, Stamford, Connecticut 06902. Subscription $60 per year. Technical, economic, and political newsletter on waste and pollution.

ESCP Newsletter published quarterly by the Earth Sciences Curriculum Project, Box 1559, Boulder, Colorado 80302. Free on request. Includes environmental education, earth sciences, largely on high school level.

Family Planning Perspectives published bi-monthly by Planned Parenthood-World Population, Editorial Offices, 666 Fifth Avenue, New York, N.Y. 10019. Free on request. Usual issue over 50 p. A new journal; well-produced, detailed and informative, wide-ranging, liberal attitude. Apparently designed for social workers, clinicians, and other professionals, but useful to anyone concerned with the population problem.

Ford Foundation Letter published by the Ford Foundation, 320 East 43rd Street, New York, N.Y. 10017. Usual issue 8 p. No price given. Grants and other program actions, other matters of general interest. Shows growing interest in environmental problems. Includes references to published books, comment, and reports.

Forest Products Newsletter published weekly by National Forest Products Association, 1619 Massachusetts Avenue, N.W., Washington, D.C. 20036. Issue 4 p., no price given. Industry-oriented.

The Futurist published bimonthly by the World Future Society, P.O. Box 19285, Twentieth Street Station, Washington, D.C. 20036. Subscription $7.50 per year. Subtitled: "A Journal of Forecasts, Trends and Ideas About the Future." Consciousness of the environment, implicit or explicit, pervades responsible futurism.

Great Lakes Research Checklist published monthly by the Great Lakes Commission, 2200 North Campus Blvd., Ann Arbor, Michigan 48105. Usual issue 10 p.+., no price given. Articles, thesis, reports, and other publications on lake research. Prepared in cooperation with the Great Lakes Research Division, The University of Michigan.

The Green Revolution published monthly by Heathcote Center, School of Living, Route 1, Box 129, Freeland, Maryland 21053. Subscription $4 per year. Subtitled "A World-Wide Effort for Decentralization and Rural Revival." Emphasis on alternative family structures, communal living, social withdrawal, as well as pollution control, population reduction, and economic devolution. Tabloid format, relatively substantial, in ninth year of publication.

HUD Newsletter published every two weeks by the Office of Public Affairs, U.S. Department of Housing and Urban Development, Washington, D.C. 20410. Available from Government Printing Office, Washington, D.C. 20402. Subscription $2.50 per year. Usual issue 4 p.

Human Ecology Forum published quarterly by the New York State College of Human Ecology, Cornell University, Martha Van Rensselaer Hall, Ithaca, New York 14850. No subscription rate indicated. For a diverse audience, particularly community and state leaders who must deal with problems of malnutrition, housing, health, and population. Not technical; will report and interpret research results.

Impact of Science on Society published quarterly by UNESCO, 317 East 34th Street, New York, N.Y. 10016. Essays on the social consequences of science and technology.

Independent Petroleum Monthly published by Independent Petroleum Association of America, 1430 South Boulder, Tulsa, Oklahoma 74101. Subscription $5 per year. Recent articles reveal defensive stance, public relations efforts of the oil industry in response to rising criticism.

Journal of Environmental Design published by the College of Environmental Design, University of California, Berkeley. Not examined.

Journal of Environmental Health published by National Association of Sanitarians, 1550 Lincoln Street, Denver, Colorado 80203. Subscription $5 per year, free to professionals in the field. Scientific and educational aspects of environmental sanitation; emphasis on waste and sewage, public health aspects of pollution.

The Journal of Human Resources published quarterly by the Journals Department, University of Wisconsin Press, P.O. Box 1379, Madison, Wisconsin 53701.

Journal of Outdoor Education published quarterly at the Lorado Taft Field Campus of Northern Illinois University, Box 299, Oregon, Illinois 61061. No subscription rate given. The Taft Field Campus is used for graduate and undergraduate teacher-training institutes and other programs in which environmental awareness is emphasized.

Journal of Remote Sensing published bimonthly by the International Remote Sensing Institute, 6151 Freeport Blvd., Sacramento, California 95822. Subscription $15 per year for nonmembers. Devoted to development of a sensitive tool for environmental monitoring.

Journal of the Air Pollution Control Association published monthly by the Association, 4450 Fifth Avenue, Pittsburgh, Pennsylvania 15213. Individuals $15 per year, institutions $50.

Journal of the American Institute of Planners published six times a year by the Institute, 917 Fifteenth Street, N.W., Washington, D.C. 20005. Subscription $10 per year. Essential to the study of the urban environment. Also cited as *AIA Journal.*

Journal of the Water Pollution Control Federation published monthly by the Federation, 3900 Wisconsin Avenue, N.W., Washington, D.C. 20016. Subscription $18.50 per year. One of the older journals (1928); files reveal development of the technology.

Journal of Wildlife Management published quarterly by the Wildlife Society, 3900 Wisconsin Avenue, N.W., Washington, D.C. 20016. Subscription $15 per year. One of the earlier publications (1937). More technical than popular, aware of wildlife as an economic resource.

Landscape Architecture published quarterly by the Publication Board of the American Society of Landscape Architects, Schuster Building,

1500 Bairdstown Road, Louisville, Kentucky 40205. Subscription $8.50 per year. One of the oldest and most influential publications in the field. Devotes a large proportion of its space to thoughtful articles on much more than the mere esthetic aspects of environmental quality.

Landscape published three times a year by Landscape, Box 7177 Landscape Station, Berkeley, California 94707. Subscription $4 per year. Thoughtful consideration of the esthetic and social dimension.

Landscape Planning Commission Newsletter published bimonthly by International Union for Conservation of Nature and Natural Resources (IUCN), 1110 Morges, Switzerland. No subscription rate indicated. Usual issue 24 p. mimeo. International in scope, emphasis on planning.

Limnos published quarterly by the Great Lakes Foundation, 2200 North Campus Boulevard, Ann Arbor, Michigan 48105. Regular membership $7 per year. Promotion of public understanding of, and research into, the water problems of the Great Lakes Basin.

Living Wilderness published quarterly by the Wilderness Society, 729 15th Street, N.W., Washington, D.C. 20005. Free to members, nonmembers $3 per year. Strong statement of "wild areas" viewpoint.

Milieu, news report of the Environmental Research Foundation, 2700 West Sixth Street, Topeka, Kansas 66606.

Man-Environment Studies published by Division of Man-Environment Relations College of Human Development, Pennsylvania State University, University Park, Pennsylvania 16802. Supplants former *Architectural Psychology Newsletter* and *Man and His Environment Newsletter. No price given.*

Mining Congress Journal published by American Mining Congress, 1100 Ring Building, Washington, D.C. 20036. Subscription $5 per year. Technical and management publication. Reflects views of the larger mining interests, who have at least a defensive interest in environmental protection.

Mother Earth News published monthly by John Shuttleworth, P.O. Box 38, Madison, Ohio 44057. This modest publication is an old-timer in the field of ecology. Emphasizes organic gardening, alternative ways of living, the "gentle revolution." Style usually humorous, non-dogmatic, self-deprecatory.

National Parks and Conservation Magazine published monthly by National Park Association, 1701 18th Street, N.W., Washington, D.C. 20009. Subtitled "The Environmental Journal." Membership $6.50 per year.

Nation's Cities published monthly by the National League of Cities, 1612 K St., N.W., Washington, D.C. 20006. Subscription $6 per year. Attentive to urban environmental problems, federal funding policy.

Natural History published ten times a year by the American Museum of Natural History, Central Park West at 79th Street, New York, N.Y. 10024. Subscription $7.50 per year. Popular, wide school and library circulation. Regularly concerned with environment.

Natural Resources Journal published quarterly by the University of New Mexico School of Law, 1915 Roma, N.E., Albuquerque, New Mexico. Legal and other coverage of resources problems.

Naturalist Notes published bimonthly by Audubon Naturalist Society of the Central Atlantic States, Inc., 8940 Jones Mill Road, Washington, D.C. 20015. Membership, no price given. 12 p., mimeo. Typical of newsletters issued by special-interest "constituency" groups that will support environmental legislation and policy.

Nature published weekly by Macmillan Journals, Ltd., Brunel Road, Basingstoke, Hampshire, England. Subscription $48 per year. Equivalent to *Science,* enjoys outstanding reputation.

Nature and Resources published monthly by UNESCO. Available from UNESCO Publications Center, P.O. Box 433, New York, N.Y. 10016. Subscription rare not indicated. Bulleting of the International Hydrologic Decade; subtitled "Newsletter about scientific research in the environment, resources, and conservation of nature."

NABT News and Views published bimonthly by the National Association of Biology Teachers, 1420 N Street, N.W., Washington, D.C. 20005. Membership. Usual issue 6 p. Reveals concern with environmental education.

NELS Newsletter published monthly by the National Environmental Law Society, Stanford, California 94305. Free on request. A vehicle for communication among law schools, student and other organizations, and attorneys interested in the protection of the environment.

News from National Pollution Control Foundation, published by the Foundation, Room 423, 866 United Nations Plaza, New York, N.Y. 10017. Usual issue 4 + p., mimeo. Emphasis on legal problems.

Newsletter published irregularly by the Association for Voluntary Sterilization, 14 West 40th Street, New York, N.Y. 10018. No price given.

Newsletter of the Environmental Mutagen Society produced at the Biology Division, Oak Ridge National Laboratory, Oak Ridge, Tennessee, for the Society. Irregular; at least every six months. Usual issue 80 + p., mimeo. Free to members. Devoted to the problem of mutagenesis, or production of mutations, in plant and animal populations subject to chemical, nuclear, or other environmental pressures.

Newsletter published by National Coal Policy Conference, Inc., 1000 Sixteenth Street, N.W., Washington, D.C. 20036. Membership. Sample issue 10 p., mimeo. No price given. Attentive to environmental legislation and regulation.

Newsletter published bimonthly by the New York State Office for Local Government, 155 Washington Avenue, Albany, New York 12210. Free on request. Usual issue 4 p. Environmental issues facing local government -- trash and traffic – bulk large in this information newsletter sponsored by the State of New York.

Newsletter published by Zero Population Growth, 367 State Street, Los Altos, California 94022. Free on request.

Oceanography Newsletter published by Mardee Enterprises, Inc., 103 Park Ave., New York, N.Y. 10017. Subscription $65 per year. News of mining, drilling, farming, populating, and otherwise expoliting the sea floor.

Oceanology published weekly by American Aviation Publications, 1001 Vermont Avenue, N.W., Washington, D.C. 20005. Subscription $75 per year. Looseleaf format, cumulative indexes. Ocean technology; detailed, informative, industry orientation.

Oryx published monthly by the Fauna Preservation Society, c/o Zoological Society of London, Regent's Park, London N.W. 1, England. Subscription (ordinary membership) $7.75 per year. Preservation of endangered species, particularly in Africa.

Outdoor Recreation Action published quarterly by Bureau of Outdoor Recreation, Department of the Interior. Subscription $1.50 per year. Available from Government Printing Office, Washington, D.C. 20402. Examples of actions taken by Federal, state, and local government, private individuals in the interest of outdoor recreation.

Parks and Recreation published monthly by the National Recreation and Park Association, 1700 Pennsylvania Ave., N.W., Washington, D.C. 20006. Subscription $10 per year. Primary concern: the economics and management of parks and recreation areas.

Planned Parenthood News published by Planned Parenthood - World Population, 516 Madison Avenue, New York, N.Y. 10022. Free on request.

Population and Vital Statistics Report published quarterly by the United Nations. Available from UN Publications Sales Section, New York 10017. Per copy, $1.00. Latest totals for entire world.

Population Bomb News Items published irregularly by Population Policy Panel of the Hugh Moore Fund, 60 East 42nd Street, New York, N.Y. 10017. Free on request. Tends to be strident.

Population Bulletin published six times a year by Population Reference Bureau, 1755 Massachusetts Avenue, N.W., Washington, D.C. 20036.

Subscription $3 per year. Articles on mortality, migration, age structure, fertility rates, etc., world-wide.

Population Bulletin published irregularly by United Nations. $2.50 per copy. Statistical summaries. English and French. Available from U.N. Publications Service.

Population Crisis published irregularly by Population Crisis Committee, 1730 K Street, N.W., Washington, D.C. 20006. Free on request, usual issue 4 p.

Population Index published quarterly by the Princeton University Office of Population Research, 5 Ivy Lane, Princeton, New Jersey 08540. Subscription $15 per year. Demography; scientific, authoritative.

Population Trends and Environmental Policy: A Natural Resources Information Service issued monthly by the Library, U.S. Department of the Interior. Available from Clearinghouse for Federal Scientific and Technical Information, Springfield, Virginia 22151. Subscription $8 per year. Monthly sampling of current comment on population and environmental issues. First edition appeared in April, 1969.

Potomac Newsletter published monthly by Potomac Basin Center, 1250 Connecticut Avenue, N.W., Washington, D.C. 20036. Free on request. Usual issue 8 p., mimeo. "Committed to citizen involvement in decisions determining the destiny of the Potomac River Basin, and to the citizen's right to full knowledge about the issues in question."

PRB Selections published monthly by the Population Reference Bureau, 1755 Massachusetts Ave., N.W., Washington, D.C. 20036. No price given. Usual issue 6 p. Single articles or reprints; scope somewhat wider than population.

The Progressive published monthly by The Progressive, Inc., 408 West Gorham St., Madison, Wisconsin 53703. Subscription $8 per year. Largely political and reformist, devotes some space to environment. See particularly full issue, April 1970, entitled "The Crisis for Survival."

Public Health Reports published monthly by the Public Health Service. Available from Government Printing Office, Washington, D.C. 20402. Subscription $6.50 per year.

Public Power published monthly by American Public Ppwer Association, Suite 212, 2600 Virginia Avenue, N.W., Washington, D.C. 20037. Subscription $6.50 per year. Official journal of the Association, which represents municipal and other publicly-owned electric utilities. Environmental references infrequent in issues examined, although Association has Committee on Environment and urges protection of national environmental assets.

Quiet, a Newsletter published by Citizens for A Quieter City, Box 777 FDR Station, New York, N.Y. 10021. No price given. Interesting, but may be defunct.

Resources published three times a year by Resources for the Future, Inc., 1755 Massachusetts Ave., N.W., Washington, D.C. 20036. Issue 24 p. Free on request. Devoted to findings and conjectures from recent research into resource development and use.

Saturday Review published weekly by Saturday Review, Inc., 380 Madison Ave., New York, N.Y. 10017. Subscription $9 per year. With its March, 1970 issue, SR began a regular monthly supplement "Environment and the Quality of Life."

Science published weekly by American Association for the Advancement of Science, 1515 Massachusetts Ave., N.W., Washington, D.C. 20036. Subscription $12 per year. A basic resource.

Science Policy Bulletin published every two months by Battelle Memorial Institute, 505 King Ave., Columbus, Ohio 43201. Free on request. Now in its third year, this publication annotates current books, reports, articles, and fugitive materials on matters of broad public policy related to science and technology, including national goals and the allocation of resources.

SFI Bulletin published monthly by the Sport Fishing Institute, 719 13th St., N.W., Washington, D.C. 20005. 8 p., no subscription rate indicated. Interests of SFI now range beyond sport fishing, take in many aspects of natural environment.

Sierra Club Bulletin published monthly by the Sierra Club, 1050 Mills Tower, San Francisco, California 94104. Usual issue 24 p. Subscription $5 per year to nonmembers. Journal of aggressive organization devoted to study and protection of national scenic and natural resources; emphasizes legislation, education, action.

Soil and Water Conservation Journal published monthly by the Soil Conservation Society of America, 7515 North East Ankeny Road, Ankeny, Iowa 50021. Subscription $7.50 per year.

Soil Conservation published monthly by the Government Printing Office, Washington, D.C. 20402. Subscription $1.75 per year. Monthly magazine of the Soil Conservation Service, U.S. Department of Agriculture.

Technology Review published nine times each year at the Massachusetts Institute of Technology. Address inquiries to Technology Review, Room E219-430, MIT, Cambridge, Massachusetts 02139. Subscription $9 per year. Not specialized or always technical, but addressed to a sophisticated audience. In recent years has devoted more than half of its pages to environmentally related material; also strong on issues of science policy.

Transactions: American Geophysical Union published monthly by the Union, 2100 Pennsylvania Ave., N.W., Washington, D.C. 20037. Subscription $5 per year. Deals with "interface of all aspects of geophysics with society."

Transactions of The American Fisheries Society published quarterly by The American Fisheries Society, Suite 1040 Washington Building, 15th and New York Ave., N.W., Washington, D.C. 20005. Published without a break since 1870, this publication is one of the principal scientific and historical references sources on the industry. Index issues are available.

Unesco Courier published monthly by the United Nations Educational, Scientific and Cultural Organization in Paris, France: available from Unesco Publications Center, 317 East Thirty-Fourth Street, New York, N.Y. 10016. Subscription to English-language edition $5 per year. A magazine for the general reader; frequently attentive to environmental issues. See particularly January 1969 issue.

Washington Letter published at intervals by the American Bar Association, Washington Office, 1705 De Sales Street, N.W., Washington, D.C. 20036. Distributed without charge to officials of ABA and other bar associations interested in legislative activities. Sensitive to current issues, this newsletter has given substantial attention to consumer and environmental developments recently.

Washington Science Trends published weekly by Trends Publishing, Inc., National Press Building, Washington, D.C. 20004. Subscription $50 per year. Usual issue 6-8 p. Brief news notes include environmental activities of government.

Water Control News published weekly by Commerce Clearing House, Inc., 4025 West Peterson Ave., Chicago, Illinois 60646. Subscription $48 per year. Water and its availability, pollution, and treatment. Tabloid format.

Water Newsletter published by Water Information Center, Inc., 44 Sitsink Drive East, Port Washington, New York 11050. Subscription $28 per year includes 24 newsletters and 12 issues of *Research and Development.*

Water Research published monthly by Pergamon Press, Inc., 44-01 21st Street, Long Island City, New York 11101. Subscription $100 per year, $40 per year for educational libraries. Journal of the International Association on Water Pollution Research. Scientific.

Water Resources Research published bimonthly by the American Geophysical Union, 2100 Pennsylvania Ave., N.W., Washington, D.C. 20037. Subscription $17.50 per year. Original research papers on the science of water, embracing the physical, biological and social sciences.

Weekly Letter published by The American Waterways Operators, Inc., 1250 Connecticut Ave., N.W., Washington, D.C. 20036. Press and Association Edition, 4 p. mimeo., free on request. Legislative and regulatory issues affecting inland waterways transportation industry;

interesting for viewpoint. This edition is made up of excerpts from larger membership edition.

World Ports published eight times yearly by Amundsen Publications, Inc., 1612 K Street, N.W., Washington, D.C. 20006, as the official organ of the American Association of Port Authorities. Subscription $4 per year. 36 + p. Emphasis on high technology, large-scale facilities, some attention to pollution problems.